Politics without a Past

POLITICS WITHOUT A PAST

The Absence of History in Postcommunist Nationalism

Shari J. Cohen

DUKE UNIVERSITY PRESS   Durham and London 1999

© 1999 Duke University Press
All rights reserved
Printed in the United States of America on acid-free paper ∞
Typeset in Melior by Keystone Typesetting, Inc.
Library of Congress Cataloging-in-Publication Data appear
on the last printed page of this book.

Contents

Preface and Acknowledgments

In 1991, as I looked at the swath of territory that had been the communist world, hoping to contribute something original while engaging my own interests for the arduous work of a doctoral dissertation, I noticed a bizarre and troubling phenomenon. From Slovakia, where the founding of the Nazi puppet state of 1939–45 was being celebrated, to Lithuania, where some of those sent to the Gulag for Nazi collaboration were being exonerated, to Croatia, where the symbols of the fascist Ustashe were being openly invoked, there seemed to be a pattern of resurgence of symbols and issues connected to World War II. And the resurgence was of symbols from the wrong side, the side that collaborated with the Nazis, the side that had been hidden beneath the myth of Soviet liberation. Referred to by one scholar as the "big bang event" for the world as we knew it until 1989, World War II remains a significant presence even as we leave behind the century so shaped by that war. Not only was I alarmed by what appeared at the time to be a possible rehabilitation of groups that collaborated with the Nazis, but this was happening in a period that looked strikingly like the 1920s and 1930s. I wanted to know how, and whether, in an odd replaying of history, we would see a return of something like fascism. I worried, through my Jewish eyes, that we would begin to see a revision of our understanding of the Holocaust as constituting a particular type of crime.

As a scholar, however, trying to make sense of the politics of postcommunism, I found myself facing a void. And this void characterized not just my subject of study but also the analytical toolkit I had at my disposal to make sense of this subject. These were polities that lacked defining myths, let alone parties, parliaments, and other common political phenomena, which were barely in the process of formation; if they did exist, they seemed to be facades, empty of content. As part of the first generation of scholars to try to analyze postcommunism, without much guidance from the past, I lacked even the words and categories to map and understand this odd reality. Political scientists studying postcommunism were pressed to draw theoretical conclusions about an extremely fluid environment and about a process that had only begun to unfold.

On several research trips from 1992 to 1995, in what at the beginning of that time period was Czechoslovakia, I came to realize that the very formlessness of the postcommunist political scene was overwhelmingly more significant than a return of fascism from the past. I began to recognize that communist regimes had impaired these societies in a particular and profound way, which in turn shaped the meaning of the return of contentious issues from World War II. These regimes had destroyed, or never built, common interpretive frameworks for understanding the past. It is the implications of trying to rebuild societies where even the leadership lacks the social and moral glue that history could provide, that I attempt to explore in this book. This "absence of history" has not been sufficiently recognized or incorporated into our theorizing about the impact and aftermath of communist regimes.

Slovakia was originally one of several case studies in which I chose to examine the meaning of the reemergence of the World War II past. It became apparent, however, that even that small country had a great deal to teach, and I opted to stay there and not go on to the other cases that were part of my original research design. This understudied case turned out to be a perfect microcosm and laboratory for a set of issues that are highly relevant for the whole region and beyond.

There are numerous individuals without whom I would have never completed this project. I mention only some of these people here. I could not have done without the day-to-day insight from my intellectual partners and co-pilots in navigating through the postcommunist void, Carrie Timko and Tomek Grabowski. Their willingness to read endless drafts and discuss the nuances of every idea made this book much better than it ever would have been. My graduate advisers at University of California, Berkeley—Ken Jowitt, Ernie Haas, George Breslauer, Michael Rogin, and Reggie Zelnik—allowed me a great deal of intellectual freedom and provided guidance at key stages of the project. The reader will quickly discover how much influence Ken Jowitt, the chair of my dissertation committee, had on my thinking. Ernie Haas's high standards and lifelong intellectual agenda also shaped my first contribution as a social scientist in important ways.

Other colleagues and friends read parts of the manuscript and helped guide me out of intellectual blind alleyways at critical moments. Here I would like to mention in particular Felicia Wong, Steve Weber, Kelly Smith, Abby Innes, and Jon Shenk. Saul Perlmutter, with his intellectual playfulness, egged me on from the beginning of this enterprise. Denis Gromb deserves special mention for combing through nearly the entire manuscript and offering invaluable advice for making the text more accessible. Jane Dawson and Kathy Moon gave generously of their time in guiding me through the publishing process.

The Slovaks and Czechs who aided in my research are too numerous to mention. I would like to thank in particular Sona Szomolanyiova, without whose help and insights I would never have been able to accomplish so much in Slovakia. Eva and Peter Salner offered their ideas, connections, and friendship over the years.

The Social Science Research Council, the American Council of Learned Societies, the MacArthur Group on International Security Studies, and the Institute for the Study of World Politics provided vital funding for this project. I would also like to thank Wellesley College and the Wellesley political science department. Through financial support and a congenial environment I was able to complete the final stages of the book.

Finally, I thank my parents, Joan and Roy Cohen. My mother in particular has been a constant cheerleader, a sounding board for ideas, and an editor. My father has served as a model of persistence in setting and achieving difficult goals.

Chronology

Ninth century. Great Moravian empire. The 1992 Slovak constitution cites this as the foundation and predecessor to modern statehood for Slovaks.

1792. First signs of Slovak national "revival" as Bernolák attempts codification of Slovak language.

1846. Codification of Slovak language by Ludovít Štúr.

June 1861. Memorandum of the Slovak nation submitted to Budapest Diet.

1863. Matica Slovenská (Slovak Cultural Foundation) founded.

1875–1918. Repression of the incipient Slovak nation-building efforts under the "Magyarization" policies of the Hapsburg empire.

October 1918. Founding of Czechoslovakia as independent, democratic state uniting the Czech lands, previously under Austrian rule, and Slovakia, previously under Hungarian rule.

August 1938. Jozef Tiso succeeds Andrej Hlinka as leader of the Slovak People's Party, the major force pushing for Slovak autonomy during the period of the First Czechoslovak Republic. The party is renamed the Hlinka Slovak People's Party (HSLS). Andrej Hlinka had founded and led the party from 1918 until his death in August 1938.

September 29, 1938. Munich agreement between Germany, the United Kingdom, France, and Italy acquiescing to the ceding of the Sudetenland to Germany.

October 6, 1938. Žilina agreement whereby, under leadership of Jozef Tiso and the HSLS, Slovaks took full control of Slovak governmental and executive power. This new administration took the first measures against political opponents and Jews.

November 2, 1938. Vienna "arbitration" in which parties to the Munich agreement granted Hungarian demands that portions of southern Slovakia be ceded to Hungary.

March 14, 1939. Declaration of "independent" Slovak state under leadership of Jozef Tiso in exchange for collaboration with Hitler; on March 15 Czech lands were occupied and became a Nazi protectorate.

September 9, 1941. Passage of Jewish "codex" codifying anti-Jewish legislation put forward in first years of the regime; paralleled the German "Nuremberg laws." This included a racial definition of Jew and the "Aryanization" policies that turned over Jewish property to Slovaks.

March 1942–October 1942. Two-thirds of Jewish population of Slovakia (57,628) deported to Poland ostensibly for resettlement. Only several hundred of these survived. After deportations about 24,000 remained in Slovakia. They lived and worked on the basis of various economic, presidential, or religious exceptions or were placed in Jewish work camps and centers.

August 29, 1944. Slovak communists, army officers, and democrats start the Slovak National Uprising against the Tiso state and the Nazis.

October 1944. Slovak National Uprising defeated and Nazis occupy Slovakia; approximately 13,500 more Jews were deported, of whom 10,000 died.

May 1945. Germans are defeated and Czechoslovakia reconstituted; Slovak communists and democrats who led the Uprising push for federal state but eventually compromise on these demands.

December 1946–April 1947. Trial of Jozef Tiso culminating in his execution.

February 1948. Communists take power and begin to repress all noncommunist political, cultural, and religious groups.

1950. Arrest and imprisonment of Slovak "bourgeois nationalists," including the important Slovak communists and partisans Gustáv Husák and Ladislav Novomeský.

1963. Amnesty and rehabilitation of "bourgeois nationalists" and beginning of the reform movement that culminates in Bratislava and Prague Spring.

January 1968. Alexander Dubček becomes Communist Party chief and presides over the Bratislava/Prague Spring.

August 20, 1968. Warsaw Pact troops invade.

January 1, 1969. Czechoslovakia becomes a federal state, though many aspects of Slovak autonomy are not implemented.

April 1969. Gustáv Husák becomes Communist Party chief and begins the process of repressing the reform movement and restoring neo-Stalinist control. This process came to be called "normalization."

1985. Mikhail Gorbachev comes to power in the Soviet Union; signals begin in 1987 that Eastern European countries can go their own way.

November 17, 1989. Beginning of "velvet revolution" which leads to collapse of communist regime ten days later.

December 29, 1989. Václav Havel becomes president of a newly democratic Czechoslovakia.

June 1990. First free parliamentary elections; Vladimír Mečiar becomes prime minister of Slovakia.

March 1991. Split of Public Against Violence movement and formation of Movement for a Democratic Slovakia under leadership of Vladimír Mečiar.

April 1991: Vladimír Mečiar removed from post of prime minister; Ján Čarnogurský appointed in his stead.

June 1992. Second parliamentary elections; Mečiar's party is the victor and Mečiar again becomes prime minister; Václav Klaus becomes prime minister in the Czech Republic. Their election leads to the August 1992 decision to split Czechoslovakia.

January 1, 1993. The end of Czechoslovakia and formation of the Slovak Republic.

1   The Legacy of Two Totalitarianisms

Ten years after the fall of the Berlin wall, the plot line of the transition from communism in Eastern Europe and the former Soviet Union remains obscure and puzzling. The characters in the drama are themselves part of the puzzle. Former communists have become nationalists, or at least taken up nationalist slogans. But they have just as often become free marketeers. Heroic dissidents, who captured the imagination of the Western world in 1989, have all but disappeared from the political scene. Others of them have disappointed as they took up the banner of fascist periods from the past. Party labels and identifications are fleeting and have little to do with policy positions. Populations, which seemed to be empowered in 1989, remain cynical and apathetic and have increasingly turned to the 1980s with nostalgia. References to the past resurface like debris, with little apparent meaning, as these societies remain confused about the most important moments in their history. But this picture does not fit well with either of the primary paradigms put forward by analysts trying to interpret the first few acts of the postcommunist play. History has not returned from the past, either as aggressive nationalism or as a seamless continuation of the precommunist period.[1] But neither has history ended: democratic institutions and liberal ideologies introduced from outside have not pushed these societies on the pathway toward liberal democracy.[2] Observers have been deceived by the democratic and nationalist costumes and masks which hide a more important reality.

Indeed, it is the very amorphous nature of these societies emerging from communist domination that is so central to their character. While there is certainly variation across the former communist countries, what has often been missed is the very profound lack of unifying ideologies, a devastating legacy left by the fifty- or seventy-year experience of Leninist domination. These are societies trying to create new polities without common standards of moral or historical judgment. It is this absence, I argue, that should stand at the center of our analysis. The absence itself needs to be explained and its significance explored. Can democracies be built without common ideologies? Might we be misunderstanding the significance of the appearance of nationalist mobilization and even ethnic conflict by assuming a continuity with the past that is not there? What exactly has returned from the past and what did Leninist regimes succeed in wiping out? This book shifts the lens in an attempt to make the drama more comprehensible. It does this through the case of Slovakia, which is used here as an emblematic case to develop ideas that I hope can be used fruitfully elsewhere.

Past, Present, and Future

Looking Backward

Hannah Arendt, in her *Origins of Totalitarianism,* and George Orwell, in his *1984,* alerted Western readers to the novel nature of the totalitarian regimes of the twentieth century. Although neither projected what political life would look like after totalitarian regimes collapsed, these authors' insights remain useful for understanding communism and postcommunism and have been discarded by most Western analysts too easily.[3] In Orwell's *1984* the regime's control of history is the central and insidious mode of exerting its power. It is no accident that East European dissidents in the 1980s saw Orwell as accurately describing life under communism, focused as it was on wiping out all competing interpretations of history. In one scene the hero Winston Smith enters a pub in a part of town inhabited by "proles," the working classes, a place where at least some link to the period before the revolution remains in folk songs and expressions. In the hope of finding out information about the past, Smith approaches a prole and asks what life was like before the revolution. But Smith is disappointed to discover that while the old man could tell him a bit about his personal experiences, he could not locate those experiences in any larger interpretive context.[4]

This larger interpretive context—which I refer to throughout the book as historical consciousness—into which individuals can place their family stories is at the very heart of what we understand as modern national ideologies. National ideologies, with their standardized society-wide histories, create an "imagined community" in which individuals feel connected to people they do not know through a common history.[5] These narratives of history which come to be shared keep individuals connected to state institutions. They allow elites to cooperate to achieve common goals that stretch beyond personal enrichment; they cause members of society to participate; they allow for a society to move forward. Without this glue, societies would be comprised only of the individual families within them. National ideologies function this way whether they are civic—meaning membership is based on the individual—or ethnic, where membership is based on birth.[6] Family stories and even ethnic stereotypes—which often float free of these larger narratives of history—cannot integrate societies. While communist regimes did not eliminate family stories, and even fostered and preserved ethnic stereotypes, these other types of connection to the past have very different political implications than do commonly shared national ideologies.

Of course, standardized meanings of history have to come from somewhere. A process needs to take place whereby either states or groups of intellectuals articulate new ideologies to substitute for the breakdown of the face-to-face and religiously based ties of the village.[7] Articulation is what happens in a nation-building process through education and socialization, political speeches, novels, and films. If this process never takes place, collective meaning of similar individual experiences—even something as traumatic as a war—would never develop.

I argue here that like Orwell's proles, postcommunist elites and the societies they govern lack that larger interpretive context into which their individual family stories could be placed. This is particularly surprising in the case of the elites and intelligentsias, since we expect intellectuals and key political figures to share historical narratives and to define the meaning of key moments of history for ordinary people.[8]

In order to understand this striking and important legacy left by Leninist regimes we need to look backward and reevaluate what exactly the nature of these regimes was. We need to look at the imposition of communist institutions as a peculiar process of nation-building. Like Orwell's infamous "ministry of truth," communist regimes successfully rewrote history, claiming for themselves exclusive insight into past, present, and future. However, Leninist regimes were notoriously poor at winning loyalty to the newly propagated histories they tried so hard to instill. Unable to build "new Soviet men," but highly successful at keeping alternatives from developing, these regimes left much of the elite as well as the larger society without common meanings of history. It was, after all, mostly agricultural societies, with weak national identities, which became the focus of Leninist nation-building. Only small islands of continuity with precommunist ideologies remained amidst this sea of homogenization. Nowhere can we see this better than in Slovakia. However, the Slovak case is only an extreme of what happened, to varying degrees, elsewhere in the communist world.

Making the Question Concrete

The absence or weakness of ideology left by Leninist regimes is very difficult to observe. It is the actors in the play who give the best clue, once we look beneath their masks. The elites who became important after communism's collapse will be the focus of this book.[9] Elites offer a way to trace continuity through the tremendous political, economic, and cultural changes that the fall of communism represented. After all, individual people constitute one of the few constants amid the baffling institutional flux of postcommunism.[10]

In Slovakia, and across the communist world, elites with a particular profile came to dominate politics and, in many cases, to mobilize nationalism. Vladimír Mečiar, who was the major figure to mobilize the postcommunist movement for Slovak autonomy, and who presided over the split of Czechoslovakia in 1993, shares a common set of traits with Leonid Kravchuk in Ukraine, Alexander Lebed in Russia, and even Slobodan Milosevic in Serbia, just to name a few. They, and those who surround them, are all products of a communist socialization process. Beneath their ideological masks, they all embody the absence of ideology that is proving so difficult to overcome. Thus the victory of this type of historyless elite, which embodies ideological weakness or absence, is the phenomenon that needs to be explained and whose significance needs to be analyzed.

Leninism and Postcommunist Elites

If we look across postcommunist countries we find similar casts of characters, though Leninist regimes varied in their ability to destroy national ideologies from the past.[11] While noncommunist institutions were largely destroyed, small groups remained as the sole bearers of the alternatives to communism—both democratic and nationalist, both civic and ethnic.

These groups were heirs to a precommunist nation-building process through which, during the communist period, they developed or preserved historical consciousness. I refer to these elites as "ideological elites." It was these anticommunist elites who presided over the revolutions in Slovakia and throughout the communist world.[12]

But more important and more pervasive was the Mečiar type to which I just referred. I call this second type the "mass-elite," in reference to the literature on mass society associated with Hannah Arendt.[13] The masses that, for Arendt, were the fodder for Nazism and Stalinism, had been unhinged from traditional institutions and ties but had not been integrated by any modern ideological framework or interest groups. Without intermediary organizations, she argued, masses were available for mobilization by totalitarian movements. Later historians of the origins of Nazism and Stalinism have shown that in both these cases, in different ways, more group associations remained than Arendt thought. These group associations might, in fact, have been critical for the ability of totalitarian movements to mobilize, thereby calling into question her causal argument.[14] However, the products of the very regime type she tried to explain fit her concept better than ever. If masses were not present at the beginning of the twentieth century, Leninist nation-building brought about precisely this result. Even without the causal link made by Arendt about the availability of masses, her concept is useful for calling attention to the fact that it is unusual for elites and societies to be so impaired in their ability to join with others based on common judgments of the central elements of their national history.[15]

The term "mass-elite" sounds oxymoronic at first. But I use this unusual designation to emphasize the fact that the elites, whom we expect to have ideologies, are more like masses, in their lack of shared understanding of the past. I also use it to accentuate that this condition is the result of a historical process.[16] The mass-elite is not by definition limited to members of the Communist Party, though many were party members since that was the road to career advancement. This type is defined as elites who had no connection to any alternative ideology and who were solely formed by the official Leninist socialization process.

These elite types, mass-elites on the one hand and ideological elites on the other, have both a historical and a behavioral element.[17] As we will see illustrated in the Slovak case, the different types of elites developed through fundamentally different historical pathways, through two types of nation-building processes. Their behavior in the postcommunist period—ideologically committed, on the one hand, and ideologically uncommitted and transformable on the other—should be understood in terms of the historical pathways that formed them.

While the connection between formative history and behavior is quite easy to understand in the case of the ideological elites, the link between history and behavior for the mass-elite needs further explanation. Without any integrating ideology, the mass-elite could only be motivated by short-term personal interest. It is important to distinguish between instrumental networks for material gain and ties to others who have the same understanding of their nation's history.[18] It is also important to make the distinction between this short-term personal interest or *egoism,* and *individualism.* As Ken Jowitt points out, individualism, the cultural underpinning of Western liberal democracies, is an ideology. It is a set of beliefs which looks like, but is distinct from, the more basic egoism. Egoism is amoral. It is what is left when nothing ties individuals to one another. It is ego unrestrained by group ties or overarching societal norms.[19]

The fact that the mass-elites are not associated with any ideological tradition makes them extremely flexible in the postcommunist period. They are free to jump from idea to idea and from party to party, and to transform themselves at will. Only in the postcommunist context, for fully opportunistic reasons, do they pick up an available idiom, whether nationalist or democratic.[20] Their apparent postcommunist ideological orientations should not be taken as defining. Instead, knowing their past, we can understand the ephemerality of their ideological guises in the present. They are opportunists but they are historically created opportunists.

That the mass-elites are historically created opportunists is critical to the argument here. While simple opportunism is a characteristic of politics everywhere, the pervasive and all-encompassing opportunism behind what looked like a return of ideology in postcommunist politics is what needs to be better understood. The opportunism of the mass-elite differs from that of a figure like Bill Clinton. Whereas some would call Clinton the consummate opportunist, in contrast to the mass-elite, Clinton is linked to an identifiable ideological tradition. In contrast to the postcommunist setting of extreme fluidity, Clinton operates within the context of well-established institutions. In addition, the mass-elite dominate politics at a founding moment when ideology is essential for building and consolidating new institutions. In the U.S. Democratic Party, for example, it is possible to find both ideologues and opportunists. In postcommunist politics, in Slovakia and elsewhere, the mass-elite tends to come together to dominate entire parties. The ideological elites tend to be marginalized not merely as individual politicians but as a group or type. The perpetuation of this opportunism is what makes democratization so daunting in the postcommunist world, as we will see illustrated in Mečiar's rise in Slovakia.

Slovakia, an Emblematic Case

In each former communist country it is possible to find ideological democrats, ideological nationalists, and mass-elites. In each country the coalitions they form, the power relationships within those, and the particular ideological labels that are adopted differ. This depends on how prevalent the mass-elite is relative to the ideological elites. But the Slovak case is an appropriate one to develop this framework because the mass-elite appear here in a purer form than elsewhere. It is only if we isolate this elite type and develop this framework in a clear case that we can then use the same approach to try to understand less clear cases. Thus I use Slovakia as a single *theory-developing* case.[21]

As we will see in the next section, the argument rests on the fact that Leninist regimes came to power in societies with weak nationalisms and in societies that were largely agricultural. But Slovakia, even in comparison to other countries of east central Europe where communism took hold, had a very weakly articulated nationalism at the time communism appeared.

Slovaks brag about the fact that they experienced three different regime types in the course of the twentieth century—democratic (1918–38) as part of the First Czechoslovak Republic, fascist (1939–45) as a quasi-independent Nazi puppet state, and communist (1948–89) as part of a reconstituted Czechoslovakia.[22] Two aspects of Slovak history stand out, making it a particularly good case with which to develop my argument. First, Slovakia had its only period of statehood as a Nazi puppet state during World War II. The nationalist party, headed by Catholic priest Jozef Tiso, opted to trade collaboration with the Nazis for Slovak independence. The Czech lands were occupied and made a German protectorate. Since the leaders of that state willingly deported much of the Jewish population and since this state was aligned with the Nazis, statehood itself is inherently tainted.[23] World War II is both a moment of glory and a moment of great shame. It is the central moment in Slovak national history but is forever associated with the Nazis. There is one aspect of Slovakia's World War II experience that could be rescued—the antifascist uprising in 1944. However, as we will see, that experience is controversial as well since it was embraced by the communist regime. There is no agreement on other formative moments in Slovak history, as evidenced by a 1992 survey of eight historians. When asked which historical experience was a moment of glory for Slovakia, they gave eight different answers.[24]

In addition to this problematic legacy of fascism, a second aspect of Slovak history that makes it an appropriate case study is that Slovakia modernized and went through a nation-building process within the communist context. Like many countries in Eastern Europe, its social structure was largely agricultural before 1948. It also had a weak national identity: a small national intelligentsia and little experience of self-administration during the period of Hungarian domination. The fascist period made it easier for communism to wipe out alternative ideologies since the strongest one was tainted. Thus communism prevented the preservation and articulation of alternative meanings more effectively here than in many other places. However, while Slovakia is an extreme case, it is not so extreme as to be unique. The mass-elite is particularly pervasive in places where there was little to withstand the communist assault upon competing ideological traditions.

Cases across the communist world vary according to how strongly rooted alternative modern ideologies were. Some countries in Eastern Europe had a more significant precommunist period of independent statehood, or a larger or more influential nationalist intelligentsia, or more institutions in which the past was preserved to withstand communist domination.

Clearly we see a less dominant mass-elite in a place like Poland, where even the Communist Party was shaped by the struggle with the Solidarity movement in the 1980s.[25] However, much of the former communist world, like Slovakia, modernized and built nations within the communist context. In most of these countries opposition to communism was extremely weak. Any society with a weak national experience before communism and which went through the Leninist modernization process would have a significant mass-elite. This would include, to varying degrees, several of the East European cases, including Romania, Bulgaria, and parts of the former Yugoslavia. Ukraine and Belarus and the central Asian republics in the former Soviet Union also share this background. Even the Czech Republic has its own version of a mass-elite, though the Czech version did not become nationalist and tends more toward the technocratic.[26]

Though in many ways a more complicated case, Russia is a perfect place to look for the mass-elite.[27] As Steve Fish points out, Russia's seventy, rather than forty, years of communism made the attempt to reconstitute ideologies in the postcommunist period even more daunting than in Eastern Europe.[28] Russian elites all were products of a Leninist regime that went even further than did the one in Slovakia in wiping out alternatives to communism and preventing these from developing. One of the most difficult tasks in analyzing Russia is trying to tell who is who among the elite. Almost every key figure in postcommunist Russia regularly switches parties and idioms. (Even the identifications of those who do not switch as frequently should be examined in terms of whether they were formed exclusively by the Leninist nation-building process.)[29] While clearly Russia has a more developed and richer history than does Slovakia, that country's tainted Stalinist legacy, the ambiguity surrounding its imperial past, and even the victory in World War II offer little clear basis for reconstituting a new society-wide ideology.

Armed with the categories I set up in the Slovak case, and with the questions they raise, we can look at other cases and try to determine exactly what the relative impacts are of the communist versus the precommunist nation-building experiences.[30] Rather than assuming a return of history, we can sort out exactly what is returning and how significant that return is.

Using the ideas developed in the Slovak case, we can look behind party and ideological self-identifications and see how shallow these identifications are. We can ask what they really mean. We can make more sense of the switching of idiom and fluidity of personnel that continues to characterize politics in these countries. We can begin to understand odd alliances between seeming ideological opposites. We can also begin to ask the larger and longer-term question about the significance of the absence of an overarching ideology in societies that often resemble the mass-elite more than they do the ideological elites and continue to elect the mass-elite through democratic politics.[31]

Historical Consciousness of World War II

Within the Slovak case I have chosen to trace historical consciousness regarding the World War II legacy in order to assess the extent to which national ideology was preserved, developed, or erased during the communist period. But each of these choices—historical consciousness as a stand-in for ideology and World War II as the central facet of Slovak history— must be justified by way of introduction.

The theoretical justification of the link between historical consciousness and national ideology is discussed at length in chapter 2, but here in brief is why it is so central to national ideology. First, history (or memory) is the central part of identity that allows a person or a group to understand themselves as maintaining particular characteristics over time. It is at the core of national ideologies for just this reason. The critical role that history plays in ideology was recognized by the dissent movements that formed in response to Leninist regimes. They preserved national ideology through their focus on history and memory. They believed that state control of history—which became known as "organized forgetting"—meant state control of identity.[32] Second, history, or historical consciousness, functioning as it does to provide group identity, allows for common judgments and learning from the past. Third, the *consciousness* part of historical consciousness calls attention to the fact that national ideologies are products of a process of articulation, of making individual family stories into a collective history.[33]

Slovakia's World War II legacy can be broken down into several controversial issues. How responsible were the leaders of the Slovak state for the deportation of Slovakia's Jewish population? Was the Slovak state and its ideology legitimate or imposed from outside? What was the character of the resistance to Nazism?

While the main focus of this book from a comparative perspective is communism's legacy, the World War II legacy is a particularly interesting one to use to demonstrate the argument, because so many countries shared it.[34] While Slovakia and Croatia had traded statehood for collaboration, Baltic nationalists, the Ukranian nationalist movement, Romania, and Hungary had also collaborated with the Nazis. Occupied countries such as Poland continued to struggle with this legacy. Of course East Germany had to contend with the legacy of two totalitarian regimes in the most direct way. World War II divided democrats, nationalists, and communists in each of these countries.[35]

Throughout this region, World War II was important on a number of levels. It was a battle between ideologies—fascist, communist, and democratic. It was an overlay on top of particularistic ethnic conflicts in each country—Czechs against Slovaks, Croats against Serbs. It was also a story of national sovereignty squashed by either Nazi or Soviet imperialism. But at the center of the difficult process of coming to terms with this past, from a moral perspective, is the Holocaust, and in particular the fate of the Jews.

The Jewish deportations at the hands of the Slovak state receive particular focus in this book. The contribution to Hitler's effort to exterminate Europe's Jews, more than the severing of the Czechoslovak state, is the central moral issue that taints the Slovak wartime state. The Jewish issue is clearly at the heart of the Western understanding of what made World

War II different from other wars. The moral catastrophe of the Holocaust was such an important part of the postwar intellectual discourse in the West that it is particularly dramatic to see how cut off the East actually was from this discussion. That these events happened on the territories of these countries makes their isolation from the postwar debate even more remarkable.[36]

The word *holocaust* did not enter the Slovak debate until 1989 (though small groups of nationalists and democrats discussed it). On the territory of that small country whose leaders traded nominal independence for collaboration in one of the century's greatest crimes, this history was never made meaningful. Even members of the elite were never exposed to the interpretation of the Holocaust that intellectuals in the West take for granted—that this was a European or human tragedy.

The Jewish deportations might, at first glance, make the 1939–45 period an odd one to use to demonstrate my argument. This is a history which elites might well try to forget anyway, even without the pressure and coercion of a Leninist regime. After distinguishing between the reasons for forgetting this difficult past in communist countries as opposed to countries of Western Europe, I offer several reasons that make the 1939–45 period a good choice in spite of this problem.

The literature on coming to terms with fascist pasts in Western European countries like Germany and France tends to use the metaphor of repressed memory rather than state-organized forgetting.[37] While repressed memory suggests denial, but also the possibility of accessing this memory, organized forgetting results in something more like amnesia and thus ignorance of events from the past. Contrast, for instance, a case like Austria, where debate about the fascist past only took off in the late 1980s and early 1990s, and the postcommunist cases. In the Austrian case, collaboration with the Nazis is not remembered by the elites because its content is difficult. In the communist cases, it is not remembered because of the state's effort to create a new elite that remembers no other history. Thus, while the fascist past is likely to be "forgotten" even in societies without Leninist regimes, there is a clear distinction between these different reasons for forgetting the past and the implications of these different types of forgetting. The divide between the ideological elites in Slovakia paralleled the divide we see in Western European countries. Anticommunist nationalists made arguments resembling those made by apologists for Nazi collaboration for the purposes of preserving national image. Democrats, like their counterparts in Western Europe, were set on condemning that collaboration in the interest of promoting tolerance and democracy.[38] The mass-elite, on the other hand, lacked any shared interpretation at all beyond their personal family experiences.

Several factors make World War II a useful case to illustrate the results of the Leninist nation-building process in Slovakia in spite of the ambiguity about reasons for forgetting the fascist past. As we already know there was little to compete with World War II as a key nation-forming experience in Slovakia, given its lack of independent political history and weak national development. The anticommunist nationalists, composed of two streams—émigrés from abroad and the small Catholic dissident community who formed the Christian Democratic Movement (KDH)—in many ways continued the legacy of the Slovak state even though it left a problematic basis for a national myth. Particularly the émigrés, who, in many cases, had been associated with the fascist Slovak state, continued to see that state as a glorious moment of Slovak autonomy.[39] They avoided admitting responsibility for its leaders' willingness to collaborate in the deportation of Slovak Jews or to impose a fascist dictatorship. The democrats—the dissident and Western oriented intellectuals of Public Against Violence (VPN)—saw Nazi crimes and the Slovak fascist state as part of a larger human tragedy that served as a benchmark against which to judge other regimes, such as the communist one.[40] They used it to warn of the dangers of dictatorship and the unprecedented immoral actions that these regimes could carry out. They saw the 1944 Slovak National Uprising against the Nazis as human resistance to dictatorship and thus as the true legacy on which a modern democratic Slovak national identity ought to be based.

World War II was also at the center of the Communist Party's claim to legitimacy and to the national myth the Party tried to build among communist elites. This was true not only in Slovakia but also throughout Eastern Europe.[41] As Pavel Campeanu puts it, "the victory of the Soviet Union in the Second World War became the improvised substitute of the worldwide revolution. The historical mission of the international proletariat was assumed by the national army of the great victor."[42] Thus, World War II, given its centrality, illustrates the striking effects of communism in destroying (or failing to build) historical consciousness quite well. The entire population was affected by the war and everyone had personal family stories about the Slovak fascist state, about participation in the Slovak army, or about the Uprising against the Nazis. In addition, society-wide meaning was given to these events only in the communist context since communist domination followed the war so quickly. National history writing in Slovakia really began during the communist period.

Competing Theories

The book falls into two parts—communist and postcommunist. The first part should be understood in contrast with two prevalent arguments regarding the effects of Leninist regimes. These are *return of history*—conflicts from the past reemerged once communist repression was lifted—and *historical institutionalism*—communist regimes inadvertently created and strengthened nationalism through a particular approach to dealing with multiethnic societies.[43] The first part of the book also has a bearing on debates about collective memory. Finally, it is a detailed examination of the World War II legacy in Slovakia and thus begins to bring the countries of Eastern Europe into the growing literature on the legacy of that war. The second part, in chapters 6 and 7, looks at postcommunist Slovak politics through the lens of the weakness of ideology embodied by the mass-elite. Those chapters are in dialogue with the literature on transitions to democracy and the literature on nationalist mobilization.

Reinterpreting the Communist Period

Both historical institutionalists and advocates of the return-of-history approach tend to look backward to find a nationalism which seems inevitably to exist. Yet neither raise the question of how strong or significant this nationalism is. Return-of-history arguments tend to see an undifferentiated return of issues and conflicts from the precommunist past which were frozen by communism. Debates regarding Slovakia's World War II past would be understood as having been pushed underground. When it became possible to engage in the free exchange of ideas, these debates simply resurfaced.

But, as I argue at greater length in chapter 2, it is essential to actually trace the mechanisms through which ideas about the past were preserved during the communist period. Analysts who contend that history has returned tend to assume that resistance to communism was more significant than it in fact was and that nation-building was more developed than can be shown to be the case.[44] The small groups that resisted communism, often in emigration, shaped the understandings of communist societies that developed in the West and gave an exaggerated sense of the importance of resistance. A second shortcoming of return-of-history arguments is that they fail to distinguish between shared national ideologies and separate family stories. By failing to make this distinction, these arguments therefore fail to assess the significance of exactly what is returning from the past.

I argue that two factors must be taken into account that allow us to see that only the small groups of democrats and anticommunist nationalists represent a return of history in the sense of a return of national ideologies from the past. The first factor that must be understood is the nature of Slovak society; it was largely agricultural in 1948 and its national identity was not strongly rooted. Second, we must pay attention to the particular approach the communist regime took to nation-building.

The weakness of Slovak national consciousness in 1948 and its socio-economic composition is the subject of chapter 3. The Slovak intelligentsia was very small in 1948 and much of that group was repressed as a threat to the communist regime. Much of the modernization process in Slovakia happened during the communist period, not before. Thus most of those who became the elites after 1948 had to have come from the parts of the population less subject to the partial processes of modernization and nation-building which took place during the years of the first republic and the wartime Slovak state. Members of the generation that became the elite after 1948, and especially of the one that entered the elite after 1968, often did not have ties to families that would have been conscious of preserving history. They were not from families that might have had prewar history books in their libraries or might have been tied in to Western networks or sources of information or even to prewar associations with the Communist Party. They went from peasant households directly into the communist socialization process.[45] While all families had some personal experience from the war, it was up to the communist regime alone to integrate the wartime experience into a new Leninist ideology.

What about communist nation-building? Historical institutionalists argue that Soviet-style nationality policy, which was aimed at muting differences between nationalities, inadvertently created nationalism where it did not exist and strengthened it where it did. This was particularly true in multiethnic federal states—the Soviet Union, Yugoslavia, and Czechoslovakia. Institutions, from academies of sciences to ethnic dance troupes, were set up with national facades and socialist substance to buy the loyalty of local elites; the intention was for their socialist content to be absorbed. But historical institutionalists point out that elites who were products of these institutions emerged from the experience of Leninist regimes with nationhood as their primary frame of reference.[46]

The historical institutionalists focus on only one side of the institutional legacy of communist regimes. They fail to take into account the atomization caused by elite purges and the regime's approach to history teaching. Thus, even if nationalist idiom is available to these elites because of their having operated in Soviet-style national institutions, these elites might still be motivated by egoism, and the nationalist idiom they adopt might well be shallow. The focus in this book is on the other side of the institutional legacy of communist regimes. While the failure of communist regimes to brainwash is commonly accepted, the effects of this failure in combination with the regime's stunning success at preventing alternatives from developing, even in the face of profound alienation from the regime, is what is less often appreciated. The Leninist nation-building process combined periodic purges with a particular approach to the presentation of history.

In the case of World War II in particular the communist regime devoted a great deal of effort and resources to creating a communist myth that would win supporters. This included official history texts, elaborate commemorations, holidays, museums, research institutes, novels, and films. According to the communist version of the war, which can be recognized with some variation across Eastern Europe, fascism was bad, but its dictatorial nature was underplayed and was said to derive from its being a product of the highest stage of capitalism. The resistance against the fascists was good, but this applied only to those aspects linked to communist parties and the Soviet Union. Deportation of the Jews and Hitler's focus on Jews in his all-European extermination project was not emphasized.[47]

But the methods the regime used for presenting history—what came to be known by East European dissidents as "organized forgetting"—made history meaningless for the people who were products of the communist education and socialization processes. Official histories not only left out and distorted key events and personalities but also shifted in what they left out and distorted. This left people unable to judge the meaning of important historical events. These methods are demonstrated in detail in chapter 5 through an analysis of the history texts, novels, and films that each generation since World War II encountered.

That chapter will also show that even though the changing and diluted Party version of the war became either suspect or meaningless for its members, alternatives did not develop. This was mostly due to the fact that the regime periodically engaged in purges—in 1948 with the coming of communist domination, in the 1950s with Stalinist purges, in the 1960s with de-Stalinization, and after 1968 and the invasion of Soviet troops suppressing the Prague Spring. The alternatives that did develop, in 1968, were too ephemeral and were expunged so quickly that they reached few people.[48] For the next generation, born after the war, these twists and turns in the Party interpretation, and the elite purges they justified, served to strip the World War II history of meaning. The failure of the Party to make the fascist past meaningful was particularly acute for the generations that lacked an independent memory of the war. Following the suppression of the Prague Spring, the Party began to be dominated by this generation.

The Party version had become hypocritical or meaningless even for those whose personal experience it reflected. And personal stories from the war were never discussed outside of the home. Those who wanted to move ahead in the Party probably ignored what they heard at home, if they heard anything, especially if it was at odds with what the official interpretation said.[49] Once the Party had lost its ability to motivate, all that was left were individuals and instrumental networks driven by egoism.[50]

While communist institutions had concealed the egoism of the mass-elite, when these institutions collapsed, the mass-elite—who were concerned solely with their reputations, power, and enrichment—became free to survey the scene and transform themselves into businessmen or politicians of various ideological colors. This picture of an elite driven by egoism is different from the historical institutionalist angle, which sees a logical ideological transition from communist to nationalist. However, for the historical institutionalist argument to be convincing there would have to be a clear correlation between an individual's connection to a particular communist institution (one of the co-opted national ones) and the taking on of national ideology in the postcommunist period.[51] In Slovakia this was very difficult to demonstrate, especially since there was so much fluidity in the positions taken by leaders like Mečiar.[52]

The identifications picked up by mass-elites had more to do with the dynamic of postcommunist politics than leftover ideological links to communist era institutions. Once we look at who the mass-elites were, in terms of their socialization process, we can see the randomness of the fact that some ended up in the Mečiar wing of Public Against Violence, some in the Slovak National Party, and some in the Slovak Democratic Left, the reformed and renamed Communist Party.

The Ideological Elites and Alternative Meanings of the Past

Chapter 4 traces the continuity with noncommunist nation-building processes embodied by the small groupings of democrats and nationalists who presided over the revolution in Slovakia. While the democrats and nationalists did embody a return of history, they were weak, isolated, and divided. As we will see in chapter 6, the divide between the democrats and nationalists over the fascist past was one of the few real cleavages from the past that became important after communism fell.

The lack of strength among the most ideological groupings in Slovakia only adds power to the argument that ideology was absent in the rest of the elite and society. In addition, in a point missed by historical institutionalists, these elites, in the postcommunist period, played by an entirely different set of rules than did the mass-elites. While the dominant socialization process can be understood through composite data, unusual circumstances allowed individuals to escape from this process. The only way to establish whether individuals could be categorized as ideological democrats or nationalists is to look at personal biography.[53] Chapter 5 relies on a combination of interviews and an analysis of the historiographical debates about World War II carried on in samizdat and in emigration.[54]

The Democrats

In Slovakia there were only a handful of true dissidents with democratic leanings. Instead, what became known as "islands of positive deviance"— loose networks of intellectuals—began to develop in the late 1980s and to discuss views critical of the regime.[55] For those who were part of these networks, the most important truth about the fascist past, and the one that the regime was keeping from society, was that Czechoslovakia was similarly dominated by two totalitarian dictatorships even though communist rule was touted as liberation from fascist rule.[56]

These networks were informed by a notion laid out by Havel that individuals could carve out spheres in which they "lived in truth" in their private lives or participated in "parallel" structures. He thought that these private acts of integrity, including the belief in ideas about history that were counter to regime nonsense, would translate into an alternative identity. But the Slovak democrats were overly optimistic that the rest of society shared these views, as were their Czech counterparts.

The Anticommunist Nationalists

The Catholic nationalist dissidents, associated with the underground church, were the only group inside Slovakia to embody continuity with prewar Slovak nationalism and the wartime Slovak state. The organizations that might have preserved this link were the Catholic Church and Matica Slovenská (the Slovak cultural organization), both of which were repressed and co-opted by the Communist Party. The regime cast all traces of

Slovak nationalism as "clerico-fascism," and its association with the fascist regime (and later with the communist regime) tainted the Catholic Church.

The Catholic nationalists tried harder to come to terms with the fascist legacy than did the Slovak émigrés, with whom they did not have strong ties. Organizations like the World Slovak Congress supported and produced a nationalist historiography sympathetic to the wartime regime, some of which was circulated in samizdat. The émigrés reappeared in Slovakia after 1989 searching for allies and planting their ideas in the press.[57] However, they were less successful than nationalist émigrés in other countries like Croatia.[58]

The problems I faced in trying to trace continuity or demonstrate lack of continuity through the communist period are themselves illuminating. Information is difficult to obtain for both elite types, but this is true for different reasons for each type. In the case of the mass-elite, it is hard to procure biographical information. This is, in many ways, another aspect of their character. Their individual pasts are obscured due to their lack of specific commitments and their desire, in the postcommunist period, to hide their pasts for the purpose of transforming themselves. Moreover, they are products of a society in which sociological and historical information was simply not known (the research was not done) or was falsified. This made it difficult even for individuals themselves to know "who they were" on anything larger than a family scale.

Information is also poor in the case of the ideological elites. First, because of the nature of dissent, records were not kept. For those who were not specifically connected with dissent and, instead, were connected to "islands of positive deviance" it is even harder. These "islands" were, in many cases, unconnected and unaware of one another. However, because the Bratislava elite is so small, it is possible to piece together who participated in these networks.

I carried out interviews with individuals from both types of elite asking about what sources of information formed their understanding of World War II (see interview list in the appendix). Interestingly the ideological elites were more willing than the mass-elites to reveal their pasts. Because they have ideologies, they also find it easier to articulate what their own ideological development was.

The Politics of Postcommunism

In the second half of the book we see the implications of the pervasiveness of the mass-elite, and the absence of ideology they personify, for democratization and for nationalist mobilization. Using the lens developed in the chapters on elite formation, I interpret the postcommunist story in Slovakia. My account is based on a combination of sources: a wide range of press accounts and debates, parliamentary debates at both the Slovak and federal levels, and interviews with key players, including figures in all parts of the political spectrum, newspaper editors, and analysts.

First, the basic outline of the story: Vladimír Mečiar, the leading masselite to mobilize Slovak nationalism, started out in the democratic camp. However, just over a year after the revolution, he suddenly struck out on his own, cobbling together a defensive nationalism along the way. By the time of the June 1992 parliamentary elections, Mečiar and his followers had captured the issue of Slovak autonomy. The anticommunist nationalists had split and lost many of their former government posts and parliamentary seats. The democrats were pushed out completely. Mečiar presided over the split of Czechoslovakia and he continued to dominate the politics of the independent Slovak state into the late 1990s.

It is important to note here that my choice to frame the question in terms of the victory of a type of elite rather than of an ideology, a political party, an individual, or a policy choice has both methodological and theoretical reasons behind it. The temptation for analysts in the first years after communism fell, as well as for political actors within these rapidly changing societies, was to name the world before them using familiar terms.[59] They named themselves as democrats, liberals, and nationalists. They also named the process in which they were engaged—a transition to democracy. But by taking these identifications at face value, by jumping to study party development or the emergence of new laws, there is also an analytical cost. By imputing a reality to what might be passing identifications and a trajectory based on a model developed in a very different historical context, what is often missed is the larger context in which political life is taking place. I argue here that the legacy of ideological weakness from the communist period, observable through elites, is a fundamental piece of this context.

Transitions to Democracy

The transitions-to-democracy literature, developed originally to understand transitions from authoritarianism in southern Europe and Latin America, has been the dominant analytical approach to postcommunist politics.[60] This literature sees two kinds of major obstacles to democratization. Irreconcilable interests about the content of policy, such as failing to find a viable economic policy that will avoid labor unrest or ethnic dissatisfaction, is one way that new democracies can get pushed off course. A second major threat to new democracies is posed by extra-systemic actors who do not agree that democratic institutions are appropriate at all. Examples are militaries or extremist groups that resort to violence.[61] While both of these problems are surely present in the postcommunist world, a more daunting set of obstacles to democratization comes from the fact that elites and societies do not have ideological commitments.[62] Even the original compromise that is usually thought of as leading to the establishment of democratic institutions has a different meaning in a world where most of the elites have no predictable orientations. Compromise is an agreement by each side, which has an identifiable set of priorities, to give up some in order to reach agreement. If one side does not have any identifiable interests as a group, it is hard for a compromise to have lasting value for predicting the likely behavior of the other side.

As we will see in chapters 6 and 7, the democrats and the anticommunist nationalists, who made the revolution in Slovakia, assumed that there was greater elite and societal cohesion than was the case. They assumed that politics was about competing solutions to society's problems and that threats to democracy were from identifiable sources. They did not adequately understand the extent to which they alone had escaped from the cultural devastation wrought by communist regimes in the rest of society. Leninist domination created a society that resembled the mass-elites much more than it did the democratic or nationalist elites.

The threat from the mass-elite was very difficult to see. Political actors could all be together in parliaments. They could all be involved in a policy process. They could all make claims about history. The problem was that the mass-elite were defined by their *lack of* commitments to any ideologies and their idiom was no clue to who they were. They could win in this environment by being unidentifiable and uncommitted. Thus, for political actors and for analysts it can be deceptive to take ideological identifications at face value.[63]

The problem was not that the mass-elite as a type of political actor was opposed to democratic institutions. It was that they operated so well in them. Politicians like Mečiar used democratic institutions and electoral politics rather than being shaped by them.[64] Institutional design is thus deceptive as a subject of study without understanding the context—in this case the political actors who inhabit these institutions. Studying parliaments and electoral rules is only useful in political environments where actors are actually shaped in lasting ways by such institutions. Analysts expected new postcommunist institutions to shape political actors before those institutions had time to gel.[65]

Absence of ideology also affected the relationship between elites and society in terms of representation and accountability, making party development a problematic analytical focus.[66] The problem in Slovakia was not that society was against democracy per se, though they feared the sacrifices that came with the new market economy, but that they were not equipped or inclined to try to assess the validity of politicians' claims. Rather than representing articulated interests in society, the mass-elite reflected a society that was just like them. Whether in the arena of more concrete efforts at liberal economic reforms, or in the arena of the more complex historical justice agenda, the ideological elites assumed that their job was to represent societies that shared their beliefs. However, the appeal of Mečiar came precisely from his ability to cast himself defensively in opposition to the proposals of the democrats on the one hand and the nationalists on the other. While he became the classic demagogue, the fact that his arguments were based on lack of commitment is what is crucial to understand.

We can see this illustrated in chapter 7, where I examine the attempt to reestablish common standards for making moral and ethical judgments—the attempt to create a new national ideology. This process of trying to right the wrongs of the communist and the fascist pasts which included punishing secret police collaborators, evaluating controversial elements of history, and restitution of property was a central facet of the postcommunist agenda put forward by the ideological elites. While judgment is always difficult regarding controversial aspects of history that different groups see differently, here all guideposts and traditions were in such flux and there were so few points of reference that there was no way to judge competing claims or develop common standards. The democrats and nationalists took clear-cut positions and expected to be supported for this. But because of the way in which communism controlled history writing and subjected it to ideological priorities, it was difficult to tell what was true in trying to assess the multiplicity of issues on the agenda that required historical judgment. The political agenda included issues of history and justice before history had been written. Archives were being opened, formerly banned memoirs were published, historians' commissions were convened, but this only added to the whirlwind of information. Mečiar was able to take advantage of the fact that judgment was truly difficult. He took a nonposition—that history should not enter politics—which discredited the historical justice agenda. The result of this was that the communist era's lack of common standards regarding history was perpetuated, albeit for different reasons, in the postcommunist period.

Nationalist Mobilization

Most common explanations of nationalist mobilization also fall short by failing to focus on the strength or weakness of national ideology in the aftermath of communism. One prevalent approach explains national mobilization as due to political entrepreneurs who play the market of ideas. Mečiar fits that model well. The mass-elite were generally good at picking up nationalist idiom and selling it. In chapter 6 we will see that not only Mečiar but the Slovak National Party, which looked like the most radical of the nationalist forces, was put together by unknown leaders, none of whom had been nationalists before communism's collapse. While there had been a Slovak National Party in the past—in fact, it was the oldest Slovak party—the new party had nothing to do with that long-standing party's history. Unlike some of the other precommunist parties that reconstituted themselves based on continuity with the past, the name of this party, like the ideology itself, was randomly selected by the one historian in its leadership.

But my approach adds a critical dimension to the political entrepreneur argument. If we look at who the entrepreneurs are in terms of whether or not they have ideology, we can ask whether every entrepreneur can create a political community. Mečiar's political entrepreneurship is based precisely on his lack of commitment; even though he did win popular support, this does not mean that he can or will define in any positive sense who Slovakia is as a nation.

Political entrepreneurs need to find arguments that will resonate or sell to society. The demand side of the equation in these arguments—why nationalism resonates—tends also to ignore what is being mobilized and the strength of the nationalism being mobilized. The literature on political entrepreneurs tends to conflate the ease of stirring up a crowd in support of nationalist messages with the ease of nation-building, forging an ideology to drive new institutions. I argue that these are separate issues. What is so strikingly demonstrated in the Slovak case is the tepidness of the nationalism that was mobilized and the appeal of lack of commitment.

Another common explanation for nationalist mobilization is that demagogues offering easy solutions in hard times have appeal. This argument can explain the rise of the mass-elite as nationalists. It shares with my approach the claim that what is being mobilized are not historically based ideologies but rather fears based on confusion and disorientation. But understanding the mass-elite as embodying a profound ideological weakness takes my analysis beyond the simple claim that elites with easy answers win in hard times.[67] It keeps focus on the daunting nature of the ultimate challenge elites face in reconstituting political communities in the aftermath of communism.

A final note must be made about the challenge of studying the postcommunist world. The choice of a single case is a result of the particular challenges that face analysts in the postcommunist period. It is not clear what categories to use, nor what actually happened. We are mapping a new empirical and theoretical reality. There is much research still to be done on this case and, more generally, in this part of the world. The argument I present here does what I think social science can do best: it casts a situation in a new light and draws out the implications of that angle. As time goes on it should become possible to substantiate or refute this approach with more data.

2 Historical Consciousness, Family Stories, and Nationalism

Leninist regimes have always been interesting to social scientists for the extreme they presented: the attempt by communist parties to replace all independent organization—economic, cultural, and political—with their own. Analysts have long speculated about how successful Leninist regimes were at destroying and atomizing. What was preserved in the face of this regime? Where can we see the effects of this destruction or preservation? These questions became critical once communism collapsed, as analysis turned to the effects of the legacy of communist regimes and the role of the precommunist past.

Generally, the literature on communist systems characterized these systems monolithically: either primarily modernizing or primarily repressive in impact. But I argue here that the communist legacy was not only an industrialized society; nor did its key legacy come solely from resistance and the preservation of old nationalisms in the face of a repressive regime. To conceptualize the effects of Leninist domination in a theoretical sense, we need to recognize the fact that these regimes were not only imposed and tyrannical but also transformative. Not only did they repress and redirect the processes of national development that preceded them, they also were nation-building regimes themselves. The pre-Leninist and the Leninist nation-building processes coexisted. Both were important once communist regimes collapsed. These processes produced very different types of political actors and the divide between these types is the one I identify as critical for understanding postcommunist politics. By looking at these competing nation-building processes, we can differentiate between the consequences of Leninism as its own development pathway and the role of Leninist regimes in wiping out or preserving what came before.

Nation-Building

While it is not difficult to see the pre-Leninist period in terms of nation-building, I argue that we should also understand the Leninist experience in terms of nation-building.[1] As a starting point, I use the nation-building literature based on modernization theory developed by Karl Deutsch, Ernest Gellner, and Ernst Haas.[2] The logic of these theories is that nationalism is the natural accompaniment to industrialization.[3] Industrialization creates an increasingly complex economy, which, in order to function, requires a common idiom in which to communicate. Thus barriers to communication posed by existing local cultures and habits need to be broken down and replaced. As people are mobilized (a passive process in these theories that naturally accompanies industrialization, urbanization, education) they need to be assimilated into a new culture to substitute for the local ties and meanings of the village. This new system of meaning must provide enough cohesion "while people are being buffeted by the strains of modernization."[4]

I am using Haas's definition of nationalism: an ideology that rationalizes or gives meaning to a modernizing society. According to Haas, whatever political ideology is competing can be nationalist insofar as it represents who the nation ought to be and how to achieve that self-image.[5] National ideologies contain ideas about origin and history, membership, the proper types of political institutions, and economic organization. This definition allows us to consider in one category civic, ethnic, and Leninist versions of national ideologies.[6] In particular, it avoids the problems of defining nationalism in distinction to Marxism or liberalism.[7] It calls attention to the modern nature of national ideologies and helps focus on the process of making objective characteristics—individuals with similar language and history—subjective; this is what nation-building is about.

If we consider Leninism as a nation-building process, we can also escape thinking of the pre-Leninist nation-building process as the real one and what came later as imposed and tyrannical. While Leninism *was* imposed and tyrannical, it was not only that. The fact that it was both tyrannical and imperialist *and* a nation-building regime is what makes it so distinctive and useful to study. This last point also addresses the objection that Leninism in Eastern Europe was a system imposed from outside and dependent on the power and control of a foreign regime. The transformations were sufficient on a domestic level in each society where communism took hold that it is reasonable to think of them as nation-building processes insofar as they were oriented toward modernization and redefining the ideas on which society and institutions were based. In many cases, Leninist regimes were responsible for the process of industrialization.[8] Even in the places where there was a well-developed industrial base before the imposition of communist rule, like the Czech republic, the Leninist regime brought a political economy that imposed a great deal of social change, albeit one that distorted the process of industrialization.

Leninist regimes should also be seen as nation-building regimes because they went to great lengths to create new myths, and to instill these in society through the types of political socialization mechanisms we associate with modern nation-building.[9] The nation-building process is about substituting and instilling a new "high culture" in place of local cultures. In Leninist regimes this process of substitution varied depending on the strength of groups representing alternative high cultures at the time communist domination was established.

This theoretical approach to nation-building, with its roots in modernization theory, has been much criticized for its implicit assumption that the natural endpoint of modernization is Western liberalism, or civic nationalism. It has also been criticized for ignoring the continuing power of ethnicity.[10] However, we can avoid such problems if we do not assume that all societies are destined to become the United States, but rather look at the extent to which national ideologies succeed or fail at integrating or rationalizing societies. Without the teleology this approach is still helpful for orienting us to a starting point for the questions that I want to consider.[11] This literature will help show why historical consciousness is a useful way to understand the distinction between the two nation-building processes and between the elites who were formed by these processes.

Why Historical Consciousness?

By *historical consciousness* I mean that part of modern national ideologies that is about connection to either a group or a state that articulates a commonly shared narrative of important historical events. These can be founding myths, key moments in the group's evolution, or moments that are significant for the moral definition of the group. By *articulation* I mean a process of linking individual experience to a larger group meaning through education, ritual, commemoration, historiography. This process of giving objective events subjective meaning creates consciousness.

Historical consciousness was the means through which pre-Leninist national ideologies were kept intact, and it is precisely what distinguished dissident groupings from the rest of the elite and society. Dissent movements focused on the control of history as a central feature of these regimes. As Milan Šimečka wrote, consciousness was impossible without memory; if the state controlled memory, it controlled identity. Self-preservation was conceived as any attempt to maintain memory: "Nowhere in the world does history have such importance as in Eastern Europe."[12]

But what do we really mean by historical consciousness? How does it differ from other sources of ideas about the past such as family stories or ethnic stereotypes?

History

History is a fundamental part of national ideologies in three ways. First, history is the centerpiece of identity. Second, history has both a strategic and a unifying function. Third, history is the modern substitute for religion as the source of a group's perceptions about national uniqueness and origin.

By *history,* I mean an interpretation of events in terms of a larger narrative, not simply events that happen.[13] On a group level, this means a narrative that connects individuals to strangers who share the same experiences.[14] History, in this sense, is central to individual as well as to group identity. If identity means maintaining over time constant characteristics that make one unique, history is what establishes that continuity. Individuals and groups define themselves based on critical moments and how these fit together in a narrative that makes them understand their lives as meaningful or continuous or distinctive. National ideologies are, in essence, about origin and events of heroism or victimhood that make a group see itself as particular and different from others. Whether about an ancient and illustrious past or about a more recent event in the life of a national group, common interpretation of history is at the center of national ideology. Understandings of history also let groups know what they are not. Competing meanings of key historical events are at the heart of national conflict.

History serves as a glue, by uniting groups around a narrative that is meaningful. And it simultaneously has a strategic element: it offers a common framework for linking cause and effect, for making decisions with reference to past experience, and for judging the present in terms of the past.[15] This is why national history writing is a fundamental part of what takes an objective group of people to a subjective consciousness. The element of judgment makes history a different sort of component of national ideologies than is language, for example.

While history can be shared without sharing language, language without history does not provide the same bond. Common history can be preserved in a language other than the group's language, as in the example of émigrés. Shared and articulated meanings of history link territory and language, which are the constants of groups, to the life of a group on that territory, which changes over time.[16] Max Weber argues that the element of joint struggle for survival makes common history such an important part of national consciousness.[17]

Finally, history has a key role in *modern* national ideologies because it is the main secular substitute for religious systems of meaning. Many modern national ideologies use religion. However, nationalism substitutes common history for divine origin as a source of uniqueness. The role of history versus religion can be confusing in trying to sort out whether national ideologies should be considered modern. As authors like Gellner point out, the distinction between modern nationalisms and traditional systems of meaning has to do with a scientific rather than religious approach to understanding the world: Are certain facts privileged? Are certain phenomena not subject to investigation?[18] While civic nationalism, with its legal and scientific approach to reality, might be clearly identifiable as modern in this regard, other types of nationalism become more complicated. In ethnic nationalisms from the historicist tradition and in Leninism some ideas are privileged and not subject to investigation.[19] In the cases of ethnic nationalism and Leninism, as in all modern nationalisms, historians, rather than priests or figures with magical powers, are the source of ideas about history. But historians do not always use the scientific method; both these national ideologies use historians as the creators and guardians of a history to sustain a national myth.

One way to clarify this ambiguity is to look at the form or the source of authority for such historical accounts. The idiom of historical method is used in civic, ethnic (historicist), and Leninist ideology, and the authority for the accounts rests not with divine sources but with history itself. As Jowitt points out, in Leninist regimes the methods were distinctly modern but simultaneously gave the Party exclusive insight into the correct interpretation of all of social life.[20]

Consciousness

The distinction between a group of people in a simple descriptive sense, and a group that can be said to have a collective interest or identity, has to do with consciousness: the process through which a common frame of reference and evaluation comes to be shared. Thus objective interests or experiences must be given collective meaning. This does not happen automatically.

Consider an analogy to individual psychology. An individual can experience an event, but unless the individual articulates a meaning to the event in terms of a larger narrative, the event might be forgotten and have no lasting significance. Consciousness raising is the process through which a collection of similarly situated individuals are made to feel that they are a group and are motivated to act based on common ways of judging reality. This idea is important to the literatures on class consciousness and social movements, on nation-building and on elites. Once consciousness has been developed, these common standards of judgment substitute for previous bases of judging—either other group associations or narrow personal interest.[21]

This process of individuals becoming conscious as a group—particularly as a group other than the family or village group from which they came—has never been well understood. It is difficult to determine whether this group identity can be created through articulating meanings to common experiences alone, or whether its creation depends on a common crisis or struggle or on a charismatic leader or organization.[22] Here I am focusing primarily on articulation as playing the critical role in the development of consciousness, since this is what Leninist regimes so effectively blocked.[23] What makes Leninist regimes interesting to study, and useful for social scientific comparison, is that they were so effective at severing this link between objective interests or experiences and the meaning given to these experiences. If this link was cut, then we need to rethink the common argument that middle classes, because of their levels of urbanization, education, and alienation from the regime, automatically developed a cultural individualism. The disconnect between objective experience and consciousness also gives analysts a rare opportunity to ask questions such as the following: What makes local village or family stories into public memory or national ideology? What keeps this from happening? What happens in societies in which these local meanings and traditions are broken down but never reintegrated into a society-wide ideology?

What happens when elites are no different from society in this regard? I will discuss this more in the section on Leninist nation-building.

Historical Consciousness vs. Family Stories, Traditional Myths, and Ethnic Stereotypes

The concept of historical consciousness allows us to wade through common confusions in the literature on nationalism in another way as well. It allows us to emphasize the difference between a modern national ideology—civic or ethnic or Leninist—and local family stories, traditional ties, and tribal or ethnic stereotypes which are not linked to an ideology.

Traditional Myths and Family Stories

National ideologies differ from traditional myths about the past in two ways. First, as we have seen, they differ in origin and mode of transmission—religiously inspired and often orally transmitted versus secularly inspired and transmitted through education systems, political rhetoric, state commemoration, and military service. Second, they differ in frame of reference. Meanings of history in the village are local and specific and based on personal ties, though they stretch in time and space beyond immediate family experience. National ideologies are abstract and place individual stories within a standardized narrative shared by strangers from many different localities and even by immigrants from outside.

Nation-building aims at making national interpretations of history, rather than village or local stories, compelling. However, there are many examples, particularly in the early twentieth century, in which the substitution had not yet succeeded. Paul Connerton gives a good example of this in his book on collective memory.[24] He tells the story recounted by Carlo Levi in *Christ Stopped at Eboli* of an Italian village in the aftermath of World War I. Levi was in a southern Italian village as an exile in 1935. Although there was a commemorative plaque to those who had died and all families were fairly directly connected to the dead, nobody ever mentioned the war. The subject was not taboo. "When questioned on the matter they answered not only briefly but with indifference. They neither remembered the war as a remarkable event nor spoke of its dead." But they spoke of one war constantly—the war of the brigands, which had come to an end in 1865, seventy years earlier.[25] Very few were old enough to remember it but everyone spoke of it as if it were yesterday.[26]

This example demonstrates the distinction between local group memories and more abstract history associated with a nation state; it appears that national ideology and modernization had not yet broken down or substituted for local stories even though individuals had firsthand experience fighting for Italy and the state commemorated it. They lived in Italy, fought for Italy, but did not feel associated with a key event defined nationally as Italian.

The story of the southern Italian peasants also illustrates another point: the nation-building process needs to progress enough to win loyalty and elicit strong sentiments. It is only if you have an ideology and have been a product of a process through which a larger meaning is disseminated that you can place your village or family stories in this context. Thus all families might have experienced World War I, but memories would differ in a peasant family from a nationally conscious family. The same memento from the past, for example an old military uniform or medal, could have very different meanings. In one case it could have only personal significance; in the other it might have importance as part of a national narrative.

Both in the case of local traditional myths about the past and in the case of modern national ideologies, family stories are tied to larger interpretive contexts. But family stories can exist free of either traditional meanings or of modern ideologies. What if traditional meanings break down and new national ideologies do not substitute? Then we might have a situation more like that of Orwell's proles. They maintain relics of past myths but have lost the traditional interpretive context; the new modern one functions only to confuse and coerce but not to win loyalty. This is the condition in much of the communist world. While traditional meanings of the past were significantly eroded through the Leninist modernization process, the new Leninist ideology did not win loyalty, leaving only family stories as the source of information about the past. But family stories alone cannot function to integrate societies.

Ethnic Stereotypes
Ethnic stereotypes are one of the most common sources of ideas about the past and, like family stories, were preserved and even fostered by Leninist regimes. But it is critical to distinguish between them and historical consciousness. As opposed to family stories, ethnic stereotypes are shared. However, like family stories, they can exist free of either traditional myths or modern ideologies. An example might be the use of anti-Semitism by communist regimes. This was not linked to a national ideology and was more about mobilizing resentments than forging an ideology. What was left over was the odd phenomenon of anti-Semitism without Jews.[27] Eth-

nic stereotypes about Jews that exist, for example, in schoolyard rhymes in a society where the people using the rhymes no longer know what Jews are do not constitute national ideology.

The distinction between ethnic stereotypes and historical consciousness is most difficult to see in the case of ethnic nationalism. But even when these stereotypes exist in the language of the nation, for example, the idea that Hungarians have always persecuted Slovaks, these resentments need to be tied into a more cohesive national myth for it to count as ideology. While ethnic stereotypes are fodder for demagogues and groups can be mobilized to kill one another based simply on these stereotypes, they must be seen as distinct from national ideology, which plays the role of social glue so important for building and sustaining institutions.

Pre-Leninist Nation-Building and the Ideological Elites

To avoid the problems that have beset the return-of-history approach, it is important to look at the status of nation-building at the moment of the inception of communism and to trace continuity through the communist period. We must also look at where these alternative ideologies were carried in the face of communist attempts to destroy them.

Each East European country was at a different stage in the development of its modern sense of nationhood after World War II. However, the vast literature dedicated to nationalism in Eastern Europe, sometimes written by nationalist émigrés who were victims of communism, exaggerated the advancement of often limited and partial nation-building processes. All of these countries fit Gellner's "nation first, state second pathway" whereby intellectuals in submerged nations in the Hapsburg, Ottoman, or Russian empires began to revive cultures and build national movements within the imperial context with the goal of controlling their own states. Having developed new nationalisms as alternatives to the repressive dominant culture, these movements used them to mobilize those who were the losers in the industrialization process.[28] With the collapse of these empires, some of these movements gained control over states. Others, like Slovakia and Croatia, did so only in the context of World War II. Communist intelligentsias also mobilized in the face of the difficulties of industrialization, and they were at odds with nationalists during the interwar period.

This rather sketchy elaboration of the precommunist nation-building experience offers a guide to the types of questions that are relevant for assessing how far national development had progressed when communist regimes took power. To establish continuity we must ask: Was there a period of national statehood? What was the size of the nationally conscious intelligentsia? Was the intelligentsia split, for example, over World War II? How strong were institutions that embodied national consciousness? Had there been national socialization through schools? Had there been national history writing? To what extent had industrialization taken off? Were communist elites primarily from peasant backgrounds?

The way communism was imposed in each country also tells us something about how and where these precommunist national alternatives were preserved. The first step communist regimes took in each country was to try to eliminate alternative ideologies and institutions that could threaten total control by the Party. What did the communist regime succeed in destroying or co-opting? (For example, what happened to the church?) Were nationalist intelligentsias linked with the fascist regime or Nazi collaboration and thereby weakened by this association? To what extent were noncommunist intelligentsias integrated into the communist elite? To what extent were alternative strands of communism wiped out?

To understand continuity during communism, we also need to examine the small networks of dissent and semi-dissent as mechanisms of preservation. How strong and widespread were they? To what extent were they linked to the West? How isolated were they from one another? To what extent did they take risks to bring their ideas to the public?

Common meanings of history were articulated in the face of the extreme constraints of the regime and partially shaped by these constraints. Interestingly, these modern ideologies were passed on orally and in private through personal networks, methods more recognizable from traditional societies.[29] They were perpetuated through samizdat and links to Western émigrés and the efforts of Western governments. But these methods of preservation, and the fact that these ideas were not institutionalized and resided in weak networks of individuals, impaired the ability of the elites who represented continuity to act politically once communism fell.[30] Because of the way these small groups developed, they were cut off from a social base and from the socioeconomic process of development. In addition, these networks were often infiltrated by the regime, as were institutions that represented continuity like the churches and cultural organizations.

While the above discussion applies to both the civic and ethnic alternatives to communism that we see throughout the region, these alternatives have slightly different bases. The ethnic alternative was developed before the war, but the civic alternative, while also present to varying degrees in the precommunist period, often came from within the Left and from the disillusioned communist intelligentsia.[31] There was also an important nationalist alternative within communist parties; this nationalism is the focus of historical-institutional arguments, which we will examine in more detail below.

Leninist Nation-Building: The Dominant Process and the Mass-Elite

What about those who were not part of these alternative networks and were, instead, products of the communist regime's particular approach to modernization and nation-building? The utopian nature of communist regimes, in combination with a priority on maintaining power, meant that they were simultaneously coercive and transformative. They destroyed all competing political groups but, established as they were in countries with predominantly agricultural populations and weak national identities, they tried to re-create society from above. Through elaborate nation-building efforts they dominated the cultural accompaniment to modernization. While analysts have long known that communist ideology did not stick, they have conflated the regime's illegitimacy with its failure to keep alternatives from developing. Here I am suggesting that the regime was both illegitimate and successful at keeping alternatives ideologies from developing, thus leaving elites and societies informed only by family stories and driven by egoism. The nation-building literature will help us understand this result.

Masses who have been unhinged from traditional peasant cultures (or smaller groupings in a larger polity) have two choices. They can either assimilate into the new modern "high culture" or secede and develop an alternative high culture. In Albert Hirschman's terms, the choices are loyalty or exit.[32] Social unrest can arise when these minority groups can neither assimilate nor secede.[33]

In Leninist regimes, the new high culture does not successfully assimilate available masses, for reasons already suggested. But at the same time these masses cannot go back to their prior cultures of the village due to both industrialization and coercion. However, the reasons for this are quite different from those spelled out in the nation-building literature. Haas, in a typology of nation-building pathways, identifies an "African pathway" where individuals who have been mobilized but are not assimilated are unable to opt for the new high culture but cannot go back to their prior low cultures. Haas identifies two reasons for this. First, the multi-

plicity of incompatible low cultures would make a national polity meaningless. Second, even if the low cultures were less numerous, the problem
remains that the modernity of the new high culture is hard to reconcile
culturally with the tradition of the new "citizens."[34] In the Leninist nation-
building pathway the failure to integrate traditional populations is due to
the nature of the state or regime, a factor underemphasized in the nation-
building literature. The alternative high cultures that existed before communism are destroyed or severely limited by the Party. To the extent they
exist, the remaining low cultures are destroyed through collectivization,
which, according to Jowitt, leaves individuals further from village sociocultural alternatives than did other types of modernizing regimes, for example, in the third world.[35] In the African case, traditional society was left
more intact, and integration of the masses was difficult for that reason. In
communist societies, even though traditional society was destroyed, the
"newly mobilized" were not integrated.

We can use a slight twist on Hirschman's "exit, voice, or loyalty" to see
that Leninism presents us with a distinct model of nation-building. After
the Party loses its combat task, elites continue to be publicly loyal while
simultaneously exiting into the private sphere, since they do not believe in
the regime.[36] In Czechoslovakia, voice was precluded in 1968, when the
reform movement inside the Communist Party was crushed, and it was
difficult in the aftermath of the repression of the Prague Spring for the
Party to reclaim full loyalty of its members. However, there was no real
possibility for exit on a large scale either in the form of massive emigration
or in the formation of alternative political groups. The effect was that
individuals, including elites, were pushed into the private sphere. However, the reform movements, like Czechoslovakia's Prague Spring, were
often fragile and did not lead to continuity in politically relevant networks. Thus, though there was an exit into the private sphere, there was no
attempt to join with others to voice alternatives. This meant massive alienation from the Communist Party but no articulation of alternatives. Exit
did not mean the possibility for joining with others because the regime
was still effective at preventing alternative groupings from forming and
had already destroyed or weakened precommunist competitors. The process of "organized forgetting," which I will discuss below, contributed to a
lack of ability or even inclination for this alienation to translate into the
articulation of noncommunist ideologies. Society thus increasingly consisted simply of the individual families within it. The middle classes and
elites, the primary products of the Leninist nation-building process, were

left with only private interest as a motivating force. Of course the black market, which was encouraged by the regime, developed on a mass scale. But again, the possibilities for articulating alternative *meanings,* particularly in regime priority areas, like national versions of history alternative to the Leninist one, were effectively curtailed.[37]

If this is true, and alienation did not automatically imply resistance, then modernization theory's assumptions are also called into question.[38] Modernization theory assumes that individualism naturally evolves from increased levels of education and urbanization.[39] However, without the conscious articulation of alternative values, the cultural accompaniment to the processes of modernization was egoism, not individualism.[40] As we will see below, aggregate data on industrialization, urbanization, and education would show no difference between the mass-elite and the ideological elites. But once the lens is turned to the nature of the Leninist nation-building process, we see how misleading that aggregate picture can be.

Egoism and Dissimulation

What happened for elites produced by the regime who did not literally exit (by leaving the country or going into dissent) and who remained loyal in public but were simultaneously pushed into the private sphere? Ken Jowitt has characterized the public/private split that emerged as "dissimulation." Jowitt has described this problem both for elites and the new middle classes. Dissimulation is, according to Jowitt, "the conscious adaptation of false appearances."[41] It is based on fear, avoidance, and calculation of ways to keep an intrusive state out of one's private life. He talks about a "highly calculative and selective recognition of regime authority"; "this stance takes the form not so much of political opposition, as of a strong anti-political privatism in which family and personal interests are emphasized at the expense of regime and societal interests."[42] Dissimulation became the response to Leninist monopolization of the public sphere and failure to integrate society in slightly different ways for party elites and the broader educated classes. In the late Leninist period when the Party could no longer claim the loyalties of its own members, private interests became confused with public goals of the Party, leading to corruption. Outward public loyalty was a facade for private enrichment.[43] Thus the dominant approach was egoism.

The educated part of society who were not Party members, also key candidates for the elite once communism collapsed, tended to turn inward to private concerns as a response to the indignities of political and economic life. Different Leninist regimes took different strategies in exchanging some fulfillment of private pleasures for lack of public criticism. The end result here was also egoism.

Jowitt is most interested in pointing out that dissimulation fits culturally with traditional suspicion of public life in these societies.[44] Here I focus on how it created a practical problem in elite formation and reconstituting political communities in Leninism's aftermath. There are two practical implications of the egoism produced by Leninist regimes. First, individuals in the elites and the middle classes are connected to one another only for the purpose of pursuing private goods, not in the articulation of alternatives to regime ideology. Thus in the postcommunist period most of those who become the elite have no public identity, and when they do take on public identities they do so for reasons of individual private gain and they switch when necessary. Thus, even in the postcommunist period, they do not have a public self that is identifiable to others. It is difficult to trust or even to pin down the fleeting nature of public identifications. This theme will be explored at great length in chapters 6 and 7. Second, dissimulation meant that everyone was, in some sense, a collaborator in acquiescing to these methods of regime domination.[45] This also made trust—determining who was who—problematic after communism fell and was most evident in the efforts to punish collaborators with the former regime.

Organized Forgetting

The literature developed among dissidents in east central Europe in the 1970s and 1980s helps illuminate the link between the communist regime's approach to history, on the one hand, and dissimulation on the other. It suggests that what we saw after Stalinist terror abated was a more flexible and subtle version of totalitarianism.[46] Dissidents argue that the most important characteristic of the communist regime was its control of information and thus of independent activity and thought. Their writings are a useful reminder of the considerable efforts made by communist regimes to re-create histories and prevent alternatives from developing.

Dissident authors maintain that control of common socializing processes play the central role in regime power and legitimacy. They share this focus with the nation-building literature. But these writers argue that communist regimes went beyond the manipulation of history that characterizes socialization mechanisms in all modern regimes. As Leszek Kolakowski points out, this regime type was qualitatively different, a new civilization. The idea here, in Rupnick's paraphrase, is that we are not talking about white lies or half truths in which all politicians indulge but a Lie with a capital "L" which constitutes the very foundations of the political system. According to Rupnick, East European dissidents see two pillars of this system: destruction of memory and totalitarian language.[47]

George Orwell's *1984,* which these dissidents saw as a remarkably astute characterization of life under communism, explains the logic behind the first of these pillars. The Party needs to destroy memory for two reasons. First, what came before the onset of this regime is a link to an alternative world and alternative standards for judgment, which would include alternative historical narratives. Links to the West also need to be cut off for this reason. Second, the Party needs to be presented as infallible and to replace on a day-to-day basis information that might suggest otherwise.[48]

The destruction of memory is reinforced by the second pillar—totalitarian language—which extended to all realms of life and consisted of what one dissident called a "system of jamming information and memory."[49] The Party's incessant and falsified claims about history keep individuals from understanding themselves otherwise. They prevent groups from emerging with an alternative vision of who they are, and this is true as much for individual interest groups as for the whole society. The dissimulation and assault on the independent ability to judge becomes so numbing and atomizing that group identity ceases to have meaning. Individuals could not counter regime interpretations since they lost their ability to make critical judgments.

Milan Šimečka's writings are useful in understanding exactly how organized forgetting so undermined the formation of alternative ideologies within the communist context. Organized forgetting does not simply expunge historical events and information. Instead it works by constructing a new history that leaves out and distorts and, moreover, shifts in what is left out and distorted. As Šimečka points out, "Three generations witnessed a shift . . . in the interpretation of history so frequently, that they have become effectively immune to the moral aspects of history."[50] It is one thing to keep celebrating the same "fake" history. It is another to keep switching in which version is celebrated.

Another aspect of organized forgetting that kept alternatives from developing was that the entire sphere of history came to be viewed with skepticism. As Šimečka says, in childhood, this is generated in school; "in adulthood it is confirmed by enforced attendance at frequent celebrations of false history."[51] Even though people are alienated from official history, there is no room for or *inclination* to search for alternatives. Thus all but the most curious are left with no sense of history at all.[52]

So the very inclination to ask is eroded and even the more curious are unable to overcome the gaps—or as Šimečka calls them, "black holes"—the regime has created. Šimečka continues: "An ordinary person is helpless before them [the black holes] since unless he himself is a historian, he cannot by his own research fill those holes." Šimečka himself came to realize that he could not bridge the "black holes" since he was not even aware of them. He complains that those who are paid historians lack the courage; others lack the time.[53] Even if fear and numbness are overcome, the inaccessibility of information makes the development of historical consciousness nearly impossible.

Organized forgetting has a third critical dimension: those who remember or are repositories of information will not speak if they are not asked. But even if they are asked they might refuse to share information.[54] For a number of reasons, including fear and opportunities for social mobility, the generations who have a memory do not pass it on and the next generation has no incentive to listen. As time passes this dimension is more and more effective.[55]

Not only did these methods of presenting history confuse and alienate and make judgment difficult. As I will demonstrate, these twists and turns in interpretation of history were accompanied by changes in the people who constituted the elite. The process of organized forgetting was intertwined with the elite atomization that resulted from power struggles in the Party and its priority on political control rather than legitimacy.[56]

It is not difficult to see the phenomenon of egoism emerging from this type of situation. Šimečka sees human thought reduced to its present dimension whereby "an entire moral category, that of historical responsibility, will be erased from consciousness."[57] What Šimečka means here is that ties to a group based on any larger narrative of that group's life became irrelevant.[58] Nor was there any opportunity as a society to engage in any debate about the moral implications of their past in order to define a meaning for political community. If the past is never given meaning and its meaning is always being revised, there are no grounds for continuity in one's ties to either individual or group identity.

But the private sphere, even in the face of this lack of connection with a public ideology, does not provide resources for judgment. Information is lacking, as is the drive to find a larger identity beyond material interests.[59] What this leaves in the postcommunist period is not only individuals separated from one another or any set of political beliefs, but also individuals with no experience evaluating competing claims or the reliability of information.

What Kind of Elites?

Now that we understand the two nation-building pathways and their results, we must turn to the implications for postcommunism. What does it mean politically for the majority of the elite to have no historical consciousness? Why focus on this divide between elites and not others?

I choose the term *mass-elite* (in reference to Hannah Arendt's notion of masses) for two reasons. First, I am calling attention to the historical pathway that made them like a mass—cut off from one another and tied to neither traditional nor modern institutions. Second, I want to accentuate that this was an elite that was like a mass; elites are distinguished from masses ordinarily on the basis of power and on the basis of being qualified and oriented toward defining ideas about society. But this second distinction between elites and masses is not there in the postcommunist setting.

The implication drawn by Arendt, however, that there is a necessary link between the anomie of the masses and totalitarian movements is less clearly applicable to postcommunism and is not implicit in my use of the term *mass-elite*. For her, a mass refers to commonly situated individuals who might be difficult to integrate into any organization based on common interest—such as political parties, municipal governments, professional organizations, or trade unions—except through totalitarian means.[60] She saw the masses as available and having a desire to become fully absorbed in totalitarian movements.[61] Yet they did not identify themselves as a group: "The fact that with monotonous but abstract uniformity the same fate had befallen a mass of individuals did not prevent their judging themselves in terms of individual failure or the world in terms of specific injustice. This self-centered bitterness, however, although repeated again and again in individual isolation, was not a common bond despite its tendency to extinguish individual differences because it was based on no common interest, economic or social or political."[62] By contrast, whereas the mass-elites are anomic in the sense of lacking ideas to make them into a cohesive group, these individuals are not necessarily available. Their flexible and uncommitted behavior serves them well and it is not clear that this fluidity is an unstable state. In fact, interestingly, it might be the presence of group ties from the past that made Arendt's masses subject to totalitarian mobilization. This has been the main critique of her causal argument. William Sheridan Allen argues that it was the very complexity and density of associational life in Weimar Germany that made it possible for the Nazis to mobilize so effectively.[63] The scarcity of group ties and of independent organizations caused by communism might, in fact, prevent totalitarian mobilization.

The postcommunist setting is more like Robert Putnam's vision of southern Italy caught in a vicious Hobbesian circle—which is an equilibrium state—rather than available anomic masses or mass-elites.[64] What is absent in southern Italy—and, I am arguing, in postcommunist elites—is the social glue that he calls social capital, which creates reciprocity and trust.[65] As Jowitt put it, we can think of communist societies as being characterized by amoral urbanism: the urban equivalent of Edward Banfield's notion of "amoral familialism" for southern Italy.[66]

Something like social capital is supposed to be what nation-building creates, if not in all of society, at least in key groups like the elites. National myths are usually thought of as enabling elites to recognize one another, thereby fostering trust and reciprocity (the ability to make short-term sacrifices for long-term gains) and allowing elites to make common judgments.[67]

Ralf Dahrendorf's distinction between abstract and established elites is also useful.[68] While abstract elites have nothing uniting them except that they hold positions of power, similar socialization processes unite established elites, breeding trust and recognizability. This distinction does not have to do with political attitudes or interests, but rather with cohesion in a more fundamental sense. While Dahrendorf's categorization is useful for clarification, interestingly, in the communist world, common socialization contributed both to a similarity in style and recognizability but also to a fundamental atomization between elites. Certainly those who became the mass-elite had similar and uniform experiences of socialization during communism, as we will see in chapter 4. But while the communist socialization process created similar motivations, it happens that this motivation was egoism. Thus the mass-elite lacked the trust of Dahrendorf's established elites.[69]

Why *This* Divide between Elites?

The mass-elite as a type is difficult to characterize because absence is so central to its very definition. Needless to say, there are other forces besides historical consciousness that shape individuals even in Leninist societies where interest and identity groups were, for the most part, eliminated. The categorization I use here cuts along one key line: connection to a group that had historical consciousness or absence of those ties. The mass-elite ends up including, together in the same category, people with a variety of political traits: technocrats, those who are more corruptible, those with greater and lesser leadership abilities, those with stronger or weaker ties to the Communist Party.[70] But all of these other divides take for granted that some overall consensus exists about the nature of the political community. By looking at this divide I am trying to focus attention on the presence or absence of this more fundamental characteristic: do elites have national ideologies or do they not?

A final reason for making this distinction between elites is to question the assumptions of rational-choice theory that the short-term, self-interested actor can be found in all places at all times. Rational-choice theory, by assuming common motivations, never asks where preferences come from. If this question is never asked, it would not seem odd to have an elite of short-term opportunists untied to any political tradition or system of thought. I see the short-term, self-interested actor in postcommunist Eastern Europe as a product of an extreme historical institutional setting, not as a matter of course. And this absence raises the possibility that it will be difficult to build the "social capital" to escape Putnam's vicious circle.[71] This point will be developed more in the post-1989 part of the book.

The Historical-Institutional Argument

My argument focuses on one key historical institutional legacy of Leninism: the absence of historical consciousness. But as we saw in chapter 1, a more common argument about the origin of postcommunist nationalism focuses on a different historical institutional legacy of communist regimes. Historical-institutionalists are most concerned with the *existence* of postcommunist nations and the role of Soviet-style national institutions in producing these nations. I care more about the *strength or weakness* of these nationalisms and what this means for the ability of these societies to get through difficult transformations. Historical-institutionalists improve on the return-of-history argument by paying attention to cleavages and sociocultural realities created by the communist regime for its own purposes. But just as with arguments that assume continuity with the precommunist past, they are not always careful about specifying what kinds of ties to the past were perpetuated by communist institutions.

What follows is an example of the logic of this argument:

Soviet nationality policy, despite its professed goal of subverting ethnic loyalties and destroying ethnic differences, promoted and accelerated the process of nation-building. During the Soviet period various populations, which had not previously developed national consciousness, acquired national identities and turned into nations. The Soviet state erected virtually impenetrable barriers between the different nationalities and by way of bureaucratic means tied individuals to their national groups. National cohesion was further reinforced by the creation of firm links between nationalities, their territories, and their political administrations.[72]

This argument is also made for Yugoslavia and Czechoslovakia.[73] Institutions that were designed to be "nationalist in form and socialist in content" through unintended consequences gave nationalism the chance to take on a life of its own. This nationalism remained when communism collapsed. Former communists could easily make the shift from an implicit to an explicit nationalist ideology given the compatibility of the ideologies and availability of ideas. The ideas come from a nationalist intelligentsia that turned out to be socialist in form and nationalist in content rather than the other way around.

The historical-institutional argument exists in a weaker and a stronger form. In its weaker form, it is not too different from the perspective taken here. That is, once communism collapsed, national institutions were available to elites, who might or might not have had national identities and who appealed to societies (or did not) based on any number of messages including a national one. This is an argument about disintegration and the form disintegration took. It addresses questions such as: Why a peaceful breakup in some cases and ethnic violence in others? Why necessarily nationalism or the nation state as a format?[74]

In its strong form, as argued by Rogers Brubaker, and, to some extent by Zaslavsky, communist institutions actually were fundamental in not just structuring but in *constituting* identities. Something more lasting was left over and was politically significant once communism collapsed.[75] Not just intellectuals in academies of sciences but also elites shared the national ideologies generated by communist institutions.

A Critique of Historical Institutionalism

There are several dimensions to the counterargument I offer to this stronger form of the historical-institutional argument. First, in its stronger form, this argument focuses on some institutional legacies and not others. It explicitly ignores terror and atomization and the processes of organized forgetting that were so central to these regimes. While national institutions might exist, it still might be that the people in them are driven by egoism, and are unlikely to be long committed to the identities behind those institutions.[76]

The argument also fails to distinguish between those nationalists who were products of dissent and those who were former communists.[77] This distinction allows us to see the possible weakness of the nationalisms mobilized and developed by the mass-elite. As Brubaker himself argues, we need to be looking at the process of creating nations to fill the states that were inherited from the collapse of communism.[78] But I would argue that it is difficult to understand the nature of this process by looking only at the nature of citizenship laws and minority policies. Indeed, given the types of elites and societies that continue to exist in these new nation-states, these new institutions and policies are often ephemeral.

The distinction made earlier between national ideologies and ethnic stereotypes is again important here. Often the "reproduction of ethnicity" during the communist period is seen to have arisen from the regime's perpetuation of ethnic stereotypes and ethnic dances. What the regime did in public was to develop folk or traditional culture. But ethnic dance and folk culture does not constitute a basis for political community even if these activities did have more than recreational significance during the communist period and served some sort of community-forming role. This folk culture was not integrated into a meaningful narrative of who the national community was. The regime also perpetuated ethnic stereotypes such as anti-Semitism. But ethnic stereotypes can exist in any number of types of societies and contexts, as mentioned above, and, like family stories, do not add up to or constitute national ideologies.

Conclusion

The divide between elites over historical consciousness is critical to understanding postcommunist politics. I see postcommunist elites (and societies) as products of two types of nation-building processes. These processes can be distinguished analytically even though they are, in fact, intertwined and affect one another. One represented continuity with precommunist nation-building and the ideological cleavages of the past. The other, a Leninist nation-building process, produced a mass-elite, without historical consciousness.

This conceptualization helps disentangle some of the key confusions that have plagued analysis of postcommunist politics. Rather than seeing emerging trends in postcommunist politics as a continuity with what these countries' fates otherwise would have been, or viewing post-1989 developments as beginning from scratch, we need to look more closely at how communism combined with national trajectories—how it selectively destroyed and preserved—to produce the types of political groupings we can observe in communism's aftermath.

The phrase "return of history" was widely used and dominated the framing of post-1989 transformations. But what got lost is a more careful discussion of which aspects of the post-1989 period can be understood as having returned from the precommunist past, and which aspects might be a product of the communist regime. Even if we agree that *something* returned from the past once Communist Party control was lifted, there continues to be confusion about what has returned. Is it ethnic hatreds that are returning? Is it family stories? Or is it society-wide ideologies that had a broad-based hold over individuals' loyalties and which could easily become the ideas around which societies could be reorganized? Once we distinguish between ethnic hatreds, family stories, and national ideologies, we still need to ask whether *Leninism* reinforced or produced them. We need to ask where these ideologies or hatreds resided during communism. And we need to ask how they were preserved or reproduced.

3   Weak Nationalism in Slovakia:
The Precommunist Period

We now turn to Slovakia as an emblematic case. While surely nation-building took place before World War II, Slovak national consciousness was extremely fragile and underdeveloped when the communist regime came to power.[1] Thus communist nation-building had particularly pronounced effects, owing to a combination of circumstances. Slovakia remained a largely agricultural society until 1948, modernizing only within the communist context. The nation-building that began before the First Czechoslovak Republic, established in 1918, was weakened by Hungarian assimilationist policies and remained limited to a small elite. Although this process expanded during the 1918–38 period, nation-building was still in an embryonic stage. Slovakia's main precommunist period of nation-building, including its only period of self-administration, was in the context of the wartime fascist state. Thus the communist regime had added license to destroy the key national institutions, like the Catholic Church and the Matica Slovenská, and members of the nationally conscious elite and intelligentsia, all of which were tainted by collaboration with the Nazis.[2] Most of those who became the elites after 1948 flowed directly from peasant and worker backgrounds, with weak national consciousness, into the communist socialization process.

Assessing the Level of Precommunist National Development

Slovak National Intelligentsia before 1918

Before 1918, Slovakia had a tiny national intelligentsia. As we saw in chapter 2, Slovakia fit the typical pathway of national development in the Hapsburg empire in which a national intelligentsia developed first through a cultural revival and only later tried to establish statehood. The first evidence of a national revival in Slovakia can be found in the late eighteenth century. At that time a handful of intellectuals surrounding Anton Bernolák, partly motivated by an effort to educate the peasants who spoke a variety of dialects, first tried, and failed, to codify a Slovak language.[3] Lutheran teacher Ľudovít Štúr tried again in the middle of the nineteenth century and succeeded. By then, there was a slowly developing nationalist movement, mostly Lutheran and influenced by German romanticism, which began to have political aspirations beyond the cultural and language focus of the earlier group. In 1848, about fifty nationally conscious Slovaks adopted the "demands of the Slovak nation," calling for the establishment of public schools and for other symbols of autonomy. By 1869, the first of three newly established Slovak gymnasia graduated students. Matica Slovenská, the Slovak cultural foundation, was set up in 1863 with the mission of spreading national consciousness to the population. However, with increasing efforts on the part of the ruling Hungarians to assimilate ethnic minorities and thus "Magyarize" all culture, the schools were closed five years later, as was the cultural foundation.[4]

The combination of the pressure of Magyarization and the fact that the sheer numbers were small due to the level of industrialization meant that the Slovak national intelligentsia remained of limited influence before the establishment of Czechoslovakia in 1918. It is important to keep in mind that Slovakia was comprised mostly of peasants. Germans and Jews dominated industry and commerce. Hungarians primarily, but also Germans and Jews, were heavily represented in professional and public positions. In 1910, taking the ethnic distribution of labor into account, 72 percent of ethnic Slovaks worked in agriculture.[5] Census respondents in 1920 were more likely to offer regional or religious self-identifications than national.[6] Even Slovaks with higher education, such as the 1.9 percent who were state employees or professionals in 1910, could not be assumed to be nationally conscious, since higher education came at the cost of Magyarization.[7] The numbers are telling: out of a population of approximately two million ethnic Slovaks the number of nationally Slovak intelligentsia in 1918 is generally thought to be between five hundred and one thousand people.[8]

The condition that is reflected in the above numbers can be contrasted with the Czech national intelligentsia. As opposed to the largely agricultural population in Slovakia, where industrialization did not begin until the late nineteenth century, only 39 percent of Czechs were employed in agriculture in 1910, and 12.3 percent (as opposed to the Slovak 1.9 percent) were in the professions and state service.[9] Although the Czechs did not have a state until 1918, conditions were different in the Austrian part of the empire. The Czech national movement had grown during the nineteenth century and had developed a Czech-language education system as well as an extensive network of civic organizations. Czechs had also acquired jobs in state administration and government, making them better prepared to take on these positions in 1918.[10]

Compounding the effects of the small numbers of Slovak intelligentsia and the predominant peasant population without national consciousness, the Slovak intelligentsia tended to be rural and was comprised mostly of clergymen, doctors, and lawyers. The urban intelligentsia was generally not Slovak, as the cities were populated mostly by Hungarians, Germans, and Jews.[11] There was thus a geographical element in the weakness of Slovak national consciousness; the Slovaks were "a nation of peasants dispersed over the valleys and basins of the Carpathian mountains . . . [and] this lack of a Slovak urban center hindered Slovak cultural, economic and political development."[12]

The comparison with the more advanced Czechs is also telling politically. The Slovaks joined with the Czechs when the opportunity arose at the end of World War I with the collapse of the Austro-Hungarian empire. They were brought together by common Slavic culture. But more important, the formation of the state met a common security interest in the face of the surrounding states of Hungary and Germany. It was an attempt to right the population balance in both regions between Slavs and minority German and Hungarian populations. While the history of Czech-Slovak relations can be found elsewhere, it is important to realize that the Slovaks entered the union with the Czechs in a position of weaker national development and less advanced industrialization. While the attempt to create a new Czechoslovak identity was not repressive, as Magyarization had been, it did dilute efforts to build a purely Slovak national consciousness now that Hungarian domination was over. The Slovak intelligentsia was divided between those oriented toward a more ethnic Slovak ideology and a more civic Czechoslovak ideology.[13]

Slovak National Consciousness, 1918–1945: A Mixed Picture

There were certainly not, in 1918, enough Slovaks with administrative experience or education to run a modern state, and thus Czechs were brought in to fulfill these functions. However, the years of the First Republic and the period of the Slovak state brought increasing education for Slovaks, the development of Slovak culture through the Matica Slovenská, and finally, during the period of the wartime state, the experience of self administration.

Education and Cultural Development
The Czechs became particularly involved in staffing the schools.[14] Basic literacy rates were high, even going into the First Republic: 82.5 percent in 1921.[15] However, a comparison of levels of education between Czechs and Slovaks is revealing: in 1920 almost twice as many Czechs had finished secondary education as had Slovaks.[16]

Many more Slovaks were educated during the First Republic than earlier, but for example, the first Slovak technical university did not open until 1938. As Johnson points out, national socialization came more from secondary schools than from university education.[17] Comenius University had three faculties and began accepting graduates of gymnasia in 1921. But neither its faculty nor its student body was predominantly Slovak.[18] There were also two theological faculties.[19] Even given the greater tendency for Slovaks to receive higher education during this period, the state authorities in Prague did not see the need to educate Slovaks at all levels and in all fields. One of the reasons for the lack of a Slovak technical university was the assumption that enough people were being educated in those fields in Bohemia and Moravia.[20]

The university system was "Slovakized" during the period of independent statehood. For example, according to Stanislav Kirschbaum, by 1943 more than twice as many students were enrolled in Slovak institutions of higher learning than in 1938. School curricula were changed to reflect the Catholic nationalist ideology of the regime. It was only with the coming of the communist regime that the educational system at the university level really expanded.

Cultural development also took place during the years of the First Republic when the Matica Slovenská expanded its network of local branches aimed at raising national consciousness. The research divisions of the organization, which included research into history, culture, and even science, provided the information that its local organizations propagated.[21] The organization was politicized after 1932 when it began to be controlled by the nationalist Slovak People's Party.[22] As with educational institutions, during the period of the Slovak state the modernization of the publication facilities of Matica Slovenská gave added momentum to scientific and literary work.[23] A Slovak Academy of Arts and Sciences was founded in the 1939–45 period; after being ideologically cleansed of its nationalist content, this institution was expanded under the communist regime.

Self Administration and Elite Building

The period of the First Czechoslovak Republic also gave Slovaks more opportunity to serve in administrative positions even though Czechs clearly dominated those posts. Political experience developed through party politics in the only democracy in East Central Europe. Slovak elites were divided between those favoring Slovak autonomy and those oriented more toward Czechoslovakia. A spectrum of ideologies were represented from the nationalist/populist right—the Slovak People's Party, which later became the Hlinka Slovak People's Party (HSLS) and ruled the wartime Slovak state—to the communists on the left. In the middle were the Social Democrats and the Agrarians, who were clearly in favor of maintaining Czechoslovakia.

Two important developments occurred during World War II. First, politics was dominated by the HSLS and other parties were eliminated or absorbed. Second, the 1939–45 period, in spite of the status as a Nazi puppet state, gave educated Slovaks their first opportunity for self-administration. Even those who opposed the state grant this development. Gustáv Husák, in a frequently cited comment, wrote that in spite of Czechoslovakia's position as Nazi puppet state, and the fact that a war was going on, this period of self-administration played an enormous role in the development of Slovak national consciousness.[24] According to Stanislav Kirschbaum, positions in state and other organizations previously filled by Czechs were now open to Slovaks.[25] The Slovak National Uprising was also important in Slovak elite formation.[26]

Catholic and Lutheran Churches

The Catholic and Lutheran churches, particularly the Catholic Church, were critical both to the formation of the nationally conscious intelligentsia and to the development of popular national consciousness. The Catholic Church, in spite of communist persecution, remained the key institution that preserved continuity with the precommunist nation-building process into the postcommunist period. In the nineteenth and early twentieth centuries the largest number of nationally conscious Slovaks were Lutherans, while the Catholic priests tended to identify with Hungary.[27] However, the population of Slovakia was predominantly Catholic. In 1921 71 percent of the population was Roman Catholic and 12.8 percent Lutheran.[28] Catholics began to play the more significant role in the interwar nationalist movement led by Catholic priest, Andrej Hlinka. Becoming the village priest was a mode of mobility for talented children of peasants. During the period of Hungarian domination the Catholic Church was one of the main institutions promoting Magyarization. Later, Catholic priests tended to be a key part of the Slovak nationalist intelligentsia.[29] Both clergies were opposed to secularization and thus to the Czechoslovak state building process.[30] There were nationalist parties during the period of the First Republic associated with both Catholics and Lutherans. However, the Lutherans are generally seen to have been more closely associated with the Czechs, another divide that weakened the Slovak elite.

National History Writing

As we saw in chapter 2, a key element of modern nation-building is the writing of national history. History books and particularly textbooks are an important source of historical consciousness. However, the Slovaks had no historian like František Palacký, who wrote a history for the Czechs that "had a profound impact at a crucial moment in their national development in the nineteenth century." The Slovaks did not have "historians of equal stature until well into the twentieth."[31] In fact, it was only under the communist regime that the process of national history writing really developed, though two journals were started during the Slovak State: *Historika Slováka,* started in 1942 by the Slovak Academic Society, and *Historický Sbornik,* started by the historical section of Matica Slovenská in 1943.[32] When the communists came to power the writing of the history of the First Republic and before had hardly begun. Certainly no history had been written of World War II.[33]

In addition, this lack of scholarly articulation of what constituted national history was exacerbated by a dearth of sociological and historical records. Historical accounts written before 1938 did not rely on archival material, which was not available yet.[34] The Slovak archival system did not exist until 1945.[35] According to Johnson, statistics were scarce and often unreliable and Czech and Slovak statistics were not separated from one another.[36] Sociology as a field was also underdeveloped before the war.[37] The weakness of the fields of history and sociology continued into the communist period when they fell under Party control. These two fields, critical to the self-knowledge of a society, hardly existed in Slovakia.

Popular Consciousness

Popular consciousness of any modern national ideology was almost non-existent before 1918. But this changed in the context of the modernization and nation-building process of the First Republic and of the Slovak state. The work of Matica Slovenská, which by the 1930s reached a significant proportion of the population, and the Catholic Church were key mechanisms of building popular consciousness.[38]

Much of the population was oriented toward ethnic, not civic or leftist, parties. The dominance by the Czechs in the First Republic, the rapid social change that accompanied modernization and state building, and the economic difficulties in the global economy during this period all contributed to increasing support for the nationalists.[39] The nationalists of the Slovak People's Party, also known as *l'udáks,* argued that Czechs were responsible for the economic troubles of the Slovaks and for the destruction of Slovak religious life. They also blamed Jews and Hungarians for dominance in the economy. The People's Party was the only one clearly arguing for Slovak autonomy during those years and went from 17.6 percent of the vote in 1920 to 34.3 percent in 1925 and 30.1 percent in 1935. The Slovak National Party, the oldest party in Slovakia, also had a nationalist agenda but was much smaller.[40] Up to one-third of the population voted for the HSLS and other nationally oriented parties.[41]

The wartime state and participation in the Slovak National Uprising were also experiences that would have contributed to the building of popular consciousness. After the war, the population remained supportive of the Tiso regime, particularly through loyalty to the Catholic Church. The Democratic Party, a catchall party that worked to incorporate former HSLS members and to reach out to the Catholic Church, received the most electoral support. However, most of the population was still employed in agriculture. The systematic destruction or co-optation of the elite and intelligentsia, and the all-encompassing communist nation-building process, easily eroded the weak national consciousness developed before and during the war.

Destruction, Co-optation, and Nation-Building

After the war, the Communist Party was poised to rise, given its role in the National Uprising and the Soviet Union's role in the liberation of Czechoslovakia from the Nazis and the continuing presence of Soviet troops.[42] Other parties were severely weakened. They were discredited as fascist collaborators, or by the disillusionment connected with the Western powers' abandonment of Czechoslovakia in the 1938 Munich agreement and the fall of the First Republic. Noncommunist elites were further weakened because they were divided over the war between those who supported the

Slovak state and those who opposed it (as evidenced by the later divide in emigration). The communists played a significant role in the post-victory coalition government. This was particularly true in the Czech lands, where the Communist Party won 40.1 percent of the vote in the 1946 elections. In Slovakia the communists won 30.4 percent, while the Democratic Party won 62 percent of the vote.[43]

All parties were involved in the efforts to punish fascist collaborators, though there was disagreement about the approach that should be taken, particularly to Jozef Tiso. The communists were active in the implementation of the "Beneš decrees" (Eduard Beneš was president of Czechoslovakia) set up to punish fascist collaborators. These included the expulsion and redistribution of the property of the Sudeten Germans and the Slovak Hungarians. Together with other parties, the Communist Party was quite successful at breaking the political links to the Slovak state through the retribution trials.[44] The HSLS was banned. The top party leaders were tried, imprisoned, and in some cases executed. Others escaped behind the retreating German troops.[45] The central figures in the cultural intelligentsia also emigrated, due to their links with the fascist regime. This made it easy to severely limit the power of the remaining supporters of the HSLS—both government and cultural figures. František Mikloško cites the example of a movement called the White Legion, mostly comprised of Catholics, which emerged from the Hlinka Youth in Bratislava at the end of the war when it became clear the Slovak state would not survive. Its mission was "to look after Slovak interests after the war."[46] Members of this group were put in a labor camp (even before the formal takeover by the communists) for attacks on monuments to the Soviet army and for opposing Tiso's execution.[47] Three key leaders of the White Legion were executed in 1949. Others from this group were sent to prison or to the Jáchymov uranium mines.[48]

Slovak society and elites continued to be divided after the war, with supporters of the Slovak state still having a significant amount of influence in politics.[49] Once the communists came to power they destroyed the key bases for these sentiments: the Catholic Church and the Democratic Party.[50]

Attacks on the church were easier because of its association with the fascist regime, which was run by Catholic clergymen. When the Communist Party took over, the church was declared the most dangerous enemy of the new regime due to its association with fascism.[51] Buildings were confiscated, orders were issued forbidding priests to work, Catholic magazines were closed, and associations were not allowed to continue functioning.[52] According to Mikloško there was quite a bit of resistance against the communist suppression of the church and many were arrested during those years.[53] By 1951, the church leadership had been suppressed. This institution, arguably the most important bearer of Slovak national consciousness, was effectively weakened. It would later become the source of nationalist dissent, as we will see in chapter 4.

The Democratic Party of Slovakia, which received a majority of votes in the 1946 election, is a more complicated case. It brought together resistance fighters who were noncommunist and civic minded and simultaneously it was actively trying to attract former members of the Hlinka Slovak People's Party.[54] The Democratic Party showed greater leniency toward Slovak state leaders in part to increase their support from the Catholic part of population. Many lower-level members and officials were prime candidates for recruitment not only for the Democratic Party but also for the Communist Party.[55]

While it is impossible to get any reliable data on the extent to which important or active fascists (i.e., members of the Hlinka Guard, the Slovak equivalent to the SS) were lured into Communist Party positions, using their tainted pasts as an extra guarantee of loyalty, it is generally accepted that this must have happened. In almost every account of these years, and in interviews conducted by this author, it is claimed that people who were known to be fascists often became important and loyal communists.[56]

The communists built a strong case against the Democratic Party in propaganda exploiting that party's recruitment of former HSLS members, their opposition to the execution of Tiso, their pact with the Catholic clergy granting Catholics key state positions, and an alleged connection with an underground fascist organization.[57] Once the Communist Party came to power, there was a crackdown on the leaders of the Democratic Party and most went into exile.[58]

After destroying institutions which could have been centers of alternative ideologies, as part of its own nation-building process the regime went about quickly co-opting and even expanding cultural and educational institutions.[59] This was true in the case of Matica Slovenská, which had benefited during the Slovak state. The communists now portrayed it as an institution still supportive of "bourgeois national" ideas. The regime brought it under its control and Matica began to publish only ideologically appropriate articles in its newspaper and journals.[60] In 1954, its activities were severely curtailed. It began to operate simply as a library and ceased to be a research organization that disseminated information and spread Slovak national consciousness.[61] It reemerged briefly in 1968 only to be repressed again several years later.

The communist regime also quickly put history writing and education at the service of its socialization of new elites. In 1948 it removed the major figure in Slovak historiography, Daniel Rapant, from the chairmanship of the Slovak Historical Society, established in 1946. During the next years, the action committee of communist historians oversaw a purge process, which removed students and professors for ideological reasons. The two journals set up during the Slovak state were closed and replaced in 1953 by *Historický Časopis* from the Historical Institute of the Academy of Sciences.[62] The writing of twentieth-century Slovak history and the history of World War II happened under communist control; this process is presented in great detail in chapter 5.[63]

Conclusion

Modernization and nation-building took off under the communist regime, continuing and expanding the process that had begun during the First Republic and the Slovak state. In 1949, 1.94 percent of the population aged 20 to 29 were in higher education. By 1980 that percentage had increased to 8.76 percent.[64] In 1948, 59.8 percent of the Slovak labor force worked in agriculture and 21.3 percent in industry and construction. By 1987, 13 percent were employed in agriculture and 44.3 percent in industry and construction.[65] While the Slovak intelligentsia and elite expanded during the period of the First Republic, and particularly during the period of the Slovak state, the numbers were still small when communism began in 1948, even without the destruction of noncommunist elites. Most of those who became the elites after 1948 came from peasant and worker backgrounds and were formed only by the communist socialization process. The weak national consciousness that had developed in the nonintelligentsia parts of the population before 1948 would not necessarily have been carried to the next generation.[66]

Interestingly, the coming of communism and communist modernization brought with it opportunities for upward mobility not only because of the modernization but on an ethnic basis as well; opportunities opened for Slovaks to fill positions now vacated due to the change in ethnic composition brought about by the war. After the war the percentage of Jews, Hungarians, Czechs, and Germans had all diminished significantly in Slovakia. The Slovak percentage of the population went from 67.6 percent in 1930 to 86.6 percent in 1950.[67]

4 Islands of History: The Democrats and Nationalists

Although the communist regime successfully eradicated alternative ideologies in the years following 1948, small strands survived and developed
in the next fifty years that represented continuity with precommunist
nation-building. Most obviously, the past was preserved in émigré groups,
which could freely maintain their ideology and ideas in the democratic
societies of the West. Inside Slovakia, precommunist ideologies and noncommunist historical consciousness could be found only in the Catholic
nationalists, who founded the Christian Democratic Movement (KDH) after
1989, and the democrats, who comprised the core of Public Against Violence (VPN). Both nationalists and democrats were often from families who
already had ideologies formed before communism.[1] These families were
more likely to have had prewar books or other sources of information at
home or contacts to the West.

But even these groups, which were more connected to ideology than the
rest of the elite and society, were weak and diffuse and cut off from one
another. Modern national ideologies were preserved through people, not
institutions. The methods they used to retain ideology in the difficult
atmosphere of opposition to the communist regime impaired their ability
to function in the postcommunist period. They did not realize that they
alone had withstood the effects of the Leninist nation-building process.

Because escape from the dominant socialization process was possible
only under unusual circumstances, connection to groups articulating alternative ideologies can be best demonstrated through personal biography.
(This is primarily true for those in the communist context, not in emigration.) Aggregate data, for example the number of Slovaks who considered

themselves Catholic, would not indicate such connections since it was only through discussing noncommunist ideas with others that historical consciousness could be developed or passed on. At the same time, because records were not kept for fear of punishment by the regime, and because connection to alternative networks was so diffuse, it is difficult to establish continuity. The fact that national ideologies were preserved through personal ties and often transmitted orally also had important implications for political effectiveness after communism fell.

The Nationalists

Both the Catholic nationalists in Slovakia and the nationalist émigrés abroad defined themselves in opposition to the communist regime. They saw this regime as a totalitarian state that repressed the history and culture of Slovakia. Both groups, in different ways, were isolated in their commitments. Both were small, weak groups that engendered preservation of the precommunist Slovak nation-building process. Both tried to redeem the period of the World War II Slovak state and to make it a usable part of Slovak history, the émigrés more for national reasons and the Catholic nationalists more for religious reasons.

Catholic Nationalists in Slovakia

The Catholic nationalists were the only group inside communist Slovakia that preserved an ideology favorable to the wartime Slovak state. It was partly in response to the communist regime's framing of the danger they presented—as "clerico-fascists"—that kept the memory of the national side alive, at least for the younger generation.[2] While many people had family stories from that period—"my son fought on the eastern front," or such bits and pieces as "the economy was like Switzerland," or "Slovaks saved Jews"—the Catholic nationalists integrated these stories into a national ideology.

This was the case, for example, for the Čarnogurský family. The father, Pavol Čarnogurský, born in 1908, was a member of parliament during the wartime Slovak state and a clear bearer of national ideology at the time of World War II. The sons, Ivan Čarnogurský and particularly Ján Čarnogurský, were both important in postcommunist politics.[3] Ján Čarnogurský was the leader of the KDH, founded in February 1990; he later became Slovak prime minister in April 1991 and served in that post until the elections of June 1992.[4] The Čarnogurský family was one of the few with such a clear multigenerational profile, since most of the leadership of the wartime state left or were imprisoned and their families did not carry on a legacy of historical consciousness. This family, largely for accidental reasons that had to do with the relationship between Pavol Čarnogurský and Gustáv Husák, was allowed to return to the mainstream and the sons were allowed to go to a university.[5]

A second case is Bishop Ján Korec, born in 1924. He was not directly connected to the Slovak state but was imprisoned during the early 1960s on charges of "clerico-fascism." He was the founder of the secret church and was one of the major figures articulating the anticommunist Catholic nationalist ideology, though he maintained the clergy's traditional separation from politics and was not active in KDH after 1989.

František Mikloško also had roots in the secret Catholic Church. After 1989 he first joined Public Against Violence but moved to KDH in the winter of 1992. He held several different positions in the Slovak parliament.[6]

Ján Klepáč, until 1992, was one of the leaders of KDH. In February 1992 he became the leader of a more nationalist wing which broke off and called itself SKDH (Slovak Christian Democratic Movement). He was vice-chairman of the Slovak parliament until 1992. I will also use several examples from the stories of other key figures, for example Viliam Oberhauser, who was part of the KDH leadership and followed Klepáč when the more radical wing broke off but was not associated with Catholic dissent during the communist period.

These individuals in the KDH leadership vary in their antiregime commitments. Ján Čarnogurský, Korec, and Mikloško were among the few dissidents in Slovakia. Klepáč had been part of the secret church since 1971. His house had been used as a station that received and distributed samizdat, but he was not an activist on the same scale as the first three.[7] Oberhauser was never part of the secret church and was brought into the leadership of KDH because of the party's need for specialists.[8]

Continuity with Interwar Nation-Building

Pavol Čarnogurský was not very important in post-1989 politics, but it was through him that the continuity with the interwar nation-building process was carried. He was born in 1908, was a member of parliament during the wartime Slovak state, and was active in the Slovak People's Party before the war as a journalist. That party, founded in 1905 by Andrej Hlinka during a period of Hungarian repression, reemerged in post-1918 Czechoslovakia as the advocate of Slovak interests in the common state and, in particular, of Catholicism in opposition to the secularization represented by the modernizing orientation of the new Czechoslovak state. This issue was what Pavol Čarnogurský said politicized him as a student at the gymnasium.[9] The Slovak People's Party, a populist Catholic nationalist party whose slogan was "for God and Nation," gradually gained electoral support in the period before World War II. This party, which after Hlinka's death in 1938 was renamed the Hlinka Slovak People's Party (HSLS) became more radical and turned fascist as it moved into the Nazi sphere of influence.

Pavol Čarnogurský's pathway is typical for the Catholic intelligentsia that comprised the leadership of that party. He was a teacher (most were teachers and priests) and studied law and eventually had a key editorial position at *Slovák,* the party's newspaper.[10] Čarnogurský entered politics through the Catholic youth organization and became its general secretary from 1935. After the Munich agreement at the end of September 1938, when the Western powers granted Hitler control of the Sudetenland in the hope of appeasing his expansionist aspirations, that party centralized power as it presided over the new autonomous Slovakia. Čarnogurský was placed in an important position in the ministry of education. On March 14, 1939, one day after the Germans entered the Czech Republic, an independent Slovak state was declared. In a book on the sequence of events leading to that decision, Pavol Čarnogurský argues, as many do, that the HSLS leadership, in buying independence in exchange for collaboration, chose the lesser of several evils that included occupation or dismemberment among surrounding powers.

Čarnogurský's life and choices also embody the dilemmas of the wartime state and its legacy.[11] We will examine some of the ambiguities of this state and the figure of Jozef Tiso below. But for now, the point is that Čarnogurský was associated with this party and that he is the means through which continuity can be established between the prewar nationalist movement and post-1989 Slovakia.

The Repressive 1950s

The postwar retribution process and the communist regime almost completely broke the links to the wartime state. Its leadership and intelligentsia went into exile or to prison. Pavol Čarnogurský himself was imprisoned and lived in internal exile throughout the 1950s and 60s. Others associated with that state were imprisoned until the 1960s. The Catholic Church was severely repressed and its leadership imprisoned. Many supporters of the Slovak state abandoned their ideology, which in many cases was weak anyway, and tried to blend in or, as for Viliam Oberhauser's family, were subjected to minor harassment.[12]

De-Stalinization came late to Czechoslovakia, with trials against fascist collaborators continuing into the 1960s. For example, in 1962 there was a trial against the "Edelweiss affair," an attempt by students associated with the Slovak state to preserve its ideas. It was generally seen as a show trial with trumped up charges.[13] There was also a 1958 trial of Hlinka Guard members.[14]

After several amnesties in the early 1960s, and the beginning of reforms within the Communist Party in 1964, all political prisoners were released in 1968. The generation formed by real struggle and sacrifice—some of whom had been fascist collaborators and some of whom had not—now had to pass on the ideas to the next generation. Mikloško maintains that out of this experience of struggle in the early years of communism came the main legacy that the Catholic nationalists brought to post-1989 politics.[15]

The Window of the 1960s

During the movement for national revival and democratization that began in the early 1960s, generated from inside the Communist Party, there was some coming together of the dominant Leninist nation-building process with the nationalist and democratic alternatives. This was the one short period when a national elite could be said to have started to form inside the Communist Party and to have included some noncommunist ideas. Issues from the war entered the public debate for the first time, and even some individuals who had been long imprisoned for their connection to the Slovak state were published.[16]

However, 1968 did not bring an end to divisions over World War II. While persecutions of the church ended and were acknowledged, even during these years, the legacy of the Slovak state remained somewhat taboo and advocates of Slovak statehood were still at odds with the mainstream.[17] This divide over the World War II past was one factor that weakened the movement for national revival during the 1960s and made it easier for this movement to be fragmented during the subsequent normalization period.

The next generation to carry on the Catholic nationalist legacy was in college during the 1960s thaw. This generation was formed by the 1968 experience. In general, they needed more stamina than did their predecessors. Although they were less encumbered by the persecutions of the 1950s and by the war, they were also themselves more fully products of the regime since they had lived their whole lives in communist Slovakia. Unlike their predecessors, they did not have contacts or experience from before communism. They also had more to lose from opposition.

The Secret Church in Slovakia and Nationalist Dissent

All of the key Catholic nationalist figures in post-1989 politics came from the generation that entered the "secret church" after 1968. As we will see, this "secret church" coexisted with, and sometimes overlapped with, the official church. It was a network of religious dissenters with little formal organization. The generation persecuted during the 1950s passed on their ideology to this new generation, but the younger generation also took risks to preserve religious freedom. This resistance to the regime and their commitment to living up to the legacy of their predecessors gave them incentives to pursue alternative versions of history.

What became the secret church after 1969 emerged from a strain in the Catholic Church that began during the wartime state and was led by a Croatian priest named Tomislav Kolakovič. It is unclear whether a link existed between this small group and the official Catholic Church hierarchy at the time; the wartime Slovak state was led by a Catholic priest and its ideology was intertwined with Catholicism.[18] The Catholic Church in Slovakia had an ambiguous history regarding the collaboration in Nazi crimes.[19]

From the time it took power, and even before, the Communist Party used the clerico-fascist label to oppose the Catholic Church. Ján Korec, whose life embodies the history of Catholic dissent in Slovakia, came of age and finished his religious education just as communism was cracking down on religion.[20] He was secretly ordained in 1951, at a very young age, at a time when many of the Catholic bishops were sent to prison. During this period he was a blue-collar worker and a clerk. In 1960 he was sentenced to twelve years in prison, and he was released in 1968 when the last of the political prisoners were set free.[21] He established the "secret church" with Rome's approval on a visit to the Pope in 1969.[22]

Many bishops and priests were released in the mid-1960s, but it was Korec and several others associated with the Kolakovic group who tried to rebuild an active religious life. They did this by targeting university students.[23] Both Mikloško and Klepáč were reached through their efforts.[24] But there was always tension between the co-opted official Catholic Church and the underground church not subject to official penetration.

The early 1970s brought the beginning of unofficial Catholic activism. While the crackdown after 1968 was not as far reaching as the repressions of the 1950s, organizing opposition activities of any kind was still difficult and risky. Activists could, for example, support defendants in trials, which they could not have done in the 1950s.[25] However, there were periodic arrests, harassments, and attempts to co-opt priests.[26] With the signing in 1975 of the Helsinki agreement, public persecution was replaced by psychological pressure from the regime. Now instead of imprisonment for active involvement in Catholic activities, the regime would threaten that activists' children could not go to a university. Church attendance was detrimental to career advancement.

By the 1980s, underground church activism existed in three strands. The first was an intellectual center around Ján Čarnogurský; this group, starting in 1988, published the samizdat journal *Bratislavské Listy.* The second strand was professional and purely religious associations of believers, which focused on the adaptation of papal encyclicals to Slovak conditions and in-depth study of the Bible. The third was the movement of Christian families, which operated illegally for a number of years.[27] This last strand was comprised of communities of five to eight families which would meet once a week to read the Bible and pray. According to one source, membership was as high as twenty thousand. After 1989, this was the group from which the KDH drew its core.[28]

As the regime's policy toward Catholic observance liberalized and the lines between the underground and official church blurred, public activities began. These activities—which included petitions and pilgrimages during which masses were held—required a certain amount of risk. During these pilgrimages it is likely the topic of Slovak nationhood and the wartime Slovak state would have been among the ideas that were discussed. The year 1987–88 was seen as the year of the church's revival.[29]

The culminating event of this period was the March 25, 1988, prayer gathering of ten to fifteen thousand people. The dispersal of the crowd by the police became a symbol of the repression by a rigid Czechoslovak regime at a time of increasing openness in the Soviet bloc.[30]

Clearly this period brought increasing unofficial church activism and mass participation as the larger events grew. With the Helsinki process, the regime was somewhat constrained in its ability to repress the movement. Also important was the recognition of Korec's struggle by the Vatican and other Catholics in the West.[31] However, the core activists were a small group. The motivations of the participants in the pilgrimages were probably varied. It cannot be assumed that the act of attendance had political relevance in the post-1989 period.

Ideology, World War II, and Catholic Dissent
How were alternative national ideologies preserved in the Catholic nationalist group? Were these ideas about the past any more than family stories? These networks had few written materials and little shared information to draw upon as alternatives to the regime version of history. How-

ever, their involvement in opposition itself provided opportunities and motivation to find such alternatives. The risks and sacrifices that came along with opposition and their ties to one another prevented them from retreating into the private sphere, as did the rest of the elite and society.

The church was the major mechanism for generating historical consciousness, though religion, not national ideology, was clearly the priority. Religion was likely perceived as less dangerous during communism. For example, Klepáč, who became a leader of the more nationalist wing of KDH in 1992, said in an interview that it was not preservation of ties to the Slovak state but preservation of religious belief that brought him and others to the secret church. In other parts of the interview, however, he talked about church and nation being fundamentally intertwined. He said, "Christianity and matters of nation are like two railways on which the locomotive of Slovak history goes."[32] Mikloško, too, in his book on the secret church, sees church and nation as interrelated, though he himself was involved because of religion and ethical opposition to communism.[33]

What brought individuals from the younger generation to the church and to this version of national ideology? In the case of the Čarnogurský family, the father was a clear source of information and motivation. Not only had he been a player in the wartime Slovak state but by the 1960s he was writing a historical memoir of the Slovak state period using personal documents.[34] Ján Čarnogurský wrote a doctoral dissertation in law on the anti-Jewish laws.[35]

For others, whose families were not clearly involved in the wartime Slovak state, there were other reasons for joining the secret church. František Mikloško had come from a religious family in Nitra and said it was natural that he was attracted to the secret church after he came to study in Bratislava. His parents were teachers. His mother in particular was persecuted by the regime, and the house was searched several times by the StB (the secret police). His grandfather saved Jews, and Mikloško heard about the Jewish tragedy from childhood.

Ján Klepáč heard about the Slovak state period from his parents throughout his childhood. Whereas they saw it favorably as a period of economic success and self-realization for Slovakia, they were apparently also involved in hiding Jews.[36] For Klepáč, these family stories were supplemented by an old history book he found in his parents' house.[37] But he came to an alternative ideology after the failure of 1968, when he said he "had the feeling that it was necessary to do something for this nation."[38]

Beyond family stories, these individuals also had occasional access to unofficial information. No histories that integrated the Slovak state period into national ideology were written by this group during communism. While there was an active discussion during the 1970s in Czech samizdat about the Sudeten German expulsion, there was little equivalent debate about World War II in Slovakia.[39] This had partly to do with the scarcity of dissident historians. Moreover, the communist regime was successful in persecuting this strand of dissent in the postwar period.

Some of the works written by émigrés sympathetic to the Slovak state circulated in samizdat. Klepáč gained access to such books in 1968.[40] Pavol Čarnogurský was another source of information. Mikloško was close to Korec and other founders of the secret church. In addition, he had contact during the 1980s with other antiregime circles. He supplemented family stories about the Jewish issue by reading the manuscript of Ivan Kamenec's book, finished in 1971 but unpublished until after 1989. (Kamenec was the only Slovak historian to write seriously about the wartime fate of the Jews.) His consciousness regarding those issues developed through his frequent conversations with Jews.[41] Partly due to these contacts, Mikloško became an initiator of a 1987 declaration of apology to Jews for the deportations and for the involvement of Slovaks and the Slovak state in these crimes. This was signed mostly by Catholic dissidents and circulated by that group.[42] However, as is apparent in Mikloško's own book, which was put together in the last years of communism and published afterward, it was only in the process of writing the book, and bringing together the separate stories and memories of the participants of the secret church, that he was able to give meaning to the war and bring it into the next generation.[43]

The Nationalist Émigrés

The other grouping that represented continuity with the precommunist nation-building process, and whose members were active in the post-1989 period, were émigrés from all three postwar emigration periods—1945, 1948, and 1968. They were important mostly for supplying ideas by writing articles and giving lectures on history.[44] Some functioned as advisers, some ran for political office; some participated through émigré organizations, though they tended to be active as individuals not as groups. As we will see below, they generally had an ambiguous reputation in the minds of Slovak politicians and were less important than were émigrés in other postcommunist transitions.[45]

The 1945 emigration consisted of political elites and intelligentsia connected with the Slovak state of 1939–45. Some left with the German troops in 1945. A large proportion of the Slovak state elite spent the postwar years abroad, mostly in the United States. This included those who were involved in that state's crimes against the Jews and those who were merely supportive of its ideology.[46] The main leaders were executed or imprisoned and some were tried in absentia.

The 1945 group found support in the already existing U.S. émigré organizations, which had been active throughout the century. The main one in the United States was the Slovak League, a federation of American Slovak organizations.[47] There was a long tradition of foreign Slovaks taking an active role in Slovak affairs; most important was when the Slovak League became a party to the Pittsburgh agreement of 1918.[48] The key American and Canadian organizations supported an independent Slovakia during the war.[49] They opposed the execution of Tiso and even pressured the U.S. Congress on behalf of this cause. In the immediate postwar years, the Slovak exiles, the most active of which were those in the Slovak National Council Abroad and the Slovak Liberation Committee, worked for renewal of independent Slovakia.[50] They continued to be devoted to the cause of an independent Slovakia throughout the communist period.[51]

These organizations wrote histories devoted to preserving Slovak nationalism and the legacy of the wartime Slovak state. They celebrated the anniversary of the declaration of the Slovak state and tried to smuggle their literature back into Slovakia. In 1970, two years after the 1968 invasion by Soviet troops, the World Slovak Congress was founded to unite all Slovak émigré organizations and to focus their energy on preserving Slovak culture and an independent and noncommunist Slovakia.[52]

Over the course of the postwar period the émigrés set up several scholarly journals.[53] In the 1970s the journals were taken over by the children of the postwar émigrés. This younger generation created the Slovak Studies Association in 1977, and one of their more important publications was the proceedings of a 1984 conference on Slovak history.[54] While still committed to the Slovak cause, they were often less dogmatic than their parents and had greater access to archives in Czechoslovakia during the communist period. In addition, some non-Slovak academics working on related topics began to be invited to conferences and to publish in their journals.

There was another important émigré wave after 1968. However, these often did not join émigré organizations, and if they did they sometimes joined Czechoslovak rather than Slovak organizations.[55] The 1968 émigrés were not as cohesive a group and had emigrated for numerous reasons. At the same time, the fact that they had left so recently made them closer to events in Slovakia.[56]

The Ethnic Nationalist View of the Slovak State of 1939–45

The communist regime's methods for presenting World War II, whereby the story changed frequently and facts were presented with no context in dogmatic fashion, led most of the elite to distrust that history and thus to rely instead on family stories. In the case of the émigrés and the Slovak Catholic nationalists, the argument is different. In these groups there was a relatively stable position on the key issues of World War II. This position integrated the events of the war into a view of Slovak national development that saw the wartime state as the main event in modern Slovak history. This view is ethnic nationalist in the sense that it argues that Slovakia should be run by Slovaks, who are a natural cultural entity fighting for self-determination. The ideology of the wartime Slovak state clearly saw membership in the nation as limited to ethnic Slovaks.

While there was more opportunity for the articulation of this view in émigré circles abroad, operating as they were in an environment of press freedom and opportunity for debate, a similar view was articulated by the Catholic nationalists in Slovakia, partly based on the writings of the émigrés. However, neither of these groupings openly debated or weighed different points of view against one another. Slovak dissidents were, of course, isolated and could not engage in public debate. The émigrés were isolated in their own small circles and did not see their positions as subject to debate.

The general approach in these groups was that the wartime state was a long-awaited moment of Slovak self-determination and that its negative aspects had to do with the circumstances of the war.[57] While the argument appears in different variations, these writers generally argue that the Jewish tragedy and Nazi collaboration did not define this state. The views presented here are a composite picture of a number of writers.[58]

The Character of the Slovak State
These authors argue that Tiso's decision to declare independence at Hitler's urging, which was part of a Nazi strategy to destroy Czechoslovakia, was the lesser of evils in a difficult situation. Some go further to contend that "Slovak independence was as much an act of national self-determination as one of self-preservation."[59] They see the government as

authoritarian but not dictatorial or totalitarian, less repressive than the communist regime and certainly not fascist. According to these writers, the new state was generally supported by all parties and had wide popular support. It finally gave the Slovaks an opportunity to control their fate and non-Jewish citizens survived the war in peace and prosperity as Europe burned all around them.[60] The 1939–45 period was one when Slovak culture flourished, economic development took off, and Slovaks gained confidence that they could govern themselves.[61] Nationalist authors point to the fact that Slovak opponents of the regime—for example, communists—were allowed to publish and, to some extent, avoided imprisonment. A common claim is that l'udáks and communists sat together in the cafes of Bratislava.[62]

Catholicism and the church, according to nationalist authors, functioned mostly as a source of opposition to the policies the Nazis wanted to impose, particularly the Jewish deportations. Tiso, and other clergymen in political roles, did the best they could on moral grounds under trying circumstances.[63] Vojtech Tuka and Alexander Mach and the nonclerical wing of the HSLS were seen as immoral and responsible for acquiescing to Nazi policies. Had Tiso resigned, the Nazis would have had freer reign.[64]

The Jewish Issue
Anti-Jewish legislation, modeled on the Nazi Nuremberg laws, started even before the establishment of the Slovak state and came in pieces throughout 1939 and 1940. It was finally codified in September 1941 and deprived Jews of rights and property. The émigré writers do not deny the imposition of the anti-Jewish laws and some even see the seizure of property as justified.[65] These authors tend to pay no attention to the fact that some of the new Slovak prosperity during those years came directly at the expense of Jews and that some of the popular support for the regime came as a result of the distribution of Jewish property. Kirschbaum says that the confiscation of Jewish property was "unfortunate and tragic" and that the Aryanization policy, which was introduced just after independence, "was voted on by the Slovak parliament in response to a mood that existed in popular circles."[66] The anti-Semitism of the HSLS is also ignored and is attributed again to a minority of the more radical leadership. There is some debate about whether anti-Semitic laws were imposed by Germany or imposed voluntarily by the HSLS leadership.[67]

The issue of the deportation of the Jews is the most controversial and is dealt with in a variety of ways. Most generally, nationalists argue that the decision to deport the Jews was imposed by the Germans and agreed to by the radicals Tuka and Mach. Tiso did not at first know about it and could not officially oppose it when he found out. Tiso's passing of the deportation legislation is justified in that this allowed him to grant exceptions, which he did, according to this argument, in large numbers.[68] The émigrés use lower estimates for the number of Jews deported. They claim more Jews were saved than do other observers, thereby bolstering the argument that had the Slovak state been run by another regime, the Slovak Jews would have had a worse fate.[69] They also emphasize that initially the fate of the Jews was not known and that once information reached Slovakia that Jews were being killed in Poland, there was pressure for stopping the deportations.[70]

Another argument invokes the wartime context in which all the surrounding countries were deporting their Jews.[71] In addition, once the deportations stopped, Slovakia became a haven for Jews from other countries. The argument then goes that it was during the Uprising that the fate of the Jews who were saved through exceptions was sealed. Thus, without the Uprising, the Germans would not have occupied Slovakia, and more Jews would have survived. In addition, they do not fail to mention that there was anti-Semitism among the partisans and among communists.

The Slovak National Uprising

The émigrés and the Catholic nationalists generally also agree in their interpretation of the Slovak National Uprising, though they vary in seeing it as a conspiracy, a tragedy, a civil war, or a war against one's own state.[72] The Uprising was a complex event, bringing together fighters with a variety of motives. Even though some Catholic nationalists participated in the Uprising, which they saw as anti-Nazi, not anti-Tiso, they do not share the democrats' evaluation of the antifascist resistance as a moment of Slovak heroism and as a sign of commitment to democracy.[73]

The Democrats

In the case of the democrats, it is even harder to establish continuity than with the nationalists. The Catholic nationalists were a more clear-cut group of dissidents. In this sense they were more similar in style, if not ideology, to the dissent of the mostly Czech Charter 77 group.[74] The founders of Public Against Violence were shallowly connected to groups that articulated a civic ideology.

There were three pathways to this form of historical consciousness, coinciding, in general, with generations. The first was actual continuity with the democrats of the wartime period. The few who were involved in postcommunist politics from this generation were important mostly as a source of ideas. The second path was that of the transformed communist true believers of the 1950s, who were generally born in the 1930s. The third and most common road into the leadership of the postcommunist democrats was from the generations born in the 1940s and 1950s. Networks of artists, sociologists, and members of the environmental movement with unofficial ideas began to develop in the last years before 1989. Whether through exposure to friends, family, or associates who had access to unconventional ideas or perspectives, or through their own curiosity, this group, while sharing the dominant experience of communist socialization, came to the postcommunist period with an ideology. The more rooted ideology of Czech dissent strengthened these networks of Slovak democrats.

In all cases this was a Czechoslovak civic ideology committed to returning to Europe, and to continuity with the democratic First Republic before two totalitarian dictatorships pushed it off course. In this ideology, World War II figured prominently, although, as we will see below, it was important in different ways for different generations. Slovak democrats associated democracy with the union with the Czechs in Czechoslovakia. There was not much of a tradition for a civic Slovak identity.

The Democratic Party of 1945–48

As we saw in the last chapter, the Slovak Democratic Party was set up after World War II by a combination of supporters of Czechoslovak resistance and Catholics. They sought voters from the former base of the Tiso party and won a strong majority in the 1946 elections. The party existed for only three years and was something of a catchall party, comprised as it was of several ideological streams. Civic ideology, even in the Czech portion of Czechoslovakia, with its more solid civic traditions, was weak after World War II. The civic alternative was weakened after six years of Nazi occupation and had been discredited by the failure of the First Republic to withstand the Nazi onslaught. After 1948, the leadership of the Democratic Party was tried and key figures went into exile.[75] Instead of joining the émigrés from the Slovak state, they joined the Czechoslovak exile community and the Council for a Free Czechoslovakia. This was a small, select organization, which was tied to U.S. government efforts to penetrate the iron curtain with the beginning of the cold war.[76] Martin Kvetko, the one figure from this group who returned to politics after 1989, as honorary chairman of the newly constituted Democratic Party, had been part of the council.[77] He had also worked as co-chief of the Czechoslovak desk for Radio Free Europe. According to Kvetko, one-half of the three million Slovaks abroad were represented by the council. Others were part of Slovak and Czechoslovak organizations.[78]

This group of democratic Slovaks, along with the Czechoslovak exiles, was at odds with the Slovak émigré community discussed above. The Slovak civic tradition was again tied in with Czechoslovak opposition as it had been before and during World War II.[79] Central to this group's ideology, built mostly by Czech intellectuals in the West, was that Czechoslovakia was the only democracy in east central Europe; it was thus particularly tragic that it fell victim first to Nazi then communist domination.[80] In the post-1989 period, the wartime democrats were more important as sources of ideas than as participants in politics.[81]

Transformed Communist Intellectuals

Civic ideology also developed among "true believer" communists who fought fascism (or were its victims) only to be later persecuted by the communist regime.[82] In a fascinating collective biography of communist intellectuals, Peter Hrubý characterizes this transformation that came from the realization, once they became victims of the communist regime, that it was the nature of Leninism itself that had led the regime eventually to destroy its own supporters. The privileging of the Party above all else was as problematic as privileging the nation above all else in fascist regimes. They began to think instead of general moral principles and humanism as the antidote.[83] Jewish communists frequently took this route.[84] In the Czech case, many of these transformed true believers became the leaders of the reform movement from within the Communist Party in 1968 and then went on to become members of Charter 77.[85]

Interestingly, this same profile of the communist fighting fascism only to then be persecuted by the communist regime also fits Gustáv Husák. After fighting in the communist resistance, Husák was jailed in the 1950s as a "bourgeois nationalist." His imprisonment and that of other national communists was what mobilized the reform movement in Slovakia in the 1960s. But his later incarnation—Communist Party chief that presided over the post-1968 normalization—was quite different from the transformed true believers. In Slovakia, the national communists generally did not continue in dissent.

The civic orientation among disillusioned communists was a smaller stream in Slovakia.[86] One of the few Slovaks who went in this direction was Miroslav Kusý, a key figure in VPN after 1989.[87] After 1968 his earlier antifascism was bolstered by anticommunism. He became one of the articulators of this ideology of civic dissent.

Born in 1931, Kusý came from a communist family; his father was a worker and a communist before the war. He says he was formed by his family's experience from World War II, even though he was only ten at the time. While his father spent one year in prison under the Tiso regime, he and his mother participated in the Uprising. He studied in Prague during the 1950s and himself became a communist because he saw the Party as "the first barricade against fascism." He was in the university when Stalin died and when word of Stalin's crimes came out in Khrushchev's "secret speech." The shock of these revelations led him to begin to change in the early sixties when he was a professor at Comenius University.[88] By 1968, he was one of the major philosophers questioning communist orthodoxy.[89]

Kusý was part of a more civic wing of the reform movement, as opposed to the dominant group concerned with federalization and Slovak autonomy.[90] He was expelled from the Party in 1970, after a four-month stint as Slovak Communist Party ideological chief under Husák. Until 1977 he worked in the archives at the university. In 1977 he was among the first signatories of Charter 77, one of only a handful in Slovakia.[91] After this he was demoted to blue-collar jobs and subjected to police harassment.

Kusý wrote for and circulated samizdat journals and traveled frequently to Prague.[92] In samizdat he argued against communist suppression of Slovak culture and history.[93] Also, together with Milan Šimečka, he articulated a critique of communism similar to Havel's.[94] He was isolated in Slovakia, where the charter was perceived as a Prague project, but was in contact with Catholic dissidents.[95]

Kusý, Šimečka, and others who fit this profile provided contacts for the younger opposition-minded intellectuals in Slovakia. The ideology that they personally embodied was passed on mostly orally though their writings were also circulated. They also provided the tie to Czech samizdat. The main bearers of postcommunist civic ideology, however, belonged to the next generation.[96]

Islands of Positive Deviance

The majority of the leadership of VPN was from the generation born after the war. Only a few of them can be shown to have had lasting contact with groups that developed or preserved alternative ideologies. They were slightly more tied in to networks that provided access to information and discussion than were other members of their generation of similar educational levels. The term "islands of positive deviance" was used by Slovak sociologists to describe this type of opposition that became the core of Public Against Violence.[97]

Unlike the situation in the Czech lands, where intellectuals active in 1968 lost their jobs, in Slovakia they were often allowed to keep their jobs, even if they were not allowed to publish.[98] Unlike their Czech counterparts who went into dissent, they had something to lose. This difference had two effects. The first is that the potential opposition was less isolated from the rest of society in Slovakia. The idea of positive deviance was that even while working at official jobs it was possible to try to live morally and to explore unconventional ideas. For university professors, like Soňa Szomolányiová, it meant providing unofficial information to students both in lectures and in private meetings. For Peter Zajac, who became the ideologist for VPN, it meant proposing unconventional projects for official literary conferences.[99] However, while they were less isolated from the rest of society than their counterparts in the Czech lands, the fact that post-1968 repression was less harsh in Slovakia kept opposition groupings from forming until quite late. The other islands and their ideologies were hard to identify. Eventually the separate networks among the sociologists, the artists, and the environmentalists began to interact.

The publication of *Bratislavský Nahlas*—Bratislava Aloud—in fall 1988 was a key moment in the development of these islands. This document was a description and analysis of environmental conditions in Bratislava produced by environmentalists and natural and social scientists.[100] Leaders of the November 1989 revolution came from this group, which became a major platform for independent thinkers.[101] But it was really only in the summer of 1989, with the trial of a group that became known as the "Bratislava Five"—a cross-section of the handful of Slovak dissidents—that greater mobilization took place.[102] This event generated unprecedented response in the form of petitions with many signatories from "official structures" including Communist Party members. The trial mobilized and integrated the islands of discontent that had, until then, been isolated.[103] Two separate meetings—one by artists, the other by sociologists, environmentalists, and other intellectuals—marked the beginning of VPN in November 1989.[104]

While these groups overcame the egoism that characterized most of their generation, their links to one another and a common ideology were weak. Only a handful was truly involved beyond the signature of petitions. Others were inclined in this direction and tied through personal connections; they were willing to sacrifice by acting against the regime openly once it was clear that communism was collapsing. That the most ideological of the post-1989 democratic elites of this generation had such shallow ties to noncommunist ideologies further bolsters the point about the rest of elite and society who were even less committed to seeking alternatives. As we will see in the discussion of elite formation in the postcommunist period, these islands of positive deviance were limited in size and did not always lead to appropriate choices for new government posts or even political allies. They were also very much subject to penetration by secret police collaborators.

Personal Pathways to Ideology

Three reasons can be found for joining the networks of democrats and for developing the inclination to seek alternatives to official ideology: family background, activism during the 1960s, and friendship and professional networks. One would have to undertake a more in-depth study of the informal friendship networks and discussion circles to determine the true level of cohesion in these networks. But here I will examine the stories of several of the most important figures in the networks that would become Public Against Violence: Fedor Gál, leader of VPN and founding member; Martin Bútora, another founding member and adviser to Havel on human rights; Peter Zajac, founding member of VPN and ideologist; Soňa Szomolányiová, VPN activist, a sociologist; Miloš Žiak, a writer, founding member of VPN, and Havel's Slovak representative; Milan Zemko, vice chairman of the Slovak parliament.[105] Zemko was initially active in VPN but became independent when the movement split in spring 1991.

Family background was the most important reason. Many in this group were the children of "true believer" communists who left the Party after 1968 or, as in the case of Fedor Gál's family, before. Their post-1968 departure from the Party meant being on the periphery and, to a greater or lesser degree, suffering at the hands of the regime. The Jews among them were even more on the periphery.

Fedor Gál was born in the Terezín concentration camp in 1945. His father and uncle were both communists and participated in the Uprising and his uncle served briefly as a diplomat after the war but was arrested and imprisoned in the 1950s. While his birth in Terezín and Jewish past did not result in a strong Jewish identity, he did come from a family that suffered and that had a history of ideological involvement and persecution by the regime. This put him on the periphery.

Both Peter Zajac's parents were devoted communists from the World War II period; his father, from a secular Jewish family, and who joined the Communist Party in 1940, avoided deportation since he was imprisoned for his communism. His mother was the granddaughter of Milan Hodža, one of the founders of the First Republic and a key Slovak political figure from that time. Both left the Party in 1968.

Soňa Szomolányiová came from a strong communist family and her uncle played an important role in the Uprising. Her parents became disillusioned after Stalin's crimes were revealed but remained active. She herself joined the Party during the normalization period.

Miloš Žiak, younger than the rest, was from a communist family and his parents left the party after 1968. He was also Jewish and found himself seeking out opposition after being removed from a job in 1986.

Activism during the 1960s was another reason for ending up in these circles. The group around the student paper, *Echo,* tended to meet to discuss unconventional ideas after the 1960s. This group included Martin Bútora and Milan Zemko. Others, like Soňa Szomolányiová, were not as active in the 1960s but were introduced to reformist ideas, in her case by a friend who brought unconventional articles to her attention. Study trips abroad during the late 1960s were also important for some of this group.

Friends or professional circles or a particular teacher were often important. Gál and Bútora both lived in the same apartment house. Soňa Szomolányiová happened to have that friend and she also had inspiring teachers, both in elementary school and at the university. Miloš Žiak came to know the Šimečka family—both the father and the son, also a writer, were in dissent. It was partly through this contact that he became motivated to seek out Ivan Kamenec's book about the Holocaust.

Articulating Ideology

Association with such networks was not enough to develop shared historical consciousness. Without access to similar types of noncommunist interpretations of history and without discussion of this information, they would have remained much like most of their counterparts in the mass-elite. Samizdat was the most likely source of information. Generally they read the works of opposition writers Havel, Kusý, and Šimečka and forbidden works of literature. What they read also depended on what languages they knew, with English and German readers having wider access. They were all involved, more or less formally, for more or less time, in gatherings to discuss what they read. Some met throughout the 1970s and 1980s, like Bútora and Zemko. Zajac began to invite people from the networks of sociologists and environmentalists to his literature institute in the mid-1980s. Soňa Szomolányiová was first brought to a meeting by Martin Bútora only in 1988, after the *Bratislavský Nahlas* came out. Throughout the 1970s Gál was tied in with Czech sociologists and economists who were exploring unofficial ideas.[106] He became an environmental activist in the mid- to late-1980s.

In some cases these networks relied on people from older generations to provide information. Milan Zemko, for example, reports talking with the former editor of cultural weekly *Kultúrný Život*—Juraj Špitzer—about World War II. Špitzer, a Jewish communist writer, had been silenced after 1968.

Admittedly, this generation's historical consciousness regarding the war and its role in a civic ideology was diffuse. Yet, as opposed to the mass-elite, they came to the postcommunist period with a shared orientation toward historical justice and shared a commitment to moral politics and truth about the past. In the postcommunist period, they were driven by ideology, however weak, while the mass-elite was driven by nothing but short-term personal interest.

World War II as Part of a Civic Ideology

As did the nationalists, the democrats developed a fairly clear and consistent approach to the events of World War II. This stands in contrast to the twists and turns and omissions of the communist history education process that we will see in the next chapter.

All three generations of democrats shared a Czechoslovak, anticommunist basis for a civic ideology but had different relationships to World War II. For the wartime democrats, the communists, and the Jews, particularly of the earlier generation, the war was still the more horrible period and it informed their approach to anticommunism. The wartime democrats of the Council for Free Czechoslovakia had fought and resisted fascism only to be faced with another tyranny. The true-believer communists had seen communism as the antidote to fascism until they discovered that it was just another tyranny and that any system built on a single commitment can lead to that type of tyranny. For the generation that grew up under communism, it was communism first, with fascism as a background of suffering or resistance that their parents experienced. For this group, the events of World War II were more embedded in an ideology that was anticommunist first and Czechoslovak second.[107] This anticommunism overshadowed the issue of what the national ideology for Slovakia should be. It was taken for granted that Czechoslovakia would always exist. So, for example, in the younger group, the World War II period was sometimes more vague, even for the Jews. Gál, in spite of his family history, never heard much about the experience except in fragments. The World War II aspect became more important for him after 1989. As Žiak said comparing fascism to communism, "One was my family; the other my life." For much of his life World War II had no personal meaning for him. But because of anticommunism he was later inclined to go and seek out the Kamenec book on the Holocaust. Zajac, whose grandfather died in Auschwitz, says he always knew about the Holocaust but was opposed to the social inequities of communism. Soňa Szomolányiová, whose uncle was a hero of the Uprising and who grew up hearing terrible stories about the Germans, knew less about the Jewish issue. Her views of this were shaped by seeing the movie *Shop on Mainstreet* (though she said that the issue of deportations for her was vague until after 1989). Bútora lived with Gál and knew about Gál's mother's past; he was more directly interested in World War II and, after 1989, was the main scholar involved in pursuing sociological projects about the fascist past and public opinion of those events.

What was this ideology and how did World War II fit in? The antitotalitarian critique of communism was the main unifying set of ideas for this group. It focused on totalitarianism's repression of individualism and included a historical source of opposition to totalitarianism: the First Czechoslovak Republic with its multiethnic tolerance, its commitment to truth, and its victimhood at the hands of the Nazis and the communists.[108] Havel's analysis of totalitarianism as an extreme outgrowth of modern society was framed as an additional lesson that Czechoslovakia, which also experienced Nazi occupation, could offer the rest of the modern world.[109]

This ideology also included a strong commitment to the principle of overcoming the communist regime's lies about history, particularly those about the horrors of both the communist and World War II periods. Finding truth about the past was a prime way of fighting the regime. This anticommunist ideology easily encompassed antifascism as well and took a consistent stance on the key elements of World War II. The ideology included the idea of tolerance, which was eroded when any single group or idea is given preeminence, whether a class or nation. It included free exchange of ideas and facing difficult aspects of the past in order to learn from them. It also included resistance as the most noble response to tyranny of any type and the need to face instances where resistance did not take place. These all fit well with Western ideas about fascism and World War II. They also fit with the focus that has accompanied discussions of the Holocaust about learning from history and the preventative role of memory.

Alternative meanings to the regime's presentation of World War II could be found in a number of sources. The most widely influential was the movie *Shop on Mainstreet.* In addition, there were other treatments in literature and in more historical/social theoretical discussions.[110] The major historical works that formed this group's ideas about World War II were the book on the Holocaust in Slovakia by Ivan Kamenec, passed around in manuscript form, and one by Jozef Lettrich, who was of the older wartime generation of democrats.[111] Both of these were published soon after 1989 by Archa Press, associated with the civic movement.[112] There was more available on the Slovak National Uprising. The main writer on this topic in samizdat was Jozef Jablonický.[113]

Character of the Slovak State

Most agree that the decision to trade collaboration for nominal independence was a lesser evil than other choices available to Slovakia. However, Czechs and Slovak democrats see the fascist HSLS as having actively facilitated this choice and the occupation of the Czech lands by the Nazis. Thus the HSLS is viewed as having contributed to the fall of the First Republic and thus to the destruction of a state which was democratic and which represented a positive period of development for both Slovaks and Czechs.[114]

The regime of Jozef Tiso is seen as fascist and totalitarian.[115] It did not allow for opposition and persecuted opponents of the regime and non-Slovak ethnic groups. The positive developments during the Slovak state, to which nationalists point, are seen as tainted and built on immoral foundations. Support for the Tiso regime was won through Aryanization of Jewish property and redistribution of positions in state bureaucracies and in other institutions.[116] While there might have been a development of Slovak culture, intellectuals collaborated in making Slovak culture conform to Nazi culture.[117] Economic advances were also at the expense of fueling the German war effort.[118]

The Jewish Issue

The deportation of the Jews was a human tragedy that stands as the black mark against this regime and offers a lesson of tolerance. It needs to be faced to avoid the repetition of similar crimes. Responsibility is clearly in Tiso's hands, not only in the hands of the radicals Tuka and Mach, whom the nationalists point to as the sole culprits. Some go further to give responsibility to a broader group in the Slovak population who benefited from the anti-Jewish policy and did not resist. As opposed to the nationalists, who do not go into detail about the anti-Jewish measures, these accounts enumerate the anti-Jewish laws precisely.[119] The focus is on the anti-Semitism in the ideology of the HSLS, which began to take anti-Jewish measures in 1938, even before the deal with Hitler.[120] These authors also object to each of the grounds on which nationalists tend to try to divert responsibility for deportations from Tiso to the radicals in the regime. On the argument that other countries were doing the same or worse, Kamenec points out that the Slovak state was the only country in Europe not occupied by Germany that implemented the deportations through their own power and administrative apparatus.[121]

In response to the point that Tiso was a buffer against an even worse fate for the Jews, Kamenec argues that when it comes to attributing responsibility ultimately it is results, not intentions that count. He says that there is no evidence that Tiso tried to intervene against the deportations. Tiso did not respond to notes of protest from Jewish organizations submitted soon before the deportations began in March 1942. His silence, as president, implied support for the anti-Semitic policy. Also, in occasional public appearances he argued that the policy was justified from a moral, Christian, and civic perspective.[122]

Kamenec disputes the frequent claim that deportations were halted in the fall of 1942 and not earlier since it was only then that Slovak state leaders could finally resist on moral grounds without risking the dissolution of the state by the Nazis.[123] He suspects that the deportations were stopped for more instrumental reasons, arguing that by then the regime no longer needed to get rid of a poor Jewish population, which had been deprived of their livelihoods and property.

Kamenec is also skeptical about the significance of the presidential exceptions. He shows that of the thirty to forty thousand exceptions pointed to by the nationalists, only one thousand managed to escape the 1942 deportations on these grounds. He argues that the rest were mostly converts and wealthy Jews who could pay, thereby questioning whether the rationale for the exemptions was moral. He maintains that Tiso was the creator of the system and was therefore the one most responsible for what happened to the Jews: "The responsibility for this development is incomparably greater than granting hundreds of thousands of exceptions to the victims of the official anti-Semitic policy of the state."[124]

Slovak National Uprising

For the democrats, the Slovak National Uprising was oriented toward re-creating a democratic Czechoslovakia and was opposed not only to the Nazis but to the Tiso state.[125] It was a return to Europe and the allied war effort. For some, particularly Czechs, it constituted a necessary moral renewal for Slovakia.[126] Unlike in communist portrayals, the Soviets were not the liberators and there were other heroes besides the communists. But even though the event was abused by the communists, it remained important for this group.[127] The Slovak National Uprising also fits in with the idea of resistance to totalitarianism as heroic: it was difficult, but still possible, to resist.

From Dissent to Democratic Politics

What kinds of groups were these islands of history? What were the implications of the fact that they were formed in opposition to the communist regime for their approach to politics after communism? The most important effect of their formation in opposition to communism was their isolation. This isolation had the following dimensions. First, they were isolated in important ways from one another even though they were linked in their anticommunism. Second, and more important, they had no social base. Third, and related to both of the above, they were isolated from the mass-elite.

Relationship to One Another

The cores of both groups—the Catholic nationalists and the democrats—were joined in their anticommunism. Thus the group arrested as the "Bratislava Five" in 1989 included civic activist Miroslav Kusý and Catholic nationalist Ján Čarnogurský. Particularly through the younger generation—Mikloško and Langoš—the Catholic activists were connected to their civic-oriented counterparts and chose to go with Public Against Violence rather than the Christian Democratic Movement.

However, because both came into their own ideologically only after 1989, the democrats and nationalists were not fully aware of the differences between them, which surfaced in the first months after communism collapsed. And these differences had to do with nationalism, symbolized by World War II.[128] There was genuine surprise after 1989 at the push to revive the Slovak state, which seemed to be coming from KDH and which scared the democrats. As we will see in chapter 6, this divide continued to plague these groups.

The Slovak democrats of VPN were also isolated from the Prague democrats surrounding Václav Havel. Except for a few direct personal connections, there were communication problems and frustrations among Slovaks about their inability to penetrate the circle around Havel.[129] In addition, the Slovak nationalist émigrés were isolated from the Czechoslovak democratic groups in emigration in a way that the two sides inside Slovakia were not. This animosity had partly to do with their freedom of expression. In addition, they did not have to compromise because they were not involved in real politics together.[130]

The nationalist émigrés in particular were isolated in a Western world, which saw the Nazi period and the Holocaust as the epitome of evil.[131] Like other east and central European émigrés who were anticommunist and supporters of nationalist movements which, to varying degrees, were involved in collaborating in the Holocaust, they were frequently under attack from groups who cared about such issues. Jewish groups, committed to finding every last perpetrator and exposing the steps that led to extermination, condemned the émigrés. According to Jelinek, the émigrés tried to persuade Jewish organizations to stop focusing on this aspect of their past, but they refused to unconditionally condemn the actions of the Slovak state.[132]

The nationalist émigrés were also isolated from the Catholic nationalists in Slovakia. One difference was that the Catholic nationalists had focused on religious dissent during the years of communism. This was well illustrated when Ján Čarnogurský turned away the émigrés in 1990 because of their insistence on pushing immediately for an independent Slovakia on the model of the wartime state.[133] Partly because of these different orientations, these groups diverged in their approaches to the issue of the Jewish deportations and in the declarations of apology each group issued during the last years of communism.[134] The difference stems from the fact that the émigrés preserved an ideology as it was in 1945 in the unusual "hothouse" atmosphere of emigration, while the Catholic nationalists had to fight to defend their beliefs in the face of great odds and were, in spite of their resistance, products of the communist system.[135] The Catholic nationalists came face to face with others who shared their anticommunism but not their views toward the wartime state.

So the strands of opposition, in addition to being weak, were isolated from one another in ways which mattered in the postcommunist period.

Most important of these was the divide between the Slovak democrats and their Czech allies on the one hand, and the Catholic nationalists on the other.

Isolation from Social Base and from Mass-Elite

Each of these groups was cut off from a social base. Interestingly, however, none of them seemed to realize to what extent they were cut off. Each imagined themselves to be the true representatives of Slovakia.

The émigrés were the furthest removed from a social base since they had lived in the West. Their development of a historiography about World War II, an activity always limited to a relatively small group of intellectuals, happened far away from a sociopolitical debate in Slovak society. This was true to such an extent that Luboš Jurík, editor of the literary journal *Literárny Týždenník,* did not know what views the émigrés would espouse when he invited them in 1989 to contribute to his journal. He says that he was surprised to see such a clearly favorable position regarding the wartime Slovak state.[136] It is striking that this debate about the events of World War II was carried out in exile and everywhere but on the territory where they took place.

The émigrés assumed that they represented Slovaks whose ideologies had simply been repressed. Their entire postwar work was to show that in fact Slovaks had supported the Slovak state and that this state had been terribly misunderstood. We can see this in Kirschbaum's concern that the West is unfamiliar with Slovak history, implying that the Slovaks naturally are aware of their own history.[137] But the idea that Slovakia was waiting for them to come and fill in the gaps caused by communist repression was unrealistic. The fact that Čarnogurský turned them away in February 1990 is again illustrative. Čarnogurský complained precisely about their lack of connection to the realities of Slovakia and that they were trying to sell the idea of independence without themselves bearing any costs.[138] Because the émigrés did not have supporters, and did not offer much in the way of resources, they ended up being co-opted by the mass-elite. Mass-elite groupings were able to use émigré ideas to add legitimacy to their own claim to represent the Slovak nation.

The Catholic nationalists, too, overestimated their social base. They expected that they would get the support of a large portion of the 70 percent of Slovaks who considered themselves Catholic. But this group did not fully realize how isolated they were in a society and elite which continued to be informed only by family stories, not ideology. They could not assess the extent to which communist domination had wiped out ideology. Mikloško, in his book, assumes widely shared common views regarding religious freedom.[139] Korec writes that one of the results of communism was a society without national consciousness.[140] But like the democrats, after 1989 they acted as if they were representative. While they clearly had access to the Catholic population of Slovakia, it is surprising that they failed to retain more of the Catholic vote since, unlike many postcommunist parties, they had local organization through the church. They lost support because of their commitment to principle in a political environment that favored lack of commitment.

The democrats, too, lacked a social base. That group also assumed it was representative of both society and elites since to them it seemed obvious that the antithesis to communism was democracy and a market economy. They assumed that the more educated part of the population shared their opposition to the regime, that there were many more "islands of positive deviance," and that more of an alternative culture existed.[141] Part of what contributed to their misperception was that they shared an ideology with the Western world: If there was a social base anywhere, it was in the West.[142]

The same assumptions—that ideology was shared—applied to the elites who became involved in politics after the collapse of the communist regime. So confident were the democratic intellectuals at the core of VPN that society and elite shared their ideology and approach to politics, that many key figures from this group did not run for office in the June 1990 elections. They later found themselves in the unfortunate position of trying to give life to democratic institutions while trying to influence politics from nonelected positions. As we will see below, the assumption that there was a society and an elite with cohesive ideologies contributed to the downfall of the ideological elites.

Antipolitical Politics

A final effect of their development in opposition to communism was these groups' belief that the ideologies developed in private and through personal networks could be translated into the political realm without parties or institutionalization.[143] Whereas they did preserve modern ideologies in private, unlike the rest of society, their mode of acting to politicize and publicize these ideologies continued to be personal. This is evident in two important ways. First, in the critical period following the collapse of communism the only criterion with which to choose allies and opponents seemed to be whether or not they had opposed the regime. And this judgment was often based on personal ties or information channeled through the networks of dissent.

Second, they assumed that their personal knowledge of history, developed in opposition networks, enabled them to make judgments in politics about historical justice questions. They ended up in an ambiguous position. On the one hand, they argued that there was a need for a public debate about important historical issues to overcome the omissions and distortions of communist history writing. On the other hand, they also brought issues of historical justice to the agenda before history had been written and before the public debate had taken place. This was particularly important in the dilemma democrats faced about the fate of former communists and secret police collaborators. While it was important in a democracy to avoid imposing a truth about history without the proper historical research, history was a weapon that could be used to keep people out of politics who were associated with the communist or the fascist pasts. Revolution is about deposing and removing an enemy from politics. Democracy is about forgiving and including an enemy in politics. As we will see, removing or forgiving requires knowing who the enemy is. The problem was that the enemy in the postcommunist period was not identifiable.

Finally, the agenda developed in dissent gave a prominent role to moral issues, which included historical justice. This assumed that there was a truth and a justice that could be found in politics.

Conclusion

We have seen that the democrats and the nationalists alone had alternative national ideologies and that World War II was at the center of these ideologies. They, as opposed to the mass-elite, were able to withstand communist socialization processes. However, they were weak and isolated from one another and from society. The weakness was due to the success of the regime in preventing dissent. It was also due to the continuing legacy of the fascist past. The history of World War II divided the weak groups of democrats and nationalists from one another. It also was the primary reason that so much of the precommunist elite and intelligentsia went into exile. The fact that these small strands of opposition initially dominated politics yet were so weak, divided, and isolated was a critical factor in the way politics developed in the postcommunist period.

5 Organized Forgetting: Elites with No History

From the moment the war ended in 1945, the Communist Party leadership made antifascist ideology, including the role of the Soviet Union as liberator and its own role in the Slovak National Uprising, central to its claim to legitimacy.[1] The official policy on the Jewish question, on the meaning of fascism, and the interpretation of the Slovak National Uprising changed quite dramatically in the years of communist rule.[2] A quick summary of these switches is striking. First, during a period when the Communist Party was officially implementing the "Beneš decrees" against fascist collaborators, it was quietly bringing former fascists into the Party. Following Yugoslav leader Josip Tito's split with Stalin in 1948, the Party shifted to condemnation of the Slovak communist leaders of the Uprising. After just having used allegations of anti-Semitism against the Slovak "bourgeois nationalists," the Party suddenly began to appeal to anti-Semitism (albeit indirectly). Then there was a flip back to a favorable view of the Slovak National Uprising with de-Stalinization in 1963. During the normalization period, which destroyed the 1968 reform movement, the Party reverted to more orthodox interpretations of history, including a renewed focus on the Soviet army's role as liberators in World War II. This, of course, followed the Soviet invasion that suppressed the Prague Spring.

While the Party shifted in its position, purging and changing personnel at each turn, it simultaneously engaged in a nation-building process. The regime went to great lengths to replicate the Soviet World War II cult, complete with days of commemoration, museums, large-circulation official histories, films, schoolbooks, field trips, and articles in the media. But the methods that the regime used to present this history included distortions and omissions. History writing was characterized by abstract phrases and lists of facts without context. There was the infamous appearance and disappearance of figures from schoolbooks and the expunging of certain events and personalities from history based on the rapid shifts in what the regime found acceptable.[3] To bolster this, the Party curtailed archival access and removed certain information from libraries.

This frequent change in position, the constant elite purges, and these methods of presenting history had the Orwellian effect of leaving those who were socialized in this system alienated from the regime and atomized from one another. It left them confused about how to judge either the activities of the Communist Party or of the wartime Slovak state.[4] The two key functions of historical consciousness in national ideology were either eroded or not allowed to develop. Historical consciousness neither served as a glue binding together members of a society and elite, nor did it serve the strategic role of allowing for common judgments and learning from the past. In this way, the regime created the *condition* of the mass-elite.

Many of the more educated and articulate members of society (whether or not they were close to the power structure) were products of the communist modernization process: they mostly came from worker and peasant families. The communist socialization process was the only source of ideology (and in many cases the only source of information) to which they were exposed.[5] The unusual cases we saw in the last chapter were exceptions. In most cases, neither families nor other institutions preserved alternative meanings of the past to challenge the official ones. Substitutes did not develop as they did for the democrats and nationalists. The mass-elite, and much of the population, was left with nothing but family stories to inform them of the meaning of World War II.

Each time period in the chronology of nation-building that follows has three parts. The first part focuses on the official Communist Party position on World War II in the context of changing Party politics, including elite purges and personnel changes. The second part illustrates the mechanisms of nation-building and organized forgetting through history textbooks and other cultural representations of these events like films and novels. The third piece in each time period shows how the above two factors meant that elites failed to cohere around any alternative ideology in spite of alienation from the official one.

Before turning to the chronology of Leninist nation-building, however, we must introduce the mass-elite according to generation.

Generational Cohorts

The basic dictionary definition of generation is: A group of individuals "regarded as having a common, more or less contemporaneous, cultural or social attribute."[6] While the end result of the Leninist nation-building process was the mass-elite, generational effects remained important even in the face of communist regimes' attempt to homogenize meaning and to eliminate social cleavages and nonstate groupings. This is true in several ways.

First, the very idea of nation-building and developing historical consciousness has a cross-generational component. Meanings of the past need to be reproduced over time. It is obvious that those generations that did not personally experience key events have to acquire historical consciousness from different sources than do generations that lived through this history. But even the latter need to articulate a *meaning* to their common experiences.

Each generation in Slovakia came to the communist period differently, the younger having been shaped by communism and the older having been shaped by precommunism. Generation is fundamental to the concept of mass-elite in just this sense. Because of their age and the fact that they came from families that lacked alternative ideologies, mass-elites were pure products of the communist socialization process. They were either children or were not alive during World War II. Older generations also can fit the category of mass-elite, but were not as fully cut off from the past.

Second, aside from the above effect of the passage of time, the regime changed its approach toward nation-building from the Stalinist 1950s, to the liberalization of the 1960s, to the repressive "normalization" of the 1970s and 1980s. Different generations of elites were thus affected differently by state-organized forgetting. Some were more strongly affected by the hiatus of 1968. But due to changing regime policies, even those who did have a possibility of cohering in 1968 were fragmented with the crackdown that followed the suppression of the Prague Spring.

Third, in east central Europe in particular there were unusal twists and turns in the history, and thus in the experience, of the populations of these countries, which had two somewhat contradictory effects. On the one hand, the major shifts of 1938, 1948, 1963–68, and 1989 had a lasting formative effect on generations. On the other hand, the fact that such significant events happened so frequently and represented such dramatic

Table 1 Generational Experiences of the Mass-Elite

Generation/Examples of key figures	Age in 1989	Age during World War II (1939–45)
Prewar Generation A. Dubček; V. Mináč; R. Kaliský; H. Koctúh; L. Ťažký; D. Slobodník	60–75	9–24 to 15–30
Reform Communist Generation I. Laluha; P. Števček; M. Kováč	50–60	0–9 to 6–15
Children of the Sixties Generation V. Mečiar; M. Kňažko; J. Markuš; V. Moric	40–50	small children or born after war
Normalization Generation J. Prokeš; A. Hrnko; V. Miškovský; S. Pánis; P. Brňák; V. Repka	30–40	born after war

changes kept cross-generational meanings of the past from accumulating over time.[7] This was particularly true owing to the revolutionary nature of the regime, which separated generations so markedly both in their socialization processes and in the very act of revolution which older generations had lived through.[8]

Thus there were several reasons that older generations did not pass on ideas about the past to their children and grandchildren or their younger colleagues. In addition to the separation of generations that is a by-product of revolution, the fear attached to the revolutionary and repressive policies of the communist regime was a deterrent. Incentives for upward mobility also contributed to the failure for ideas about the past to be transmitted from older to younger generations. Of course there are a variety of personal reasons for whether family stories are passed on that have little to do with these larger sociocultural patterns.

As we saw in the last chapter, generation was a key element in the maintenance of continuity among the democrats and Catholic nationalists. In that chapter, each generation had different reasons for preserving ideas about the past. Communication across generation was an important mechanism for transmitting and preserving historical consciousness. For

Years in school (based on when they would have been age 12); Orientation of Communist Party education	Years in higher education; orientation of communist party education	Role in 1968
1926–1940 First Republic/Slovak state	1932–46 First Republic/ Slovak state	Some were at head of reform communist movement; movement for Slovak autonomy
1941–51 Slovak state/Stalinism	1947–57 Stalinism	Some at head of reform communist movement; movement for Slovak autonomy
1952–62 Stalinism/beginning of reform	1958–68 Post-Stalin reform	Involved in youth movement during Prague Spring
1963–73 reform period/ normalization	1969–79 "Normalization"	Generally too young to have been involved

the mass-elite, however, I will show how, for each generation since the war, there was a failure to cohere and to pass on ideas about the past.

Four generational cohorts were important in the postcommunist period (see table 1). I will call the generation born in the 1920s or before, who were over sixty years old in 1989, the *prewar generation.* Those born in the 1930s who were over fifty in 1989 will be called the *reform communist generation.* The bulk of the postcommunist elites, the *children of the sixties generation,* were those born in the 1940s who were between forty and fifty in 1989. Those born in the 1950s and after, who were under forty in 1989, are the *normalization generation.*[9] The three younger cohorts are represented in the mass-elite. The oldest cohort was also important in the post-1989 story.

I will introduce each generation in terms of their relationship to the memory of the war, their educational experience and when it took place, their involvement in 1968, and how important they were after 1989. I will then foreshadow my later, more detailed discussion of why it was unlikely that any of these cohorts could develop or retain the kind of shared understanding of history that I am calling historical consciousness. Especially important is the impact, or lack thereof, of the reform movement of the

1960s, in particular the 1968 Prague Spring, in forming lasting alternative identities.

The Children of the Sixties

Those born after 1939 comprised the generation at the center of the political elite in the post-1989 period. Individuals in this cohort were socialized in communist educational institutions from 1951 to 1961 (based on when they would have been age twelve and in middle school); started university or higher education from 1957 to 1967 (when they would have been eighteen). Their parents would likely have been born approximately between 1910 and 1920.[10]

The key mass-elite nationalists after 1989 were all in this generation or a few years younger: Vladimír Mečiar was born in 1942. Jozef Markuš, who emerged as head of the Matica Slovenská, the Slovak cultural foundation, was born in 1944. The leaders of the Slovak National Party, the most radical of the mainstream nationalist parties after 1989, were Jozef Prokeš, born in 1950; Marián Andel, 1950; Vít'azoslav Moric, 1946. Interestingly, none of these figures came from intelligentsia families or even strong communist families.

After the elections of June 1992, when the political scene was dominated by the mass-elite, eight out of thirteen ministers in the Slovak government were from this cohort (one was younger). Fifty-seven out of one hundred and fifty deputies in the post–June 1992 Slovak parliament were from this age group, the most heavily represented.[11]

Most in this age group were formed by the reform movement of 1968 and were either purged and diverted by the experience or were quietly affected as they continued with their lives in the mainstream, and even with Party membership. It is difficult to determine the extent to which 1968 contributed to an articulated ideology, and I will discuss this more below. Certainly exposure to 1968 alone was not sufficient. For this generation, the events of 1968 were too short and passing. The repressive methods of the post-1968 regime were thus able to fairly easily destroy the ties forged during the brief reform period.

The Normalization Generation

The cohort born in the 1950s and later was also plentiful in the post-89 mass-elite. They were between thirty and forty years old after 1989. They came of age after 1968, and were products of "normalization." They were even more cut off from the direct memory and impact of the war. They grew up during a period of alienation. This group was in middle school in 1963–73 and entered higher education from 1968 to 1978. Some were exposed to the more open discussions and reliable information during the 1960s; others were not old enough for the sixties to be meaningful. They grew up when the experience of the war was further away in people's memories, after the Soviet troops had come and thereby tarnished the memory of the Soviet "liberation" from the Nazis, and when the regime was extremely restrictive regarding information. The parents of this cohort were likely born in 1920–35 and themselves were children during the war. Referring to this generation, Milan Šimečka wrote in 1985: "There has grown up already an entire generation in whose memory there really is no history. Its memory contains only the official reduced version which that generation seeks to forget as fast as possible."[12]

Many of the leaders of the Slovak National Party were from this younger group (Anton Hrnko, 1955; Vladimír Miškovský, 1961; Ján Slota, 1953). (That party's leader, Peter Weiss, born in 1952, is an example.) Key figures in the newly renamed Communist Party—the Party of the Democratic Left—were also from this generation. Of sixteen deputies from the Slovak National Party in the parliament elected in June 1990, fourteen were from this age cohort and a group a few years older. Of the deputies to the Slovak National Council after 1992, thirty-five out of one hundred and fifty were in this age group. In addition, some of the smaller, more extreme national-ist parties were formed by members of this generation.[13]

The Prewar Generation

Unlike any of the others, this cohort could be defined, according to my criteria, as a group based on an independent communist understanding of the war, since it was formed by the antifascist resistance. The older part of this group was educated before the communist period and grew up during the First Republic. Many who led the reform in the 1960s are no longer alive, such as Gustáv Husák. But several from this cohort—for example Alexander Dubček, a Slovak who was Communist Party chief during the reform movement of 1968—were important in the post-1989 period.

Reform Communist Generation

The generation born in the 1930s, in their fifties or sixties in 1989–92, would have been educated mostly during the communist period. They generally came of age after the war, but would still have some independent memories of the war. The oldest would have gone through higher education in the early communist period; the youngest would have had more of their education during the communist period, including, of course, Party education (which, especially during those years, was highly dogmatic). After confronting the disappointment of Stalinism and, in the case of the older part of this group, their own involvement in the Stalinist excesses of the 1950s, many in this group became reform communists in the 1960s.[14]

While most post-1989 ministers and deputies tended to be slightly younger, this cohort was a significant presence, particularly in Mečiar's party, both as parliamentary deputies and members of the government. In the Slovak government after 1992, for example, one out of thirteen ministers was from this age group, one from the prewar generation, and the rest from the children of the sixties generation. In the federal government, out of five Slovaks represented, two were from this group (one was from the older group and two from the children of the sixties cohort). Forty-three out of one hundred and fifty Slovak National Council deputies were from this cohort (Mečiar's party had the greatest proportion from this group). They were also represented in the journalists and commentators who emerged after 1989 as nationalists, some of whom had been important during the 1960s.[15]

Members of the reform communist generation, who became important after 1989, included those who were purged in 1968 as well as those who compromised with the regime and stayed in their positions after 1968. I sometimes refer to them as "national communists." I put them in the mass-elite category even though they do not fit the generational criterion of the profile. The fact that they were older and had precommunist memories, and that they had the opportunity to cohere in the 1960s, distinguishes them from the younger group. But they represent the power of regime efforts to atomize even more than the younger generation, since they had ideological ties that needed to be broken.

The communist nationalist intellectuals from the older two cohorts were, in some cases, committed to historical truth and motivated by the excesses of the Stalinist purge period. They were involved in a public discussion and evolution of an elite consensus or ideology regarding history. But the post-1968 "normalization," when it was necessary to conform in order to survive, was critical. During that period, their ties to one another and commitment to ideas was diluted.

After 1968, there was a divide between those loyal to their convictions and those loyal to Communist Party leader Husák (this was truer of the prewar generation).[16] As we saw in the last chapter, Husák himself had an ambiguous legacy. After being jailed in the 1950s for "bourgeois national- ism" and fighting in the 1960s for greater recognition of Slovakia, he pre- sided over the "normalization" process, which included the suppression of Slovak identity.[17] Aside from a group around the deposed Dubček called *Obroda* (which played a key role after 1989 but was not large), the 1968 reformers did not maintain ties. Almost none went into dissent or signed Charter 77.

Leninist Nation-building and the Formation of the Mass-elite

Nation-building did not begin until the Communist Party took power in 1948. But to give perspective to the later periods we must start with the 1945–48 period, which was one of struggle over the legacy of the war. In this context, the Communist Party began to create its legitimating myth as a way of building cohesion among the elite but also as a mechanism for pop- ular mobilization. The war shaped the alignments and the groupings that were competing for power and ideological primacy. During these years, the reform communist generation was entering high school and university.[18]

While the war shaped politics, politics also shaped the war. The con- struction of the myth of the war during the early communist years was also very much influenced by Czech primacy in the Party. Czech dominance be- came more pronounced when, on July 26, 1948, the presidium of the Com- munist Party of Czechoslovakia decided that the Party needed to be united and to dissolve the separate Slovak Communist Party. Until then, follow- ing the independent role played by the Slovak communists during the war, the Slovak Communist Party had been separately represented in the pre- February 1948 Prague coalition. After this decision, though the Slovak Party kept its name, the Central Committee was subordinated to the Cen- tral Committee in Prague.[19] This step would come back to haunt the Party and was itself important for the later building of the World War II myth.

The wartime fate of Slovak Jews did not figure much in Party discus- sions during these years. The Communist Party was ambivalent about singling out Jews as victims of fascism. The books and memoirs that were published during this period were removed from library shelves and book- stores after 1948 or 1949.[20] But, it was, in many ways, too early to write about this trauma anyway.[21] As we will see, there was no public discus- sion of the Jews' fate until after 1989.

The Coming of Communism, 1948–1960

The Party and World War II

Once they came to power, the communists took steps to eliminate the power of noncommunist institutions and parties. During these years, the justification for the destruction of nonparty groups was based as much on the side of the war they were on as it was on class background.[22] But with the Tito "heresy" in 1948–49 the Party turned in on itself. As is well known, the purges in communist parties throughout Eastern Europe at the time coincided with whether the war years were spent in the West or at home or in Moscow. Those who were not in Moscow became subjects of suspicion. While power and Soviet dominance were the primary issues, the events of World War II and the nature of individual countries' experiences of resistance were at the center of the debate. Stalin's turn against Tito was reflected within the Czechoslovak Party. This led to one of the most critical steps in the eventual developments in Slovakia: the imprisonment of Slovak leaders of the uprising against the Nazis as "bourgeois nationalists."

The argument used by Party officials was that there was a heresy analogous to Titoism in Slovakia. The bourgeois nationalists were condemned for their "abrogation of democratic centralism" and indicted with the "Yugoslav hubris" regarding their liberation struggle.[23] The Party began to allege that the "bourgeois nationalists" advocated a new separatist program and identified their nationalism with the HSLS and the Slovak state. Slovak Party leader Karol Bacílek alleged that in "bourgeois nationalism" could be seen the hand of "former officials of the . . . fascist Slovak state."[24] At another point, Viliam Široký alleged that during the 1930s it was hard to distinguish between the point of view of the fascists and certain representatives of the Communist Party. He argued that while clerico-fascism had gone underground, it was surviving there "with the help of the Husáks and the Novomeskýs."[25]

In 1950, Husák, Ladislav Novomeský, and Vladimír Clementis were forced to engage in "self-criticism" at the ninth congress of the Slovak and Czechoslovak Communist Party. They confessed to "bourgeois nationalism" regarding the Czech and Hungarian minorities and were criticized at this time (Stalin was friendly to Israel) for anti-Semitic views. Husák admitted that there was justification for the allegations about anti-Semitism.[26]

As time went on in the purge, Rudolf Slánský and the group surrounding him, the jailers of the Slovak "bourgeois nationalists," themselves became victims. During this period, with a switch in Soviet Middle East policy and now with Stalin's anti-Semitism, the main enemy of the regime became "Zionists involved in a Western conspiracy."[27]

Eleven of the fourteen leading communists in the Slánský trial were Jews, and the rhetoric included references to the war and the Holocaust, including the Jews as special victims. The prosecutor at the Slánský trial claimed that Zionists had "shamelessly abused the Czechoslovak people's traditional abhorrence of anti-Semitism . . . to infiltrate the Communist Party and to hide their faces behind the suffering of Jews under Nazi rule."[28]

In terms of the Party's articulation of a meaning to the events of World War II, this was not a random tactic. Czech purge victims were not as heavily associated with fascism as were Slovaks.[29] It is probably true that the power of popular anti-Semitism exceeded that of antifascism, especially in Slovakia. Some say that the regime linked the popular Slovak communist Clementis with the Slánský group of "Zionists" in order to tarnish a popular figure. The Party might have thought that arresting Clementis alongside Jews could dilute the effects of his execution.[30] In a classic example of Orwellian distortion of history, the "bourgeois nationalists" were associated first with anti-Semitism, then with Zionist conspiracy and also with leaders of the fascist state.

Nation-Building

It was during the highly dogmatic 1948–60 period that the Party began its efforts to build its myth around World War II, and the history writing enterprise began during these years. It is important to remember that up to this time very little national history had been written and there was not much of a tradition of Slovak historians. But under the communist regime history writing flowered at the Historical Institute, which was set up at the Academy of Sciences in 1950 and at the Institute for the History of the Communist Party. (Both of these had equivalents in Prague.)[31]

Political control in history education was clearly evident during these years. At Comenius University, it became possible to be named a docent without the "habilitation," and this led to a decrease in the quality of teaching.[32] There were no university textbooks during these early years, especially regarding twentieth-century history.[33] The only professor teaching about the twentieth century was a product of the Party ideological school rather than a trained historian.[34] That same professor wrote the first official history of the Uprising just at this time, and by the time it was going to press, he dutifully rewrote the part on Husák and Novomeský to portray them as traitors rather than heroes.[35] The reform communist generation was going through university and higher education during these years.

I focus here on history textbooks to portray the content of the Party line on World War II and its methods of nation-building. The textbooks engender a distillation of how the issues I am concerned with—the meaning of fascism, the character of the Slovak state, the responsibility for the Jewish deportations, and the meaning of the Uprising—were officially treated. Official propaganda and the media were also important but are not analyzed here; the content would have been the same and the prevalence of media depictions of the official line would only strengthen my claims about organized forgetting.

Textbooks began to be written after the first law on schools in 1948 and particularly after 1951, when a Party resolution complained that curriculum reform was not happening quickly enough.[36] During these years many books were translated directly from Soviet texts. There was little local history included; instead these books were about the history of the international communist movement.[37] This changed in later years.

The textbooks analyzed are from a number of types of schools. There were three educational tracks after the eight- or nine-year basic school: gymnasium, whose graduates could go on to university; trade schools, which also prepared students for higher education at the various institutes; and the manual labor or the apprenticeship track.[38] Mostly, those who became the elite would have been in either gymnasium or trade school.[39] While the history texts used by these two types of schools were similar, students in the trade school track were exposed to a more superficial history curriculum (fewer history lessons per week). The history classes for those on the worker track were almost nonexistent and their texts were extremely sparse and simplistic.[40]

While into the 1950s there were no textbooks at the university level, once they were written students in the philosophical faculty at Comenius University, who had courses in general history, used them. In other types of higher education—from medicine, to law, to economics—students would learn the history of their particular disciplines. The law school curriculum included more history, and history tests were required to get in. All of these schools had courses in Marxist-Leninist ideology. One of the three parts of this course—scientific communism—included a history of international communism, which would have provided students with some information on World War II.[41]

Before turning to the texts from the 1950s, it is important to point out that there are two reasons for presenting the texts throughout this chapter. First is to show the content of the changing communist myth about World War II and what information was available to whom and from what sources. But even more important is to illustrate, and give a flavor for, the regime's methods of presenting history. The main point here is that this presentation of history was not only not compelling, thereby failing to create a widely shared communist ideology regarding the war, but it was also numbing and eroded the ability to come up with shared noncommunist judgments of the past.

Although the methods will become evident through the presentation of the texts, a word about the communist myth of the war is in order. The communist position on each of the issues from the war remained constant in the basics, and in fact was the same throughout the socialist bloc. But it switched frequently in the specifics. This is why it is important to look at the evolving approach to the war in each time period, as opposed to the stable views of the democrats and nationalists. The general view was that fascism was bad, and a product of the highest stage of capitalism, though it often is not clear exactly why it was bad; its causes are emphasized at the expense of its character. The resistance to fascism was heroic but was led by communists and particularly the Soviet Union. The Holocaust is downplayed and often the fact that Jews were particular victims is not emphasized.

The specific approach to these issues in Slovakia, however, shifted over time. Democrats and nationalists disagree about whether to label the Tiso state fascist, how repressive it was, and how popular. The communists vary in the extent to which the regime is presented as dictatorial or totalitarian and whether the content of its ideology—racist, anti-Semitic—is presented at all. Treatments differ in terms of how much emphasis they place on the imposition of fascism by Germany, and how much support the regime had and from whom. Most of the time the Western imperialist powers are implicated.

On the Jewish deportations the main controversy is about responsibility, but unlike the debate between the democrats and the nationalists, the distinctions between Tiso and Tuka and Mach are not made. In communist texts it is assumed that Tiso was the main villain. The only remaining question is whether the Germans pushed the Slovaks into the policy or whether the Slovaks willingly enacted and participated in the deportations. Whereas for democrats and nationalists the debate is about the Tiso exemptions, and under what conditions the regime pushed to halt the deportations, for communists the issue is who were the main victims of fascism. Was it communists? Is the particular place of Jews as victims acknowledged? Is their ultimate fate presented? Where does the Slovak involvement in the deportations fit in the larger history of World War II? Again there is a different concern for communists, who do not point to all the other countries that deported their Jews. Here the concern is whether or not the Holocaust is placed in the larger context of the entire Nazi extermination effort.

The communists also have a different concern than do the democrats and nationalists when it comes to the Slovak National Uprising. Instead of debating whether or not it was a civil war, communists care more about who played the main role in the resistance. Was it the Soviet Union or Slovak communists? Did any groups besides communists play a role? What was its purpose: the restoration of democracy or to prove the antifascist role of the Soviet Union as opposed to the continuing militarism of the capitalist West?

The following summaries are from several textbooks from the 1950s.[42] Interestingly, the children of the sixties generation, most represented in the post-1989 elite, was in school during this period. It is illuminating to look at the textbooks that they would have had.

On the nature of fascism. In the books from this period there is really no mention of what fascism meant. Fascists were simply the enemy. In addition, the population was against fascism, no one wanted an independent Slovakia, and the leaders of the Slovak state were puppets of Germany. According to these books, responsibility for fascism in Slovakia lay as much with foreign capitalists as with the leaders of the Slovak state.

On the Jews. The issue of responsibility does not come up, since in these books there is no mention at all of Slovak Jews. Jews are only mentioned in the part of the book about the occupation of the Czech lands where, after the assassination of Reichsprotektor Reinhard Heydrich by Czech resistance fighters, the Nazis "unleashed terror against the population." In this context it is mentioned that Jews were separated from the rest of the population and later were sent to death camps where they were exterminated. It says that Terezín became a concentration camp. No numbers are mentioned; nor is it mentioned that sending Jews away to camps like Terezín was part of a Europe-wide Nazi attempt at extermination.

On the resistance. As was appropriate to the atmosphere in the Party during this time, the "bourgeois nationalists" (who by the time these textbooks were written were in prison) were working with the London government, which was in the hands of capitalists; they wanted to return to the pre-Munich bourgeois republic. Husák and Novomeský favored the bourgeoisie, not the people, and betrayed the party of which they were a part. While Viliam Široký—then prime minister—was portrayed as heroic, Husák and Novomeský were traitors. At the core of the resistance were the Soviet Union and the Communist Party of Slovakia.

As we can see in the texts from the 1950s, the place of the Soviet Union is given great priority and the "imperialists" and "bourgeois nationalists" are represented as equally evil and worthy of blame for wartime suffering and crimes to the Germans, let alone the Slovak fascists.

During these first years of communism students would also have been exposed to a proliferation of literature and film on the World War II period. There were numerous films on the Soviet liberation, probably mostly imported. There was also an outpouring of socialist realist novels on the Slovak National Uprising.[43] But this was a period of such conformity and the official line was so clear that it is not necessary to elaborate on the content. Official information policy was so strict during these years that it is fairly easy to be certain that other sources of information, which did not conform to these very specific contours of the myth of the war, would have been unavailable.

Elite Cohesion

In the dual story of the creation of the World War II myth and of elite atomization, 1948 to 1956 (and really until 1961) was a critical period. And this was true both for the generation in power and for those being socialized during this period, who would later become the mass-elite. Official meanings of history shifted quickly and were inconsistent, making it difficult for one to become widely accepted.[44] In addition, Slovak communists were alienated by the condemnation of the Slovak heroes of the resistance. The atomization in the Party and the distortions of history lasted for ten years, longer than in other bloc countries.[45]

The atmosphere during this period is often characterized as one of moral collapse, as symbolized by the phenomenon of children informing on parents. As Heda Kovály strikingly illustrates in her memoir of the period, the moral collapse and the collapse of morale that happened during World War II set the stage for the period that followed, including the purges.[46] Milan Hauner points out that the "Nazi terror shook the belief of the population in essential moral values of western civilization."[47] Collaboration led to more collaboration rather than to resolve and resistance.[48]

Karel Kaplan, one of the major Czech historians of the period, writes that the purges created an atmosphere that encouraged the rise of informers and ruthless careerists, causing extensive changes in Party and state personnel, and that "it is possible to talk about the emergence of a certain social class recruited or promoted by this situation."[49] He says elsewhere that not only were they guilty of terror but "they were also mediocrities not only unwilling but *unable* [author's italics] to think in a wider context."

De-Stalinization and Reform, 1962–68

The Party in the 1960s

It was, in part, due to this atomization in the elite that the influence of the 1956 Soviet twentieth Party congress came more slowly to Czechoslovakia than to any other Eastern Bloc country. No one emerged to lead a revitalization of the Party.[50] But the official Party line became subject to challenge in Slovakia in the early 1960s from inside the Party itself—mostly from Party intellectuals: writers and journalists of the prewar and reform communist generations. The interpretation of the World War II period was central to the evolving process of Slovak self-assertion, and to the calls for a reckoning with the purges of the 1950s. Best known among emerging critics are Dubček and Husák, who both became prominent in leading the reform. Commentators and writers like Vladimír Mináč (born 1922), Roman Kaliský (born 1922), and Miroslav Kusý (born 1931), all of whom were important in the post-1989 period, came of age and became important voices during this period. During this period Mečiar, born in 1942, was just entering his twenties, attending law school in Bratislava, and beginning to be active in the Young Communists.

Starting with demands for reinterpretation of the Slovak National Uprising, the Party myth about the war began to change. The main problem from the past that needed to be faced was one within the Party itself: the purges of the 1950s. But World War II, which was intertwined with the purge issue because of the bourgeois nationalists (if not the Jewish communists), was also still a dominant issue. In the field of history, issues connected with the war became the main subjects of debate and study.[51]

The call for truth about the excesses of the 1950s, particularly about the fate of the Slovak "bourgeois nationalists," was suggestive of links to the war in a more peripheral sense as well. It was a complaint about regime *methods* as well as about the falsified *content* of the official account of the Uprising. Much of the push for change was couched in terms of a struggle for truth.[52] These were demands for a change in the regime's approach to all aspects of history, not just the history of the 1950s.

Since de-Stalinization in Slovakia was largely focused on the interpretation of the Slovak National Uprising and the rehabilitation of the "bour-geois nationalists," at the twelfth Party congress in 1962 a commission was established to investigate "violations of Party principles" committed in 1949–54.[53] Novomeský and Husák, who had been sentenced in 1954, were rehabilitated in 1963.

The newly rehabilitated Husák took a leading role in calls for rein-terpreting the Slovak National Uprising.[54] Until then, it had been depicted as a communist undertaking directed from Moscow. At the time of the twentieth anniversary celebrations in August 1964, a campaign in the Slo-vak press called for a revision of this interpretation. Revisions included calls for recognition that the Uprising had been primarily a Slovak under-taking; that Czech participation was limited to individuals serving under Slovak leadership; that antifascists from all parties had participated in it (not only communists); that disaffected units of the Slovak army had initi-ated and presided over the military side of it; and that the leadership was not Moscow or the Moscow-based exiles but, instead, Slovaks at home. Party leader Anotonín Novotný, still in power at the time, attended the anniversary celebrations but repeated the orthodox interpretation.[55]

The debate over the interpretation of the Uprising and, to some extent, the nature of the Slovak state itself was really embedded in a larger and continuing debate between Czechs and Slovaks about Slovak autonomy.[56] This debate resulted in the formal federalization of the state. Husák, who became a major figure in this debate, claimed that the Czech public had been told that the leaders of the Slovak Communist Party in the 1940s were separatists. He complained that in the mind of the public, Clementis, Novomeský, and Husák were probably no different from the earlier fascist separatists.[57] He said that a campaign had been waged against Slovak na-tionalism for thirteen years and that when it was reversed, in 1963–64, the Czech public was barely informed of it.[58] He also said that he and his colleagues had wanted a federal model for the Czechoslovak state in 1944–45.[59]

In 1968, an explicit debate started about the Czech allegations that Slo-vak demands for autonomy harkened back to the Slovak state. These themes emerge again in the post-1989 period, often through the writings of the same individuals. The editor of *Rolnické Noviny,* frustrated with Czech delays regarding the federalization issue, for the first time within the Marxist-Leninist framework, raised the possibility that the Slovaks would be better off on their own. *Pravda* came back a few days later alleg-ing that this was a veiled attempt to rehabilitate the wartime state. *Rol-nické Noviny* called this "demagoguery," saying it was obvious they did not mean the creation of a "l'udák" state.[60] Pavol Števček, on August 2, 1968, called for recognition of the one occasion when Slovaks had had independence (1939–45).[61] While he conceded this state had both been the product of great power politics and had brought to the surface the worst of the Slovak nation, he said it was important to realize that "the idea or recollection of the Slovak State's independence is alive in the national memory. It cannot be ignored forever in examining the alternatives in the solution of the perspectives of a small nation."[62]

Slovak communist nationalists began to argue that the wartime state was important in giving Slovaks a sense of autonomy and confidence in their ability to run their own affairs. Allegations during the 1950s trials of links between the goals of the fascist leaders and those of the bourgeois nationalists were political rhetoric. But during the 1960s, the communists themselves began to speak more openly about the importance of both the Uprising and the Slovak state for providing a significant experience of autonomy. In these arguments, the question of autonomy existed outside of (and possibly in defiance of) the moral character of the wartime regime. But still, these writers were careful to dissociate their position from any type of non-Marxist separatist or fascist nationalism of the past.[63] Émigrés and other figures from the Slovak state still living in Slovakia were not part of the debate.[64]

It is important to remember that this was a debate inside the Party, though in 1968 even some non-Party voices began to be heard. From the standpoint of the Communist Party, the war and the resistance were about a Slovak struggle against fascism, albeit as part of a pro-Soviet and pro-worker ideology. Slovak communists were much more concerned with the legacy of the war as an underpinning for Slovak autonomy than as a moral lesson about the depths to which modern Europeans could descend, the interpretation given by the democrats.

Slovak collaboration in the deportation of the Jews—the central moral issue from the war—was addressed in the increasingly active fields of culture and history. However, in the proliferation of historical studies, nothing explicitly on the Jewish question came out. As historians began to study fascism rather than simply condemning it, the meaning of fascism was treated less abstractly; for example, more emphasis was placed on Slovak participation and collaboration. But the reexamination of fascism also meant a new appreciation of the fact of autonomy, if not the character of the regime.[65] During this period, the Jewish issue, according to one historian, was a lower priority and there was not much time to focus on it. While other aspects of the debates from this period were officially incorporated into the Party interpretation of the war—particularly the Slovak National Uprising—the Jewish issue faded after 1968, with the official anti-Semitic wave following the 1967 Middle East war. Between 1948 and 1989, it was only during these few years that any real discussion of these issues took place.

Nation-Building

Although de-Stalinization came slowly to Czechoslovakia, by the end of the 1950s there were some changes. Another law on schools was passed in 1960, and historians began to push to revive the teaching of history. A slow opening began as early as 1959. In textbooks from the early 1960s more information appeared on the nature of fascism, on the Jewish question, and on the Slovak participation in the resistance. Those born in the early 1950s would have encountered these books which came out in 1962–64.

I will be referring to three textbooks, one of which was written in Czech. (While it is not clear if it was used in Slovakia, it provides an interesting comparison.) The first Slovak book, for the final years of basic school, came out in 1962. The second Slovak book, for the second year of second-ary trade school, came out in 1964. The Czech book, also for basic school, came out in 1963.[66]

Overall, there is more information in these texts than there was in the texts from the 1950s. But the point about lack of context remains impor-tant. The books vary in terms of what is emphasized and what is under-played and omitted. (This is partly due to the fact that this was a period of change in interpretation.) For example, in the Czech book we hear nothing about Slovakia and almost nothing about Jews, but we do hear about the existence of Auschwitz and the all-European Nazi effort to bring people to concentration camps and in some cases to exterminate them.[67] In the Slo-vak books we hear more about Slovakia and the Jews but little about the larger Nazi extermination project.

Nature of fascism, German Nazism, and the character of the Slovak state. In the Slovak books from 1962 and 1964 there is much more information than there was in the 1950s about the nature of Nazism in Germany and thus about the nature of fascism as an ideology. These books write that it was a doctrine based on racial hatred with superior and inferior races. Within this doctrine, the Germans deemed themselves superior and Slavs inferior and that the inferior groups should serve the superior. There is explicit reference to the centrality of anti-Semitism in German Nazism: it is referred to as "the most disgusting manifestation" of this set of beliefs and it is stated that the Nazis named the Jews as the biggest enemy of the German people. The explanation was that this was a way of distracting the German people from the struggle against the real enemy, the big capitalists and landowners. In the 1964 book there is description of persecution (deprivation of all rights) and extermination by gas of the Jews of Germany.[68]

The causes of fascism are said to be the economic crisis of the world in the 1930s and high unemployment, particularly in Germany.[69] As in the 1950s, the Western powers are blamed for doing nothing to prevent the growing influence of the Nazis, who had the support of the German imperialists. This was because the West was opposed to the working class movement and to the Soviet Union.[70] In contrast to the books of the 1950s, there is also more information here about the causes of the rise of the HSLS. According to these books, it was the poverty caused by the bourgeois government and the fact that the Slovak people as a minority should have gotten full equality that allowed them to fall under the influence of fascism.[71]

The Slovak state is said not to have been really independent and to have fulfilled only the demands of the Germans, who gave Slovakia the appearance of independence so that they did not have to waste troops there.[72] These accounts are ambiguous about how much support the regime actually had. One book says that while there was initial support for the fascist regime, the Communist Party exposed the regime's hypocrisy and many soon renounced their support, especially when the regime really began to implement Nazi policies and methods.[73] The high Catholic clergy is blamed for misusing the religious feeling of the population for its own political ends. Everything was in the interests of German capitalists who took over Slovak industry.[74]

The bourgeois parties were also to blame and acquiesced to single-party dominance in the hands of Tiso's party and allowed them to fascisize the country, including prohibiting the Communist Party and setting up the Hlinka Guard on the model of the Nazis.[75] The books also emphasize, in the list of the fascist regime's deeds, the exacerbation of the Czech-Slovak conflict. The fascists sent away all Czech state and public workers in Slovakia. The Germans, with the help of the fascists and church hierarchy, deliberately opened a rift between the Czech and Slovak peoples.[76]

Slovak state and the Jews. While these books put prohibition of the Communist Party at the top of the list of the evil deeds of the fascist state, they are much more explicit than were the 1950s books about the activities of the fascists regarding Jews. The fascists formed the Hlinka Guard, "which

persecuted Czech and Jewish citizens and all progressive people, especially communists."[77] So Jews are mentioned. But they are part of a list
of victims.

These textbooks are clear about who made the decisions: the HSLS em-
barked on the persecution of the Jews in response to German command.
The Jews were sent to concentration camps. The fact that these were death
camps is not mentioned; nor are the numbers, nor that it was primarily
Jews. The failure to mention numbers makes it particularly difficult for
students, who are living in a country with almost no Jews left, to tell what
the significance of the deportations was.

It is hard to tell why some facts are introduced and not others, but in
each book only one piece of the story is given. While the earlier book does
not mention the "Aryanization" of Jewish property and the passage of the
"Nuremberg" racial laws before the deportations, the later book does mention that the HSLS garnered support by giving away Jewish property.[78] But
this later account does not mention the deportation of the Slovak Jews or
who was responsible.

The 1964 book tells more specifically about the fate of Czech Jews but
not Slovak Jews ("Czech Jews were sent to concentration camps, where
most were killed with gas").[79] The Czech book does not mention Slovak
Jews at all and only in passing mentions that "they [the fascists] were
particularly cruel to communists, whom they set up as their key enemy;
they also treated the Jews very brutally."[80]

Another example of the method of presenting some events abstractly
and others with great detail is in the 1962 book. In contrast to the brief
mention of Jews being persecuted and sent to concentration camps, this
book gives a much more explicit description of the suffering of people who
died in the resistance: "Thousands of people who helped the partisans
found death in concentration camps and mass graves."[81] The book says
explicitly that it was not just the Germans who fought the partisans but
also members of the Hlinka Guard. But in neither book is it specified that
both the Germans and the Hlinka Guard were involved in the Jewish deportations, and thus the reader could think that it was just the Germans.[82]
Whereas the rounding up of Slovaks in several towns is described, there is
no detail at all about the much more extensive rounding up of Jews.[83]

Resistance. Here, as opposed to the 1950s, no names are mentioned in
connection with the resistance in Slovakia. Slovak communists Husák and
Novomeský are not mentioned at all. While the role of the Uprising was
central to Party debates during this period, the official position on Husák

and Novomeský had not yet been decided. According to these books, the message of the Slovak National Uprising was that the Slovak people under the leadership of the Communist Party rejected the fascist Slovak state, showed the world their resistance to "the Nazi occupiers and the domestic fascist traitors," and took charge of the liberation of Czechoslovakia.[84] A base was established for a new government power: "the power of the people."[85] The Uprising was for the reuniting of Czechoslovakia and friendship with the Soviet Union.[86] The struggle did not stop until the arrival of the Soviet army—the true heroes of the story.

As we can see, much more information about all aspects of the war was provided for students exposed to these books than during the 1950s. Still, these books are full of the kinds of omissions and distortions we see in both the earlier and the later more repressive periods. One example of this is the treatment of the atom bomb dropped on Japan. Here, a specific number of victims is given. No mention is made of the fact that the Japanese were on the other side of the war. And this number is given while, for example, the number of Jewish victims of the Holocaust is not. Thus, for a reader of these textbooks, it would be hard to tell what the difference was morally between the activities of the fascist regime at home or even of the Nazis, and the dropping of the atom bomb by the Americans.

Forming a public consciousness of the Jewish deportations. During the 1960s there were other sources of information as well, and we will look here at the two major fictional, and widely distributed, works that formed the public consciousness of the Jewish aspect of the wartime state. One was Rudolf Jašík's 1959 book *St. Elizabeth's Square.* Throughout the communist period, there were required reading lists for secondary school students. Many of the books on the list were connected to World War II, mostly to the Slovak National Uprising.[87] The Jašík book, which was on the official lists from 1959 until 1989, was the only one of these that dealt with the Jewish question and Slovak responsibility for Jewish deportations.[88] It remained officially acceptable even after the post-1968 crackdowns. The other was the 1965 movie *Shop on Mainstreet,* which was banned after 1968 and not viewed widely again until after the 1989 revolution.[89]

It is illuminating to examine and compare these works for a number of reasons. Because there was such a general dearth of information about the Holocaust, it is possible to isolate how impressions of these events were forged. In addition to revealing the images that shaped most people's understanding of this aspect of the war, this comparison also shows what was permitted and promoted (the Jašík book) and what was controversial (the movie). This mirrors the general ambivalence throughout Eastern Europe about the Jewish issue.

St. Elizabeth's Square, in many ways, deals explicitly with the persecution of Jews in Slovakia during the war. However, several interview subjects told me that *Shop on Mainstreet* (a much less stilted depiction than the Jašík book) was the first time that the issue was widely addressed in public since the war. Until then they had not understood the extent to which Slovaks supported anti-Semitic measures and were responsible for rounding up the Jews for deportation.[90]

The Jašík book is a love story between a Slovak boy and a Jewish girl (some people remember the book primarily as a romance). The girl is rounded up and shot by Germans; the Slovak boy joins the communists in the resistance at the end. *Shop on Mainstreet* is about a Slovak who is given a Jewish shop through the "Aryanization" process. At the center of the story is the relationship that develops between him and the former owner, an old Jewish woman who never understands that he is the *Aryanizer,* not her assistant. She treats him like a son. The Jewish community pays him to preserve this illusion. When the Jews are finally gathered for deportation she is, inadvertently, left off the lists and he is faced with the decision of whether to turn her in or not. He is so troubled by the situation and the choice that he kills himself.

Whereas the Jašík book tows the line we find in the textbooks—that the fascist regime was mostly something despised and imposed from outside (the entire town is sympathetic to the plight of the Jews)—in the movie we see how much of a local base it had. A reader of the book would certainly have been conscious that Jews were randomly separated from humanity just because of their ethnicity, but the issue of *responsibility* is avoided and fudged. In addition, the Jews who play heroic roles, as we might expect, are less religious and are not attached to their background. In fact there is a surprising amount of anti-Semitic stereotyping: the book depicts the Jews as like sheep in not resisting (whereas the communists were the ones fighting back); the typical stereotype of Jews caring more about money than about morality comes through clearly in several incidents in the book. The Slovaks who enthusiastically benefited from the Aryanization are shown to be on the margin and the most opportunistic and morally depraved characters. In the scene in which the local Hlinka Guard is organizing to go out to round up the Jews, most of the Slovak participants are depicted as abandoning the group so that only a small number of the worst Slovaks take part. But the dirty work is done by the Germans, who are characterized as insects.

In *Shop on Mainstreet* there is not a German in sight. It is clearly Slovaks who round up the Jews. In addition, the film depicts how central anti-Semitism was to the regime's ideology. Slovak collaboration is presented in a much more complex way, and collaboration is not limited to the most reprehensible characters. The main Jewish characters are presented as essential members of the community and, for the most part, as skillful shop owners rather than as moneygrubbers. In the Jašík book the towns-people go to the train station to bid farewell to the Jews; in *Shop on Main-street,* while individual Slovaks find the deportations tragic, a very different picture is painted. In the film, a white flag was hoisted on a structure erected with great fanfare to show that the town was "judenrein" (cleansed of Jews).[91]

Data is not available on how many people saw *Shop on Mainstreet* and, of course, such movies have different meanings for different viewers. The generation that came of age after the 1960s did not see *Shop on Mainstreet* and were only exposed to the Jašík book. In theory, even those who were exposed to the movie would not necessarily have known what the fate of the deported Jews was or that it was part of an all-European extermination effort by the Nazis.

Beyond textbooks. While these two works were widely seen and read, someone looking further could have read, during the 1960s, a number of other fictional and nonfictional works that touched on the issue.[92] At the same time, increasingly open discussion of historical issues took place in the pages of intellectual journals like *Kultúrny Život,* which began to have a relatively wide circulation, and *Historický Časopis*. Still, as mentioned above, the discussions tended to be about issues other than the Jewish one.

Some teachers during the increasingly open 1960s took more and more initiative to supplement the material in the textbooks with other materials being published at the time in the press and in intellectual journals. Depending upon the teacher and school, students would have been exposed to increasingly open discussion. Those who had the motivation and curiosity had greater opportunities for learning more during this period, as we saw in the last chapter. But the debates about history, the idea of historical truth, and the questioning of what had been the official story were mostly limited to Party circles. They did not reach the broader population, including university students, until 1968. Even so, anyone who read intellectual journals like *Kultúrny Život* would have had access to these discussions.

Lubomír Lipták's *Slovensko v 20. Storočie,* the most serious history of twentieth-century Slovakia, which had all the detail that had been missing in earlier histories, came out in 1968 and was briefly used as a university text. However, it was withdrawn after 1969, to be reissued only after 1989. Problems of Czech-Slovak relations and the Jewish question, as well as other aspects of the Slovak state, were treated with real documentation. In the scholarly world, however, nothing came out during this period explicitly on the Jewish issue. Ivan Kamenec, whose work on the Holocaust in Slovakia was cited in the last chapter, was working on his dissertation, which was published after 1989.[93] But he did not finish it in time for it to be published before the post-68 crackdown. It was circulated in samizdat.

Elite Cohesion
During the 1960s, for the first time since the war, something like an ideology and an elite cohesion began to reemerge in Slovakia, particularly for the prewar and reform communist generations. They were certainly united by the drive to end the distortions of history of the 1950s. The emphasis by the leaders of that group was on the issues important and controversial with regard to their position and struggle within the Communist Party and with the Czech party. In the more open discussion among this group in the 1960s, the Jewish issue was still underplayed. As a new elite ideology began to take shape among Slovak communists, a different rationale began to drive the ignoring of the Jewish issue. Now the nationalist desire to find a usable past caused the avoidance of responsibility for the deportations, much as it has in the countries of Western Europe; this was in clear contrast to the 1950s, when organized forgetting and elite atomization were the causes for avoidance.[94]

We can understand this last point with the help of Ken Jowitt's ideas about the changing stages Leninist regimes go through in their relationship with society.[95] During the first two stages—transformation and consolidation—the Communist Party is concerned most with eliminating threats to its power. Legitimacy is not an issue during those periods, and thus the question of whether or not the past is usable is irrelevant. The leadership decides (in accordance with the dictates of the Soviet Union) on the interpretation to be given to history and there is no input from other sources. However, once the regime is more secure in its power and in the revolution's success, it becomes more interested in building legitimacy. During Jowitt's inclusion stage, the regime begins to consult and broaden the opportunity for input from experts, in this case about history.[96] Once the question of legitimacy becomes more important, the nationalist drive to cover a difficult past becomes the new reason for elite forgetting. The debates about Slovak collaboration with the Nazis during World War II, had they continued, would have begun to resemble those in Western Europe, where the main divide is between those who want to ignore, versus those who want to come to terms with, the difficult aspects of this past. At the same time, the reform communist cohort themselves represented an ambiguous type of remembering and consciousness, since many were educated and socialized at the height of the Stalinist period.

The children of the sixties generation would certainly have had access to information and to a context in which real discussions of historical events were taking place. This would have been true especially in 1968, when what had been a discussion within the Party broadened. As we have seen, many of the future democrats were formed by this period. At the same time, it would have been possible to live through this period without absorbing much. This is particularly true for the younger part of that cohort and the normalization generation.

The seven-year period of debate that has been discussed in this section, while extremely influential later in terms of people and ideas, was ultimately outweighed by the power of post-1968 atomization. The crackdowns after 1969 went a long way toward reestablishing that overall trend. The dramatic end of the 1960s reform movement placed it prominently in the public consciousness. But the period became idealized partly because it ended quickly enough that its inherent disunities did not become apparent. (Imagine if the postcommunist revolution had ended sometime in 1990.) Its actual importance in creating a community of meaning was minimal since it was too ephemeral. In the absence of continuing discussion, the common meanings of history generated during this short interlude were never institutionalized.

The Return to Atomization, 1969–89

The Communist Party and World War II
After the crushing of the Prague Spring, the regime tried to re-create a loyal elite and intelligentsia just as it had in the post-1948 period. Even though the purges were not as violent as the Party's attempt to eliminate potential rivals in the 1950s, they affected many people, especially among the intelligentsia.[97] No longer was the crackdown carried out, as it was in the 1950s, in terms of which side people were on in World War II. However, official anti-Semitism reemerged in the period after the Soviet invasion as part of the crackdown's rhetoric.[98]

Aside from the treatment of the communist leaders of the Uprising as heroes and the greater attention given to the Slovak National Uprising in general, this period resembled the 1950s in the way it treated history. Fascism dropped out of the picture. So much official credit was given to Soviet heroism and military prowess that in 1975, on the thirtieth anniversary of the liberation, newspaper editors were ordered to eliminate the caption "30th anniversary of the victory over fascism" and replace it with "30th anniversary of the liberation of Czechoslovakia by the Soviet Army." In the same year, the annual celebration of the anniversary of the founding of the First Republic on October 28, 1918, was suspended. Until then, this day had been accepted even by the regime as the Day of National Independence.[99]

Husák presided over a period when the federalization he fought for was weakened. Whereas Czechoslovakia became a federated state in 1969 and in its original formulation considerable powers were granted to the republic level governments, by 1971 many of these powers were reduced.[100] In addition, in the early 1970s, the national revival in culture and academia that he himself had led in the 1960s was stopped. The Slovak cultural foundation, Matica Slovenská, which had greatly expanded its activities and membership during 1968, was reduced to a national library.

Nation-Building
During the normalization period the Party reimposed control in the field of education and over the school curriculum. It reversed the developments in historical research from the 1960s, and historians, purged after 1968, lost their impact on history education. The teaching of history was overtaken by a new "scientific discipline" called the "didactics of history," which proposed pedagogical experiments and guidelines for teachers. Starting in 1970, a new magazine was published by the ministry of education on the ideologically correct teaching of social sciences. Teachers lost their independence and even they themselves demanded further instructions from the authorities, including an exact timetable of what should be taught in each class.[101] This was also a period when the regime began to put more focus on technical education and less on social sciences and humanities.[102]

I will start with an example of a textbook, this time for gymnasium students. Though the book is from 1987, it resembles those that came out earlier in the normalization period.[103] (The 1960s did not last long enough to produce a revised textbook.) The younger part of the normalization cohort would have been taught from books such as this one. The book is highly ideological and spare in its treatment of the key issues from the war, such as the meaning of fascism. It is even more limited than the 1950s texts with respect to discussing who was responsible for the deportations. It does not even mention the Jews.

Character of Slovak state and meaning of fascism. The 1987 textbook depicts the Tiso regime as willingly carrying out the will of Hitler.[104] But while the main responsibility for the war and fascism was in the hands of the fascist states, the Western powers, which "followed their narrow imperialistic interests," were also at fault.[105] The cold war theme creeps back in. The deeds of the fascist state are listed, including joining the war against Poland; passing racist laws (this is the only veiled reference to Jews); establishing concentration camps; liquidating political parties, trade unions, and all democratic organizations; and privileging the German minority. The regime is characterized as fascist, antidemocratic, and antisocialist. Communists were the main victims. Six hundred were placed in Ilava concentration camp, the only specific number given for victims of the Slovak regime.[106]

Whereas the lives of the broad strata of the population worsened during the Tiso state, the Slovak bourgeoisie benefited and were its major supporters. Again, as in earlier textbooks, this one says that Germans controlled everything: the army, police, Hlinka Guard, security, office of propaganda, and the economy. While less emphasized than in earlier textbooks, the Roman Catholic Church is mentioned as a key supporter of the fascist regime.

The Jewish issue. In the description of what the Slovak state did there was also no mention of Jews or of Aryanization, and even Nazi terror is depicted with no mention of Jews as specific victims. All that is said is that the Nazis brought terror to occupied lands and threatened many peoples, first of all Slavs, with physical annihilation.[107] In the Czech lands, the goal was Germanization and physical extermination of the Czech people.[108] Even in a context where the books from the 1950s mentioned the Jews, this book does not. Instead, after the Heydrich assassination, according to this book, the Nazis began concrete preparations for "final solution of the Czech question." A number is given here: twenty thousand Czechs were sent to Nazi concentration camps.[109] But this number stands alone.

Resistance. With Husák in power, many more details about the Uprising are included than in earlier textbooks. The main goal of the Uprising was to throw out occupiers and native fascists and restore Czechoslovakia on a socially, politically, and nationally equal basis.[110] The Slovak National Uprising was the first stage in the "people's democratic revolution" in Czechoslovakia.[111] Again, the Soviet connection is emphasized.

As in earlier textbooks, certain numbers are presented while others are not mentioned. For example, the book mentions that 160,000 Soviet soldiers died in the liberation of Czechoslovakia, and specific numbers are given of participants in the Czech uprising. Again a specific figure is mentioned for victims of the atom bomb in Japan. But the specific number of victims of concentration camps, and of participants in the Slovak National Uprising, are not included. Since Jews are not mentioned at all in this book, there are, of course, no numbers mentioned of Jews deported.

This book is a classic illustration of organized forgetting. With its clear omissions, its vague references, and its facts without context, it leaves the reader with little information or sense of history. Even if the student had read the Jašík book, with its story of Jewish suffering, the larger context would be missing. It would not be clear even who the Jews were or how the Jašík book connected to events that really happened only a generation before. It would seem fictional or so abstract as to be unconnected to that person's sense of her own country's past. The same would be true for field trips to locations connected with the Uprising, the Heydrich assassination site, and to concentration camps. Of course some teachers continued to supplement the information from textbooks.[112] However, especially during the 1970s, teachers were monitored.

The only exceptions to the dramatic shift from the 1960s were the university and law school history texts. They provided more information on the Jewish issue. The law school history text from 1976 included details on the racial laws, the Aryanization, and the deportations. However, Germans were still held to be responsible for all crimes and no numbers of victims were given.[113]

Other works that had been available during the 1960s were withdrawn. The Lipták history of twentieth-century Slovakia was even removed from libraries. In addition, the purges affected the writing of history, and some of the best historians lost their positions or were unable to publish.[114] Historical discussion continued only in samizdat.[115]

The normalization generation faced more than just a lack of information. Parents and teachers were themselves further away from the actual events of the war. Because of the alienation after 1968 there was less inclination among the older generation to talk about the past or for the younger generation to think of asking. This was made more acute by the tarnishing of the Soviet role in World War II; Soviet troops were now remembered as invaders, not liberators. In addition, as people became older, and without the reinforcement of historical sources, it became less possible to tell whether their memories were any more accurate than the regime's depiction of history.

Elite Cohesion

It is only in the light of the normalization that we can understand the legacy of 1968 for the prewar, the reform communist, and children of the sixties generations. First, while the Prague Spring was memorable, it was not important for perpetuating communities of meaning. The children of the sixties cohort could have lived through the experience, and even been caught up in it, but exposure alone did not constitute a lasting identity.[116] Even if they were exposed to information about the past that was at odds with the normalization-era official version, they might never have discussed this information. They could have seen the movie *Shop on Main-street,* and thus been aware of the events depicted there, but might never have gone further to articulate a meaning with others that connected the information in the movie to a national ideology. In most cases, this generation did not have the chance to cohere, since the ties from 1968 were never institutionalized and were easily broken. As indicated in the last chapter, the networks that did last were fragile and weak.

A second reason that potential group identities forged in 1968 did not last was the disappointment of the Soviet invasion. This event was atomizing in the sense that people lost their motivation for opposition and turned to their private lives. Or they gave up on their ideals and collaborated with the StB (the secret police). The variety of responses to the crackdown itself atomized former allies or friends. There was no way to predict who might become a collaborator and who might adhere to their principles. In addition, the reform movement in Slovakia was intrinsically prone to fragmentation since it consisted of some oriented toward democratization and some more oriented toward Slovak autonomy.

As we will see, the disparate responses to the invasion, and the attendant atomization, had clear implications in the postcommunist period. It was difficult for members of the reform communist and the children of the sixties generations to assess one another's likely ideological orientation. It was not clear who would emerge as a democrat and who an advocate of Slovak autonomy. It was also difficult to know whether former allies from the 1960s could be trusted, since they might have collaborated with the StB during the normalization period.[117]

Third, as we saw in the discussion of "islands of positive deviance," in the last chapter, the effects of the purges in Slovakia were less harsh than in the Czech lands. Activists from 1968 were more often demoted than prevented from continuing work in their professions; compared to the Czech lands, fewer professionals became stokers or manual laborers.[118] In general, fewer were purged from the Party. So these Party members had greater incentive to collaborate with the regime. That they had something to lose gave them incentive to break ties to former political allies or groups to which they might have been connected in 1968.

The reform communist generation was the most likely to maintain group cohesion since they had developed the strongest group identity in the 1960s. But they belong in the mass-elite category for several reasons. Reform communism, an identity tied to the past, was not applicable to post-1989 conditions. Thus reform communists needed to search for new ideological possibilities after 1989. Except for the few who had been engaged directly in the discussions of history during 1968, they, as much as the younger generation, lacked an articulated identity regarding history. Many were economists or technically trained and were not concerned with identity issues.[119]

The question of the Slovak state was particularly complicated for those reform communists who did care about history. Because they were communists they were automatically antifascist and did not consider themselves akin to the Catholic nationalists, who were connected to the legacy of the Slovak state. During the 1960s and after 1989 they had to distinguish themselves from that group and that legacy.[120]

A final reason that the potential of the 1960s for creating an alternative historical consciousness did not come to fruition is less supportable by evidence. In his account of normalization, Šimečka says that in writing his book even a few years after the Prague Spring, he could hardly remember the events of 1968 as real. This was because change was so dramatic following the arrival of Soviet troops and because official accounts of the events were so pervasive and so different from his own experience.[121]

Conclusion

Carole Leff, in the best book written on Czech-Slovak relations, argues that separate and parallel elites were created in the Czech and Slovak parts of the country during the communist period, and that Slovak elites developed nationalist sentiments in the communist context.[122] She is impressed by the continuities in the shapes of national conflicts with the Czechs. But she tends to see communism as merely a gloss on top of what was really a story of nation-building and national conflict. However, when we take the nature of Leninist domination into account, a different interpretation is warranted.

The effort by the Leninist regime to build a national myth with World War II at its center had the odd effect of leaving the individuals who became the elites after 1989 with little historical consciousness. The fate of Slovak Jews during World War II fell out of the public discussion almost completely during the years of communism. Only during the 1960s did the development of an elite identity begin. It was only then, for example, that the nationalist incentives to forget the fascist past became more visible than the effects of organized forgetting and elite atomization. But I suggest that we cannot think of the nationalist issue as having simply gone underground. The nationalism of the 1960s was qualitatively affected by the post-1968 normalization. While individuals who had been connected with 1968 might have preserved an identity, they did not do so in the context of a group and the cohesiveness of the 1968 group was impaired. Thus the products of the official socialization process were not an elite as such; rather they were individuals separately driven by the egoism left over in the absence of ideology.

Although the focus here has been on elites, the effects of organized forgetting were likely even more powerful for the non-elite parts of the population. This calls into question the common claim that national identity was preserved in society in general or that it was developed inadvertently in the communist context. Instead, family stories and ethnic stereotypes remained, never having been integrated into a national ideology.

There is a methodological point here as well. Many analysts point to a poll from 1968 as evidence for the high levels of historical consciousness in society and thus for opposition to communist suppression of national history.[123] (In this poll people were asked to rate as positive or negative different aspects of Czech and Slovak history and different important individuals.) But the conclusion is misleading. First, it is a snapshot taken at a time when it was fashionable to care about history. But even if respondents did have some ideas at the time about these historical personalities and time periods, it is questionable if these add up to a national identity that was formed and then repressed, in the years after 1968. As I argued especially regarding the post-1968 period, there were many reasons, official and unofficial, why these pieces of association with the past or family stories did not get passed on. Without making analytical distinctions between these different types of connections to the past, and without carefully tracing continuity and lack thereof, we are misreading the effects of Leninist regimes. In the next two chapters we will see how important the absence of ideology was for postcommunist politics.

6 Nationalism without Nationalists?
Democracy without Democrats?

If the Leninist nation-building process left the majority of the elite and society without historical consciousness, what does this mean for the practicalities of building a new polity on top of Leninism's legacy? While there is a continuing debate about whether democrats are necessary for building democracy or nationalists are required to mobilize nationalism, here we are considering the question of what happens when the elite (and society) is neither.

We ordinarily think of the major threats to new and fragile democratic institutions in the aftermath of dictatorship as coming from recalcitrant militaries, from economic distress generating irreconcilable economic interests, or from antidemocratic cultures. But analysts have generally not taken into account the implications of lack of ideology, particularly at founding moments or moments of democratic transition.

Once democratic institutions are set up, they function to clarify the rules of the game: that politics is about competing solutions to society's problems. But just as important in defining the political landscape are ideology and interest groups. Ideological commitments allow elites to recognize and trust one another in order to cooperate to make decisions that postpone personal gain for a longer term goal. Interest groups also imply predictable orientations; they make or break deals with one another based on clear political stakes. Both signal that elites are acting based on something other than egoism.

In the countries of southern Europe and Latin America out of which the transitions to democracy literature came there were groups with interests that were identifiable—labor, the military. While political incentives changed, pushing authoritarian elites to "join the democratic game," those elites continued to be tied to their group interests.[1] In postcommunist Czechoslovakia, there was, in some ways, a blanker slate due to the particular legacy of Leninism. The only groups that remained identifiable were the democrats and the nationalists—embodying competing ideologies. Since the Communist Party collapsed and hardly anyone continued to claim that as a group association, it was difficult to predict group orientations.[2] Thus the first years of postcommunist democracy had a different dynamic than we would find in a transition in which ideology and interests do exist.

Because the democrats and Catholic nationalists dominated politics at the outset, and because they did engender an ideological cleavage, it was difficult for them and for their Western advisers to notice the lack of ideological commitment in the rest of the elite and in society more generally. Democratic institutions themselves, and the expectation that threats to democracy would come from clear opponents who sought to undermine the new system, only made it more difficult to see and respond to this.

In this chapter we will examine the process whereby the mass-elite came to dominate politics and to push out the ideological elites. In some ways the chapter tells a familiar story. The more politically savvy and populist politician, in this case Vladimír Mečiar, wins power and support through a divide-and-conquer strategy. However, if we stay focused on the disparity between the elites and the process whereby elites identified allies, opponents, and themselves, we will see that the mass-elite did not form parties and interest groups. Instead they remained uncommitted, changing political masks when necessary and appealing to a society whose votes could be won based on populist responses to short-term fears. They did not come to represent a victorious policy or ideology or constituency in society. The following account will elucidate the way in which democratic politics favored the uncommitted and allowed the mass-elite to co-opt democratic institutions and to marginalize the groupings that had ideologies that might have served to integrate Slovak society.

It is important to keep in mind that generally opportunism, as opposed to ideological commitment, is seen as important for successful functioning of democratic politics. Democratic institutions rest on the ability to compromise. However, opportunism is destructive at a founding moment, since some ideological consensus or interest beyond egoism must exist to give life to these institutions in the first place. While competitive politics rewards flexibility, the victory of the opportunist has different meaning for the consolidation of democracy in a setting where opportunism is so pervasive, where it is so cut off from any ideological tradition, and where institutions are in such a state of flux. In this context parliaments and elections and other new institutions served only to exacerbate and perpetuate the egoism of the mass-elite. Without ideology these institutions will remain unconsolidated, serving only the interests of opportunistic elites.

Because the account in this chapter aims to reveal a political process that is difficult to see through conventional lenses, and because absence is the central phenomenon under scrutiny, it is important to say what this account is not. The focus in this chapter and the next is deliberately narrow. It intentionally plays down two key facets of the post-1989 story: the process of deliberations and negotiations over the future setup of the state and the economic aspects of not only Mečiar's success but of the split of Czechoslovakia more generally. Whereas the disagreements with the Czechs over the constitution contributed to Mečiar's success, his appeal was not just based on his program. After all, the Catholic nationalists did not succeed. While broad-based fears that arose due to Václav Klaus's determination to implement rapid market reforms won political allies and popular support for Mečiar, I deliberately direct the spotlight away from this facet of his appeal and toward the victory of lack of ideological commitment. Thus I do not pay much attention to elite groups and networks that tried to retain power through their opposition to the marketization process, though it is significant that these groupings did not evolve as ideologically identifiable players in the democratic game.[3] Mečiar was not only a populist politician who tapped social fears, though that is consistent with my argument and maps well onto the demagogue/populist explanation for nationalist mobilization. I suggest that even if the particular economic challenges that arose from the structure of communist economies were less acute, the pervasiveness of the mass-elite would still pose the same daunting challenge of a lack of integrating ideology.

The victory of Mečiar is also not just a story of national mobilization. We will see clearly that the major mass-elite nationalists took on this ideological label only in the postcommunist context. The fact that the democrats and Catholic nationalists set the political agenda from 1989 to 1992 provided opportunities for the mass-elite to emerge, and thus shaped the types of groupings that came together and the idiom these groups picked up. But the very fact that the mass-elite became nationalists through this process, and not as a result of previous identities, is further evidence of the ephemerality of their nationalism. Thus this account deliberately concentrates on the distinction between the two types of elites. To do this we must recall the difference between what I refer to as *idiom* and what I call *ideology. Idiom* refers to words picked up and dropped—as ideological debris, plucked randomly out of the rubble of the collapse of communism, or the atmosphere of postcommunist efforts to join the West. The *ideology* of the democrats and nationalists, on the other hand, is an outgrowth of longstanding beliefs and constrains the actions of those who use it. Thus all political discourse cannot be understood as equally significant.

Not only are Mečiar and other mass-elite nationalists political entrepreneurs, picking up ideas that competitors failed to market. Not only is Mečiar a demagogue appealing to social fears in uncertain times. Knowing that the mass-elites are driven by egoism, that they win based on short-term resentment, and that their ideology is so shallow pushes us to confront the problem that once resentments are mobilized the building of political community remains difficult.

Because of the extent of collapse in 1989, and because Leninist domination destroyed groups representing alternative ideologies and interests, it was difficult to tell who to trust as allies, and what interests or political orientation could be expected from the elites who entered the political scene. The criteria used by the ideological elites, who made the revolution, to assess who represented a political ally or a threat (and on what basis) were, therefore, limited.[4] Two criteria were used by the ideological elites to make these judgments. The first criterion was membership in the networks of colleagues and acquaintances who comprised the opposition (that is, personal knowledge of commitments). Beyond these personal ties, the second criterion they used was reputation with regard to history. History and one's past were among the few markers in an environment without clear indications of who was who. And the history that mattered was one's communist past, where one was in 1968, and one's World War II past.

The ideological elites were aware of, and focused on, the obvious divides between communist and noncommunist, and between themselves over sympathy with the wartime fascist state or with the resistance to fascism. The first part of the chapter shows that a preoccupation with this divide led the democrats to bring Vladimír Mečiar onto their election list and appoint him prime minister. It was difficult then, and particularly later when Mečiar broke off from his former allies, to determine who he was and what the source might be of his danger. This was true of the transforming mass-elite in general. The people who were most difficult to identify (in terms of their likely political leanings, loyalty, predictability) were those who were not part of the original semidissident networks or were only peripherally so; people who gave up their Party cards immediately and joined the victorious groupings; people who were never connected to the Party and whom no one could identify (based on the available criteria) anyway.

The second part of the chapter examines the other obvious identifiable source of threat—the communist past. The complex problem of trying to identify former collaborators with the StB (the secret police)—which became known as "lustration"—provides a good illustration of the difficulty of identifying the nature of the threats to democracy in the post-communist context. The mass-elite—who might or might not have had collaborationist pasts—could fall between the cracks. We see this most explicitly in the case of Jozef Markuš, who became head of the Matica Slovenská.

The mass-elite thrived in this environment of suspicion and flux. This was not because of any planned conspiracy but instead because without ideological constraints they could survey the new environment based on short-term personal interest. They were a moving target, while the ideological elites were standing still. Of course it was a gamble where to put oneself and which idiom to pick up. But they remained flexible and could switch if necessary. They could pick up idiom in response to the mistakes or unintended consequences of the positions taken by the ideological elites as did the Slovak National Party, the subject of the third part of the chapter. They could become part of the movements that made the revolution and then depart when it became convenient as did Mečiar, to whom we return in the fourth section of the chapter.

The Emergence of Historical Divides and the Rise of Vladimír Mečiar

In the first months after the revolution, though many communists remained in their old positions (including membership of parliaments and governments), the agenda was set by the broad movements who made the revolution—Public Against Violence (VPN) in Slovakia and Civic Forum (OF) in the Czech Republic. Under the slogans "return to truth" and "moral politics" and "return to Europe," a range of issues forcibly frozen by the communists first in 1948, then in 1968, were brought to the agenda. The major orientation was toward reestablishing basic freedoms, preparing for the first elections, beginning to transform the economy, and righting wrongs of the communist past.

It became apparent almost immediately that the symbolism of coming to terms with the past meant different things for the different small groupings of ideological elites. The process of removing communism from all spheres

of society had both a symbolic and a practical side. Both sides were complicated. From a practical perspective communists had to be removed from
positions of power, particularly from the interior ministry, and the press
had to be detached from communist control, as did the remainder of Party
property. The symbolic side included everything from name changes and
taking down statues to removing communist symbols from the mastheads
of newspapers, to changing the form of address used in the military. It
included publishing previously banned works and personnel changes.
Those elites who had ideologies had oriented themselves around different
time periods and saw historical justice as meaning a return to different
precommunist legacies and traditions; thus the symbolic side quickly became the focus of attention.[5]

Catholic Dissent and the Fascist Past

As we already saw, the majority of the few outright dissidents in Slovakia
were Catholic. Among the first issues on the post-November 1989 agenda
were religious rights and restoration of bishops and the Catholic hierarchy.
Differences in anticommunist priorities can be seen in the fact that while
the federal government in Prague was busy investigating the November 17
events, in which security forces were used against demonstrators, Bratislava authorities began to investigate police actions against a gathering
of believers in 1988 that led to the arrest of the group known as the Bratislava Five.[6]

In early 1990, Ján Čarnogurský formed the Christian Democratic Movement as a Catholic nationalist party. Čarnogurský had originally been
united with the democrats in VPN and was appointed in December as
deputy prime minister of the federal government. KDH was formed from
several streams of Catholic dissent, which united in November of 1989
and began to form local clubs.[7] It also included some Lutherans, though
many Lutherans were wary because they feared that the Catholics would
rehabilitate the wartime fascist state.[8] But the links of the KDH to the Slovak
state were complex. The party's constituents were divided on the matter of
rehabilitating it, and from the beginning many in KDH saw the collapse
of communism as an opportunity to revive the HSLS. These people were
referred to as "l'udáci" (the historical reference to members of the fascist party).[9]

Most prominent of these "l'udáci" was Čarnogurský's own father, Pavol
Čarnogurský, who was one of the first in the post-1989 period to call for
rehabilitating that state.[10] In the first months after November he was a key

contact for émigrés, including František Vnuk, one of the main figures responsible for disseminating a sympathetic version of the history of the Slovak state.[11] The fact that Čarnogurský's father took this position added to other political observers' concerns about the ties that party had to the fascist past. During this period, when it was difficult to tell what political actors stood for and whether they should be trusted, history was one of the only labels available. Personal history, in this case, was used to assess political orientation. This mode of identification seemed obvious to the ideological elites, since historical consciousness was carried during the communist period in the form of individual people and the networks surrounding them.

Ján Čarnogurský tried to distance himself from his father's orientation.[12] As indicated in chapter 4, the younger Čarnogurský had been personally responsible for some of the efforts during communism to bring to light that state's crimes against the Jews. The links in dissent to others that were victims of fascism and the experience of dissent itself (as well as living in a society where the regime was genuinely focused on that state's crimes) were responsible for Čarnogurský's inclination to deal with this past.[13]

The émigrés, like Vnuk, who arrived from the United States, Europe, Canada, and Australia, many of whom were associated with the Catholic nationalism of the Slovak state, were less wary about openly using this legacy and calling for Slovak autonomy and even independence. At the founding congress of KDH in Nitra on February 17, 1990, this gap came out into the open. Čarnogurský deliberately kept the émigrés from taking the stage, thereby alienating many potential supporters from abroad and keeping his movement from being linked outright to the fascist past.[14]

But Čarnogurský's caution did not keep other key political groupings from continuing to make this association.[15] The ideology of the democrats (and of the Czechs) led them to be wary of the Catholicism, nationalism, and potential links to the fascist past of KDH. This was true even though the Catholic group was one of the least penetrated by communist-era collaborators. Thus, as a result of the continuing legacy of World War II, the natural alliance between anticommunist democrats and nationalists was fragile and allowed the mass-elite to steal the political agenda.

The Democrats, History, and a Critical Choice

For the democrats, the 1989 revolution was about forming a democratic Czechoslovakia with roots in the First Republic of 1918–38. The slogans of anticommunist dissent focused on overcoming, and learning from, the legacy of two totalitarianisms. But in Slovakia, as throughout the communist world, rethinking the communist judgment of the World War II past threatened rehabilitating the fascist past. For example, the political prisoners' organization was comprised not only of anticommunist democrats but also of those who were imprisoned for their alleged connections with the wartime state.[16] Rehabilitation of communist victims raised the problem of how to judge the meaning of the Soviet "liberation" of Slovakia from the fascists.

When references to the wartime state entered politics in the post-1989 period, democrats and Czechs were alarmed. Even though all political actors knew that the lost promise of the federalization of the state and of recognizing Slovakia's national aspirations would become important, the nationalist movement of the 1960s had carefully avoided harkening to the history of statehood in 1939–45. The realization that the wartime experience of statehood would now be on the agenda would not have been quite as alarming had KDH not begun to capture support just as VPN seemed to be losing it. After the founding congress of KDH, and particularly after the visit of the pope at the end of April, KDH seemed to be doing very well in the polls going into the first free elections of June 1990. With Čarnogurský promising to win the votes of the 70 percent of the population that considered themselves Catholic, and given the actual numbers in the polls, VPN's chances looked increasingly bleak.[17]

In addition to the links to the fascist past, KDH also threatened the secular parts of the population who feared its conservative social policies and antiabortion stance. Some raised the specter of a clerical totalitarianism.[18] Election propaganda against KDH by VPN was based on this threat. One ad portrayed a woman calling in worried that KDH would blackmail or punish those who did not vote for them by publishing their names in the Catholic paper and refusing to christen their children or to perform last rites. The VPN announcer assured the woman that democracy meant a secret ballot. But the link between KDH and communist tactics was clear.[19]

Although VPN and KDH were united in their anticommunism, the VPN leadership decided to invite candidates from a group of 1968 reform communists onto their election list. This group shared their concern with the possible rehabilitation of the fascist past (and many had been associated with the antifascist resistance).[20] In this choice we see a combination of the criteria used by the democrats to make judgments about the reliability of other elites. Milan Šimečka, who was a well-known dissident through the personal networks of the democrats, and had been a communist from

1968, helped the democrats convince Dubček to agree to be on their election list. Dubček could be identified because of his obvious link to a historical period.[21] The VPN leadership also wanted Dubček because he was a popular personality.[22]

In turn, Dubček gave the intellectuals of VPN faith that they could trust the group of 1968 communists called Obroda.[23] Moreover, the newly reformed communists, once they were rid of the Stalinist and "normalization" legacies, were also a natural ally against the fear of nationalism and the fascist past. It was the communist press that was the first to be alarmed by the appearance of new versions of the history of World War II sympathetic to the Tiso state.[24]

The choice to bring in the Obroda group helped VPN sweep the June 1990 election in Slovakia.[25] However, while Obroda clearly contributed to VPN's electoral victory, this group also proposed Vladimír Mečiar as prime minister in June 1990 and had proposed him in January for minister of the interior of the caretaker government.[26] And this group followed Mečiar a few months later as he split from VPN and created a new party with an increasingly nationalist agenda. The Mečiar group went on to win the 1992 election and presided over the split of the country in January 1993.

Thus the initial entry of Mečiar into a powerful political position came from a choice made based upon the historical divide in the Slovak elite over World War II. The VPN democrats chose 1968 communists as allies rather than the anticommunist nationalists of KDH. This historical divide continued to weaken the potential for cooperation between the democrats and the nationalists. The coalition between VPN and KDH after the June 1990 elections continued to be difficult. Neither the democrats nor the anticommunist nationalists were able to articulate a viable ideology, taking into account Slovak interests, as an alternative to the mass-elite.

What Was Obroda and Who Was Mečiar?

At the time the decision was made to bring Mečiar and other members of Obroda onto the VPN list there was no reason to suspect people with this profile. Mečiar appeared to have a past associated with 1968, which included study in Moscow, involvement in the Young Communists, and dismissal from his position as part of the normalization period. He was a lawyer. The fact that he was chosen from three other candidates as VPN's prime minister was due to what everyone agreed was his popularity and his political skill.[27] He was the number one leader from central Slovakia and won the highest number of votes among the VPN candidates.[28] He took positions that were anticommunist; he spoke out for responsibility and condemned extreme versions of nationalism.[29]

As we will see in greater detail, Mečiar is a good example of the lack of predictability or identifiability of the mass-elite. There was no way to tell at the time that he might break off and become the leader of a growing nationalist wave, which he began to do in the fall of 1990 and which culminated in March 1991 when the VPN split. The fact that he was the last key mass-elite figure to pick up nationalist idiom and that he had been so associated with the revolution and the democrats gave him more credibility in the eyes of the public than other nationalist figures (like the founders of the Slovak National Party).

The Obroda group had emerged in the Czech Republic and Slovakia earlier in 1989, before the November revolution, and issued some of the first statements of a program in the period after the revolution.[30] The first party in post-1989 Slovakia was established by this group and was called the Party of Democratic Socialism. However, Obroda was cloaked with mystery, in part because its activities were kept secret during the normalization period.

Miroslav Kusý—himself a dissident communist from 1968 but in the leadership of VPN—was asked, in an interview immediately after the revolution, about Obroda as a movement of expelled communists from 1968. He answered that he knew little about them because they were secret and were not "trying to establish contacts to the outside world: they are very closed groups. They are waiting for the proper situation. . . . The problem of these communists is that the opposition—namely Charter 77—has formed at a different ideological level."[31] While some members of this group were known either by reputation or through professional networks, the lack of familiarity with the group is another good example of the isolation that existed between the groupings who became the new elites.[32] Some argue that this group had ties to the former StB, and that it was more dangerous than anyone expected.[33] Whether or not Obroda had secret police ties, the 1968 legacy was complicated, as we saw in the last chapter, and that made allies from 1968 unpredictable. This was true ideologically as well, since the reform movement of the 1960s had brought together advocates of democracy and of nationalism.[34]

The influence and new importance of this group was even stronger because many VPN intellectuals chose not to run in the June 1990 election, giving the 1968 group more power and inviting later accusations that the democrats were exerting influence without being in elected office.[35] The choice not to run is another indication of the confidence the democrats had that the elites who were not associated with identifiable threats—the fascist or communist past—were engaged in the same political game. It also suggests their confidence that the support of the electorate could be taken for granted. It seemed perfectly natural that the recruitment process for key posts in the pre-election period drew upon the networks and existing groupings such as Obroda and the Democratic Socialist Party.[36]

The ideological elites later argued that the fact that Mečiar had been given the interior ministry post gave him access to a lot of information at a time when information was scarce, which would have enabled him to know about who could be blackmailed because of their pasts.[37] While his stint at the ministry of interior probably was important in his later ability to break off from the democrats and pose such a formidable political threat, that is not the focus here. Mečiar and Obroda were dangerous less because of their access to resources behind the scenes and more because of their lack of commitments and ability to be flexible and to appeal to society based on short-term fears.[38]

The Continuing Struggle with Communists

The divide with the communists could also be identified on the basis of history. But the conflict with the communists was complex.[39] The following statement by Havel expresses well the nearly impossible dilemmas that the velvet revolution left when it came to dealing with the communist past.

> How do we put together the desire for lawfulness and democratic proceedings, with the need to settle accounts radically with the past and all its dark consequences? How do we confront the intriguing followers of the old order and at the same time not make intrigues like them . . . ? How do we prevent careerists from changing coats speedily and putting themselves willfully above others, even if with a new flag in their hands? How do we break, in a revolutionary way, the old structures, and avoid in the process all the types of violence from which they were born and on which they stand?[40]

The "velvet revolution" was noteworthy for the ease with which the communist leadership gave up power. But there continued to be a real battle with communists who did not give up their Party membership over control of the media and over Party property; they also resisted personnel change in all institutions in society, from the press to the universities.[41] In an attempt to build a new legitimacy in the new environment, the Communist Party began to complain that it was being victimized in the new democracy and that there was a new VPN totalitarianism.

While the struggle with communists was straightforward, those who left the Party posed a more difficult problem. They were no longer identifiable. Some communists remained in the reborn Communist Party, which shed its Stalinist past and condemned the normalization policies and embraced the spirit of 1968.[42] Others, particularly those who remained in powerful positions, left the Party and joined new political groups or vanished from view. It was difficult to tell whether to trust the new political incarnations of former communists. It is impossible as an analyst, as it was for nearly all political actors at the time, to know exactly which networks were continuing to exert influence behind the scenes. More important than determining who had what connections, is to try to understand how the difficulty of identifying ideological orientation affected politics.

Several considerations had to be taken into account. The first problem was that everyone knew that all communists could not be equally condemned. This was frequently expressed in the statements of the leaderships. For example, Čarnogurský said as early as December 29, 1990:

> There must not be a hunt for communists. They are citizens with equal rights and there are quite a few among them who had, like the rest of the population, to keep silent for twenty years. However, precisely because they are communists, they have the responsibility for the internal renewal of their party. At the same time, there must not be quick and unprincipled changes of coats. We do not need phenomena of opportunism or, in other words, settling personal accounts. . . . We abandoned party approaches and instead of them we demand professional reliability, commitment to the cause, and responsibility.[43]

A second problem was that the new leadership needed experienced people to fill posts in government and these people were often linked with the past.[44] This was partly out of necessity—people with experience in government and the economy were linked to the old regime—and partly because of the agreements made with the Communist Party. In practice, some of the most important figures in postcommunist politics had been in positions of power in the communist government. Marián Čalfa, who became prime minister of Czechoslovakia, gave up his Party affiliation immediately; Milan Čič, who became Slovak prime minister, gave up his Party membership in March 1990.[45] Both KDH and VPN brought people into their ranks and even their leaderships because of expertise rather than ideological commitment.[46]

Third, it was difficult to tell whether even some members of the original networks of opposition had collaborationist pasts. As we saw in chapter 4, the democrats in Slovakia were not very cohesive. VPN formed from three separate streams of intellectuals who did not know one another before 1989. And even though the Bratislava elite was small, the communist system was such that even knowing someone personally did not guarantee knowledge of their potential for collaboration.

At the same time there was real openness in these networks in the first months after the revolution. The mood was such that it looked like everyone was united in overthrowing communism. There was such an assumption of consensus that the term "without political affiliation" became the preferred way to identify oneself. Needless to say, anyone could choose this label. It is not difficult to see how this would make it even harder to identify the mass-elite.

Fourth, the new political groupings feared infiltration by former StB agents and former communists from the moment the revolution took place. It was difficult to tell who joined these groups opportunistically, or with the intention of sabotage, and who was truly on their side. Leaving the movements open so that they would gain supporters came at the price of possible infiltration. And it was difficult to accept that democracy meant giving political opportunities to political forces who might be suspect. From the beginning of the revolution, as evidenced by the establishment of the "committee to investigate the events of November 17," there were suspicions about continuing activities of the former secret police. Numerous examples in early statements by the leadership of OF and VPN about the suspicion of infiltration, and of individuals opportunistically joining up because they had something to hide, indicate this.[47] The first complaints about the continuing power of the StB came as early as December 1989.[48] On December 1, OF warned that some Communist Party members were joining with the aim of creating a majority of the membership base; and that it was thus necessary to accept only those *acting* in harmony with the movement.[49] There were allegations that Obroda was trying to fragment OF. Rumors of a communist coup arose around the February 28 anniversary of the 1948 communist seizure of power.[50] The scandal that later developed around Richard Sacher, the interior minister, in which he seemed to be protecting officials of the old regime and leaking false information about dissidents, was the peak of this general mood of suspicion.[51]

These fears, and the inability to pin down where threats to the new democracy were likely to come from, shaped the assessment of some early signs of nationalism in Slovakia. Many VPN democrats claimed that among the nationalists that began to appear on the squares of Bratislava were former members of the StB. VPN members who had been politically active during communism claimed they recognized the former StB agents who had monitored them. It is impossible to confirm whether or not this is true. Several VPN leaders also publicly claimed that "dark forces" were provoking the new signs of extremism and of discord between Czechs and Slovaks. The very terminology shows the nature of the problem. At a VPN press conference in February, Ján Budaj called on the public to "dissociate itself from individual circles or groups which are trying to destabilize society."[52] Havel, at a Bratislava rally on January 12, mentioned "dark forces stirring up the mud" especially regarding Czech-Slovak relations.[53] It was not clear, however, who these people were. It was also difficult to surmise whether there were links between the continuing communist control of key positions and the mysterious forces that seemed to be sowing discord.

The Attempt to Develop a Policy on Screening

Collaborators were deemed dangerous for several moral and political reasons. From a political standpoint it was difficult to trust them since they had not had the will to resist collaboration and were not honest about what they had done. People who had information about their pasts could also blackmail collaborators, and thus collaborators in high offices posed a great danger. Even in the first months after the revolution, policy makers realized that they did not have full control over the StB files. This became a major source of conflict.

There were also moral reasons for punishing collaborators, but these were complicated. Because the Havel group and its allies in Slovakia were committed to "not being like them"—that is, not engaging in communistlike methods, such as revenge—some figures continued to be visible in politics who were suspected of collaboration.[54] From a practical perspective as well it was difficult to make the switch so quickly, especially of economic elites.[55] As the months passed, the public became impatient with the pace of the process of removing communists and former StB agents from political life, taking to the streets of Prague in May to compel the Communist Party to give up its property. Some demanded that the Communist Party be made illegal.

The decision was made, therefore, to screen candidates for the June elections. If a candidate was found to have collaboration in his past, he would be able to quietly withdraw. The screening results would only be given to the leadership of the party the candidate represented.[56] Parties could choose whether or not to screen and, with the exception of the Communist Party, most did.[57] The actual law on screening was not passed until October 1991, after much controversy.[58]

While many democrats and nationalists realized from the beginning that the screening process would be problematic, it was not until later that the ideological elites discovered the way in which it could be manipulated by the mass-elite. One reason for the lack of foresight was that both groupings of ideological elites assumed that society shared their priority of establishing historical justice. But, as we will see, this assumption of societal support and consensus turned out to be misguided. It was also hard for the ideological elites to see how problematic it would be to determine who should be kept out of politics, since it was hard to comprehend how unreliable the information on collaboration would be.

But some of the dilemmas were known even in the first months after November. As the interior ministry pointed out in May 1990, information on collaboration could easily be misused for a number of reasons. First, it was not sufficiently appreciated how difficult it would be to attribute responsibility in the aftermath of a regime that implicated almost everyone. Many were forced to cooperate with the StB; some did so only formally while others were not aware of their cooperation. And some people deliberately harmed others without being formal collaborators, that is, through anonymous letters.[59] One striking problem was that it was difficult to distinguish between levels of collaborationist activity and often the lower level collaborators were most subject to punishment. Another difficulty was that although the statute of limitations was lifted, much more serious crimes from the 1950s were not prosecuted, while individuals who were forced to collaborate in a minor way, even though they might have spent their lives fighting the regime, became entangled in the web of lustration.[60]

Second, the process of determining the nature of collaboration was slow because the information was not all in one place.[61] Third, many files were destroyed: according to a May 1990 statement, over 50 percent of the materials pertaining to active collaborators was destroyed by state security officials during November and December 1989. "Therefore, there can be no absolute certainty as to who was and who was not a collaborator of the former state security between 1948 and 1989."[62] The relevant pages of Mečiar's file were missing, thereby crippling efforts to determine his past.

Fourth, the files themselves were thought to be unreliable. The materials could be confusing and distorting and opponents of the regime could be included.[63] The problem of the reliability of information regarding collaboration later became intertwined in the Czech-Slovak conflict. Fifth, it was also easy to remain in prominent positions without ever being subjected to screening. This is what happened in the case of Jozef Markuš, to which I will turn in the next section.

But even given all of these problems it was also impossible to avoid a screening process since there were signs that "dark forces" *did* still exist in powerful places and it seemed unthinkable to create a democracy where this was the case. It was also hard to determine who was to blame for the ways in which the screening policy itself went astray. It is not clear whether, as some thought, "dark forces" from the past were pulling the strings behind the new populist nationalism that began to appear. However, one key mass-elite nationalist seems to have come to his nationalism, and to his position as head of the most important cultural institution, through an attempt to avoid the screening process.

Jozef Markuš and Matica Slovenská

Jozef Markuš became head of the most highly regarded nationalist organization in Slovakia in August 1990. Markuš took advantage of the fact that the post of chairman of Matica Slovenská was not an elected position and thus was not subject to screening. It was the perfect place to build a personal power base for someone with his profile—an ambitious political figure who had been screened and found to have a questionable past. In spite of the fact that Matica was not a political party, this organization became an important political actor. His coming to Matica is also a good example of how parties and government positions were not the only paths to power in the postcommunist environment. Emigrés, who were unlikely to run for office, saw Matica as a key channel for their interests. It was also a natural place for émigrés to go because of its historical reputation and link to foreign Slovaks. Matica Slovenská became the most important source of radical nationalist ideas. In addition, like the Catholic Church, but unlike most new political parties, the Matica had true ties on the local level.[64] The cultural foundation could be used to produce radical ideas outside of the political process, and the organization's reputation could be used to promote these ideas.

Unlike the Catholic Church, Matica Slovenská was a nationalist organization that was not directly associated with the fascist past.[65] Like the

Catholic Church, it was not only repressed but also was co-opted and many of its workers were associated with the StB. But it retained its reputation as the true voice of the Slovak nation. The fact that the former Lenin museum was made into the Matica Slovenská Museum of Slovaks Abroad attests to the continuing symbolic importance of the organization.[66]

Matica Slovenská had two wings: one was academic and involved administering libraries and museums; the other was political and had historically been involved in advocating Slovak interests and spreading national consciousness.[67] The political wing had been repressed during the "normalization" period and was now up for grabs. Its activities were, thus, difficult to predict.[68] Its political leanings began to become clear in 1990 because of its activities in the debate over the name of the country—also known as the "hyphen debate"—and the Hungarian issue.

During the Husák period, Vladimír Mináč, an ambiguous figure who was an important communist until November 1989, headed it. He was also one of the more popular Slovak writers and one of the few Slovak elites who could qualify as a nationalist intellectual.[69] Mináč was removed in 1990 as a way of giving the organization greater credibility, even though he remained in politics without much of a loss of reputation and served in the Slovak parliament before the first elections as a member of the Communist Party. He was also active as a commentator. In early 1990, a temporary new leadership of Matica was appointed. In August 1990, Jozef Markuš was chosen as its head.

Jozef Markuš was an economist (born in 1944) who had been an official in the "caretaker government" for VPN in the months between communism's fall and the June 1990 elections.[70] He had been part of the team of social scientists working on an assessment of the future of Czechoslovak society from which one stream of VPN came. VPN leader Fedor Gál knew him from that project and brought him into the caretaker government.[71]

After the June election, KDH nominated Markuš to work in the federal antimonopoly office. But he was screened and found to have collaboration with the secret police in his past.[72] Soon after being removed, he was chosen as the head of the Matica Slovenská, which, interestingly, had fired Mináč because of his *visible* communist past. Markuš was chosen because the leadership of Matica wanted someone powerful and decided that an economist would help the economic viability of the organization.[73] In addition, Markuš had developed contacts with the émigrés during his tenure in the first government.[74]

Markuš had not been connected with nationalism prior to 1989 and was not from a nationalist family.[75] The fact that Markuš was screened without the results of the screening being made public (though there were rumors), made the democrats, who knew the results, suspicious of the activities of Markuš at Matica. But it was difficult to anticipate that Markuš would re-create Matica as a rather conspiratorial organization, which would pro-pose policies such as a fall 1990 exclusionary language law.[76] The demo-crats complained about the politicization of an organization that had fought communism and was supposed to have a cultural, not a political, agenda.[77] The case of Markuš is a good example of how connections through the original networks of opposition were not helpful in establish-ing a trustworthy elite.

But the fact that the democrats, and to some extent the Catholic national-ists, made associations between "dark forces" and the nationalist activities of Matica Slovenská, gave people like Markuš the opportunity to question the very process of lustration and the goal of keeping former collaborators out of political life. It made it seem that this process was aimed at dis-crediting Slovak nationalism in general.[78]

The Slovak National Party and Other Nationalists

The unknown forces that emerged as the most vocal early nationalists are another example of the ephemeral quality of the nationalism of the mass-elite and the ease of transforming oneself in the postcommunist period. While the democrats and Catholic nationalists remained true to their long-standing beliefs, some mass-elites, unconstrained by any ideology, were able to maneuver around the ideological elites, to assess the possibilities, and to fill the space opened up by their programs.

The small groups of nationalists that appeared in the squares of Bra-tislava were discounted by both the democrats and the Catholic national-ists as extremists or as products of the workings of "dark forces." While the democrats did not take these signs seriously enough, these groups were even more problematic for KDH. The Catholic nationalists were constantly faced with the dilemma that the unknown nationalists were being too extreme and discrediting the larger cause of Slovak autonomy. KDH lead-ers maintained that Slovaks should pursue autonomy inside established channels for negotiation. Furthermore, KDH saw that some of these un-knowns had been linked to the former StB and were clearly their oppo-nents. Catholic nationalists also suffered because of their association with the fascist past, which could be used against them both by the democrats and by the unknown nationalists who were not associated with any ideo-logical tradition.

Slovak National Party, a Party of the Mass-elite

From the beginning of the "velvet" revolution, there were natural differences between Czechs and Slovaks. Disagreements cropped up in December about whom to choose as president. Many Slovaks preferred Dubček to Havel. Some leaders of VPN insisted on remaining separate from Civic Forum.[79] But no one really paid attention at first to the fact that émigrés and small groups of young nationalists, like the Štúr society, were present at the mass demonstrations after November 17.

Although not present at the early demonstrations, the most important of these groupings was the Slovak National Party (SNS). The SNS was, from early 1990, the most radical of the mainstream parties. It was established by figures who were largely unknown, but became visible during the debate over the name of the country in March 1990.[80] SNS went on to win a surprising number of seats in the June election and reached the peak of support in the fall of 1990, when that party did well in local elections.[81]

The leadership of the SNS had not been linked to a nationalist ideology or to one another before 1989.[82] They were all born after 1950; none were linked to the networks of democrats or Catholic nationalists.[83] They came together somewhat randomly as a result of looking around for people and ideas that would bring them power in the fluid environment of postcommunism. They were political entrepreneurs.

Anton Hrnko, a historian in the leadership of SNS, was responsible for the choice of the party's name. They chose the name of the oldest party in Slovakia but had no links to the historical party.[84] Interestingly, there was no acknowledgment of the fact that the link was not there. In an interview with Hrnko, when I asked how SNS was formed, he said it was originally created in 1871 and did not mention the lack of real continuity.

Hrnko, on first glance, should not be categorized as a mass-elite. He clearly had information about the history of World War II since he was a historian, but he was more an island of information than a bearer of historical consciousness (he had the information but not the group association). He said that he had always been interested in history. He became a professional historian during the years of "normalization," and his work prior to 1989 showed no indication of straying from the official line. He was the leader of the Communist Party organization in the history institute at the Academy of Sciences. The fact that Hrnko was a Party member does not tell us much about his political leanings. But the fact that he was the leader of the Party organization at the history institute is suggestive. Historians were one of the least trusted groups in post-1968 Czechoslovakia. Thus the individual chosen to head the Party organization would have had to have been considered particularly reliable.[85]

Hrnko claims that there is evidence of his nationalist leanings from before the revolution, in that he had opposed plans for a more unitary state setup, which he says, would have been implemented by the Communist Party had the revolution of November 1989 not happened.[86] He was clearly the source of historical information and interpretation behind the Slovak National Party. He was approached to join the leadership of SNS after appearing on television in January 1990 with a nationalist version of the Slovak National Uprising; that is, he questioned whether it was an event that favored reestablishment of the Czechoslovak state. He and Vladimír Miškovský (see below) wrote the party's program.[87]

Hrnko says he avoided joining KDH because of its Catholicism and its link to the fascist Slovak state. I did not ask him, nor did he say, whether the reason might have been his communist past, since KDH would not have brought him into its leadership given his past. This was suggested to me in the interview by his complaint that KDH was "stupidly anticommunist."

Another leader of SNS, Jozef Prokeš (chairman of the party, starting in fall 1990), came to them after going from party to party trying to get onto a candidate list and after he had been turned down for VPN's list.[88] Operating like others who surveyed their opportunities in the post-1989 scene and did not know which positions or institutions would become powerful, he briefly appeared as head of the new independent trade union organization but mysteriously resigned from that position.[89] He was born in 1950 and was a physicist by training. My interview with him revealed that he developed a nationalist position during the brief stint as trade union leader in early 1990.[90] He said this was due to the behavior of the Czech side.

Vladimír Miškovský was also asked to join by the founders of SNS after he wrote an article in the press calling for Slovak equality in the federation. Miškovský is an even better example of a mass-elite. Born in 1961, he was clearly a product of the period of normalization. He would have been only seven in 1968, though he claimed 1968 as the formative experience in his life. Though he was educated as a sociologist, he was not part of the networks of intelligentsia that became VPN (too young). He was fairly blunt in an interview about the fact that after 1989 he surveyed the political scene and looked for a spot to fit himself in. He was also very vague about his national leanings before 1989. When it came to his political commitments he said: "Once you find a position you go with it." Like Hrnko, he pointed out that he saw room for another party because KDH was not just Catholic but also tied to the wartime Slovak state.[91]

The Émigrés and SNS

Interestingly, the Slovak National Party became the home for some of the émigrés who had appeared in Slovakia with the end of communism and went from party to party trying to find politicians who would take up their ideas.[92] As we already saw, Čarnogurský's party was the natural first place for them to go, though they did not find a home there.

After being turned down by KDH, the émigrés went elsewhere, and even approached the democrats of VPN. But VPN was not as receptive to the nationalist message as was SNS. This is evident in the experience of Igor Uhrík, who was more involved in Slovak politics than almost any other émigré figure. He was first involved with VPN and to some extent with KDH, but went to SNS because they were the only ones willing to pursue a separatist program. He chose them even though their reputation was questionable and some did not consider them serious political figures.[93] Uhrík also describes KDH's first congress as an opportunity lost. He said "electricity was in the air" but Čarnogurský refused to tap it.[94]

There was a clear fit between the émigrés and the mass-elite of SNS. The mass-elite went looking for political ideas and groupings to associate with; the émigrés were looking for a political force willing to pursue independence at a time when that idea was taboo.

The émigrés were in an odd position. As we saw in chapter 4, they had no social base and few ties to anyone in Slovakia.[95] However, they, like the ideological elites, imagined they represented Slovak identity better than anyone. And in a sense, they did. Slovak political figures in all parts of the spectrum saw the émigrés as a source of ideas in a country where ideas were in short supply.[96] Their challenge was to connect their ideology to a social base.

The mass-elite, especially from the Slovak National Party, hoped initially that the émigrés would help them financially. The émigrés could also provide credibility and ideas. Marián Andel answered an interviewer who suggested that SNS was relying too much on the support of the émigrés by saying, "We are convinced that we must attract primarily Slovak foreign capital, that is, make use of the capital of the 3 million U.S. Slovaks. You in Bohemia will presumably center more on German capital."[97] During this first period, the SNS frequently argued that the émigrés would provide economic assistance equal to the assistance from Western countries. This was implicitly an argument for separation, since they were suggesting that the Western aid would likely end up in Prague.[98]

Hrnko and others, in retrospect, said the émigrés could not have known what the country needed. They gave support but not decisive support.[99] He also complained that the émigrés had too much connection to churches and that SNS was not in favor of clerical involvement in politics. In addition, he said that the émigrés wanted to rehabilitate the wartime Slovak state and that, unfortunately, the more nationalist wing of SNS listened to them on this. This, however, had not been enough to follow KDH's example and turn the émigrés away. The SNS continued to take stances favorable to the Slovak state while simultaneously criticizing KDH for its ties to the Tiso regime.[100]

If the SNS was disappointed in the émigrés' lack of generosity, some émigrés were disappointed in the mass-elite, and in the fact that nationalism was lost by more reputable politicians and captured by Mečiar and SNS.[101] The émigrés did not provide enough resources to have given them greater leverage. They were also dispersed and operating more as individuals than as organizations. Thus the power in the relationship was skewed toward the mass-elite, and the émigrés were left to cooperate with the mass-elite or to abandon their cause.

SNS Outmaneuvers the Nationalists of KDH

In addition to winning the support of the émigrés, limited as it was, the Slovak National Party was the beneficiary of two other issues in early 1990, neither of which KDH and VPN picked up: the Hungarians, and the issue of Slovak autonomy. With the help of the émigrés, the SNS successfully exploited the early 1990 controversy over the name of the country.

The Hungarian Issue
The Hungarian issue became problematic almost immediately after the November revolution. The 600,000-strong Hungarian minority in Slovakia had, even during the communist period, preserved its identity and had a network with which to organize. One of the few dissidents in Slovakia was Hungarian rights activist Miklos Duray. Two of the Hungarian parties came from the Committee for the Protection of Hungarian Minority Rights, which operated during the communist regime: Coexistence and the Hungarian Civic Initiative.[102] Some of the first demands from these parties were for a ministry of nationalities and for a reassessment of nationality policy, especially regarding education.[103]

While the Hungarian parties tended to be closely associated with VPN, an organization called the "Štúr Society" became the first and most vocal force opposing the Hungarian demands for minority rights. The Štúr Society was the most radical nationalist voice in early 1990. Though in the same general age group as the leaders of SNS, its founders had actually been associated with nationalist ideas before November 1989.[104] They were the first to fly a Slovak flag at the rallies in November, and began to meet on the squares of Bratislava to read nationalist poetry. The leader, Vladimír Repka, became the editor of one of the more radical and racist newspapers, *Nový Slovák*.[105] Vladimír Repka provides a clue into the outlook of this grouping. When asked about the chauvinistic and anti-Semitic leanings of the paper, Repka said, "You have to be radical if you are first," suggesting that the paper's positions had been aimed at gaining attention more than articulating strongly held beliefs.[106]

In the first days of January 1990, during a TV discussion on nationalities, the Hungarians articulated their demands regarding minority rights. The Štúr Society, in one of its first statements, complained about the lack of balance in the composition of the panel (mostly Slovak Hungarians). The Štúr Society objected to Hungarian complaints and argued that the Hungarians had more rights in Slovakia than minorities had in other countries, including Hungary. They also said that in fact it was the Slovaks in Hungarian areas that had to worry about their rights.[107] In their initial statement in the press they announced their commitment to "preventing the assimilation of foreign Slovaks in a foreign ethnic environment."[108] They continued to appear in the press, periodically opposing Hungarian demands.[109]

In general, VPN defended Hungarian interests. The policy of the government was that the Hungarians, like everyone else under communism, had suffered and that it was wrong to pursue a policy of reciprocity for the treatment of the Slovak minority in Hungary.[110] Ostensibly in response, anti-Hungarian graffiti began to appear on the walls of Bratislava. The VPN and the government linked these manifestations of anti-Hungarian sentiment to "dark forces."

In a strange incident at the end of February, at a time when there were fears of a communist coup, the VPN leadership decided to replace the communist leader of the Slovak parliament with VPN activist Ján Budaj.[111] The Štúr Society joined communists in opposing the ouster. The reasoning was that Budaj, who had a Hungarian name, favored the Hungarians. Protesters argued that Budaj was trying to claim that communists were to blame for anti-Hungarian sentiments and refused to acknowledge their legitimate concerns about Hungarians.[112] The Budaj incident brought more people into the streets, now also coordinated by SNS.

The Štúr Society issued a complaint to VPN about that group's defense of

Hungarian rights. They contended that VPN did not protect alleged abuses of Slovaks by Hungarians in southern Slovakia, saying, "Since the Slovaks, above all in southern Slovakia, could not find protection in the VPN or in other movements, *we* took up these problems to enable them to at least testify about their hardships and to provide an outlet for the Slovaks in Slovakia."[113]

The situation worsened when, in response to the tensions, the acting Hungarian president wrote to Havel voicing distress about the treatment of Hungarians in Slovakia. Slovak politicians across the spectrum were surprised by the turn to Havel and complained that the Hungarian government should address concerns to them but, in general, should not become involved. Still, the VPN leadership, including Mečiar, responded that "former normalizers and consolidators for whom a muddled political situation is rather convenient" were causing all the tension. He suggested that it was possible that "the echo of this group . . . also reached the president of the Hungarian Republic."[114]

According to a number of sources, the Hungarian issue was important for the loss of support by both the democrats of VPN and Čarnogurský's Catholic nationalist party. VPN defended Hungarian demands during the first conflict over the TV debate. They then formed a coalition with the Hungarian Civic Party for the June elections. Čarnogurský is reputed to have downplayed the Hungarian issue when asked about it at a rally.[115] Thus both of the groups of ideological elites left space for a political force to take up the anti-Hungarian cause. Vladimír Miškovský of SNS said that the groups in power underestimated national feeling, "so this is why gradually there spontaneously emerged a nationalist wave represented by SNS."[116]

The Hyphen Debate

The SNS also managed to galvanize and then capture the emerging interest in independence, which was originally represented by KDH. They used the conflict over the name of the country to bring people into the streets.[117]

One of the first and most significant symbolic moves taken by those surrounding Havel was the removal of the word *socialist* from the name of the country, which at the time was the Czechoslovak Socialist Republic. Discussions began in December about changing the state emblems.[118] In a speech to the federal parliament on January 23, Havel called for a change in the name of the state, the republics, the emblems, and the name of the army. He said that the word *socialism* had lost meaning and that ideology had no place in the name of a state.[119]

This became an important example of the unexpected ways in which anticommunism raised other issues like the differences between Czechs and Slovaks. While for the Czechs the removal of the word *socialist* seemed to be a simple matter, some Slovaks began to argue that the name of the state was evidence of Czech domination. They argued that a change was a necessary step in redefining the political constitution of Czechoslovakia and enlivening the promise of federation that was formally established in 1969. Linguists, historians, and the Union of Slovak Writers registered some of the early objections. The linguists were upset about the linguistic propriety of the name and the writers and the historians were concerned about whether the Slovaks were acknowledged in the world as a distinct nation.[120] Two people began hunger strikes on March 22.[121] Numerous different proposals for names were put forward: "czecho-slovakia," with a hyphen and with small rather than capital letters; "federation"; "federative republic"; someone even proposed "slovakoczech republic." Anton Hrnko, of the Slovak National Party, in an article on March 22, said that the name "československo" without a hyphen was a sign of Czechoslovakism and the desire to hide the existence of the Slovaks from the world.[122]

Long debates in the federal parliament ensued. Czechs called the hyphen nonsensical and raised the specter of separatism, the Munich treaty, and the wartime Slovak state. Slovaks claimed that the Czechs refused to acknowledge the status of the Slovaks as a separate and equal member in the federation.[123]

The federal parliament spent a full day in debate on March 29.[124] The outcome was a compromise, with the Czechs using "Czechoslovak Federal Republic" and the Slovaks using a hyphen and small "s" (Czecho-slovak Federal Republic). But this spurred objections in Slovakia. On March 30, several thousand people gathered in front of the Slovak National Council (SNR) to protest the decision about the country's name. Demonstrators gave the SNR leadership a petition, which said that the Czech nation does not recognize the existence of the Slovak nation before the world. They called upon the SNR to start negotiations on full recognition of sovereignty and independence of the Slovak nation.[125]

The demonstrations were organized by the Slovak National Party. Estimates of attendance were as high as twenty thousand. The demonstrators represented a range of concerns—from slogans calling for outright independence to annoyance at the failure of the Czechs to recognize Slovakia. The SNR set up a commission comprised of representatives of the major political forces and eventually, after continued debate that lasted into April, settled on "the Czech and Slovak Federative Republic."

At least part of the uproar at that particular moment in Slovakia came from a campaign put together by an individual émigré, Igor Uhrík. He wanted to publicize to Slovaks the extent to which they were being depicted in the eyes of the world as Czech. He put together a series of examples from the world press in which everything having to do with Czechoslovakia—from the velvet revolution to Alexander Dubček, Slovak leader of the 1968 reform movement—was referred to as Czech. He ran ads on television showing a montage of these references. The ads ran in mid-February. This was also the beginning of Slovak nationalists' focus on the issue of their image in the world, a theme that I develop in the next chapter.[126]

The hyphen debate came at a time when the election campaign was beginning, and not long after the late January decision to shut off arms production, which very quickly became unpopular in Slovakia.[127] According to Hrnko, the outrage over the hyphen was an expression of opposition to the arms production decision and was much more powerful because of it. The Slovak National Party consciously adopted a strategy of using the debate over the country's name as a way of gaining publicity. According to Hrnko, it was not hard to persuade people to go to the streets because they had hoped for quick changes after November 1989 and were surprised when they did not materialize.[128] SNS was the organizer of the rallies in the square and began to claim that moment, not November 1989, as the beginning of the revolution in Slovakia.

Ján Čarnogurský chose not to take a strong stance in the hyphen debate.[129] He said in a fall 1992 interview that KDH favored the national interests of Slovakia but did not want to split Czechoslovakia, did not want to be responsible for the trouble associated with a split, and did not make economic promises they knew were impossible to fulfill; "we were not populistic." Čarnogurský said that KDH was accused from the beginning by both communists and liberals of harboring separatist tendencies. He said that his party was not separatist but, because of this, SNS was established.[130]

The Democrats and SNS

Neither of the groupings of ideological elites capitalized on this first outpouring of public support for autonomy. In response to the rallies over the name of the state, VPN issued a statement on April 2 condemning expressions of extreme nationalism, which "weaken chances for democracy and prosperity."[131] VPN leader Fedor Gál acknowledged that the Czechs were being insensitive but said that the people on the square did not represent most Slovaks and that the call for an independent state would lead to a loss of everything they had spent months fighting for. Other VPN leaders were more sympathetic to the demonstrators.[132] In early 1990, when the hyphen debate took place, it was still very difficult for many political actors to believe that autonomy would become the major issue in Slovakia. At the time democrats saw the demonstrations as a manipulation of the public and complained that nationalists were bringing issues to the streets that should be decided in parliaments. Or they saw the battle over the hyphen as a product of a parliament still dominated by former communist members who would likely be ousted in the June elections.[133]

This was one way that the democrats' ideological commitments kept them from seeing even the obvious ways that society was not fully supportive of their programs. They did not adequately respond to the fact that the arms production decision, made based on a commitment to moral politics, backfired. The democrats thought society shared their opposition to communism on moral grounds. It was an easy issue for the mass-elite to pick up, and easy to make the argument that the Czechs were conspiratorially trying to push the Slovaks out of the arms market.

In addition, it was not clear how to understand the unknown figures that came to comprise the leadership of SNS. For the democrats, the SNS was indistinguishable from the other extremist and nationalist forces going to the 1990 election, since none of these groups was associated with known political figures. In assessing the threat posed by these new manifestations of nationalism, they became caught in an odd paradox. On the one hand, they did not take sufficiently seriously the genuine existence of the national issue. On the other hand, they exaggerated the extremism of the sentiments they began to see in the squares of Bratislava and linked this extremism to former communist forces and the possible revival of the wartime Slovak state. The democrats' tendency to explain behavior antithetical to democracy as either fascist or communist became a weapon for the mass-elite and a key element of their appeal to society.

The Rise and Victory of Vladimír Mečiar

Once the June 1990 elections had passed, and the VPN had won and chosen Mečiar as prime minister, it appeared that there was a mandate for the democrats to pursue their election program. This program included economic transformation, democratization, a "return to Europe," and removing communism from all aspects of life. The main problem, from the perspective of the democrats, continued to be the Catholic nationalists of KDH, who almost refused to participate in a coalition with the Czech Civic

Forum after the 1990 elections. KDH continued to propose state arrangements that appeared to the Czechs to be undermining the federation.[134]

The Slovak National Party and the reborn and renamed communists—Slovak Democratic Left (SDL)—were in opposition. On the sidelines were Matica Slovenská and a series of smaller unknown nationalist groupings that continued their activities even though they did not make it into parliament.

Mečiar's Transformation

Until the fall of 1990 and even the winter of 1991, Mečiar was very much in the democratic, pro-federation camp.[135] His speeches from the pre-election period until fall 1990 could have been made by any of the VPN activists. There was no reason to suspect him of differing in terms of his interests or his ideas about following democratic rules. In the mind of the public, he was a democrat and opposed to KDH, with its links to clericalism and the fascist past and to the Slovak National Party in the streets. Before the election his speeches included a focus on individual responsibility. He argued that communists should not be in parliament and that nationalists were StB agents, and he strongly condemned the Tiso state. When a plaque was unveiled to Jozef Tiso in July 1990, with approval of KDH, he articulated the VPN position. He said that Tiso clearly held responsibility as leader of the state that deported Jews, restricted civil liberties, repressed the popularly supported Slovak National Uprising: "Everyone who is serious about the protection of civil rights and liberties must therefore stand up and resist this wave [of Tiso's rehabilitation] in the name of our democracy. What is involved here is not an isolated local act . . . but an act which casts aspersions on the standing of Slovakia in the international public, an act which devalues the credibility of the efforts to strengthen Slovak statehood."[136]

At that time, the KDH had been the main defenders of the Slovak state, with Nitra bishop Ján Korec attending the unveiling of the plaque and the prosecutor general Tibor Boehm arguing in parliament that Tiso was not really a war criminal.[137] In retrospect, it appears possible that in July it had been to Mečiar's advantage to stay focused on KDH's link to the fascist past.[138]

In fall 1990 Mečiar joined the Czechs and the democrats of VPN in putting fascist and communist labels on what they saw as a wave of nationalist fervor at odds with democracy.[139] Mečiar, along with the democrats, remained critical of an anti-Hungarian version of the language law and the extremism of this law's supporters—the Slovak National Party and Matica Slovenská.[140]

But slowly a split began to develop between the democrats and the Mečiar group that had joined them for the June 1990 election to stem the tide of support for the KDH. In part this was a natural differentiation in the movement. A group within VPN called the Trnava group, with more nationalist leanings, was created in fall 1990. This group was concerned about the talks with the Czechs on state setup and economic reform. This group also worried that the nationalist message had clearly gained electoral support in Slovakia. SNS and KDH had done well in the fall local elections.[141] However, Mečiar apparently was not connected with this more nationalist grouping at first.[142] But Mečiar began to find the Trnava group useful as a basis for his new incarnation as a defender of Slovak interests, which he began to articulate in early 1991.[143] They supplied him with legitimacy, much as the émigrés had done for SNS.

The increasing policy divisions created tension within the VPN. However, the split in the movement was not simply over policies. It was not just that what became known as the "Fedor Gál wing" favored a federation and a continuation of radical economic reform while the "Mečiar wing" favored greater focus on Slovak interests and a slowing down of economic reform. The clash between these wings and the eventual split of VPN was a split between the two different types of elites, with their incompatible approaches to politics. It can be viewed as a turning point in the marginalization of the ideological elites. The critical moment came in March 1991. The battle was more about power distribution in the movement than it was about nationalism. The main dispute within VPN was over allegations that Mečiar had used his time in the interior ministry to doctor important files. The democrats of VPN began to try to reclaim power in the movement, and Fedor Gál was chosen as chairman in February.

The peak of the crisis came in early March. The event that precipitated the split in VPN, and marked Mečiar's debut as defender of Slovak interests, occurred on March 3. The director of Slovak TV said that officials from VPN had demanded to see Mečiar's weekly address before it was broadcast. While the VPN leadership denied they had done this, Mečiar refused to record the speech and Milan Kňažko, the Slovak minister for international relations, appeared in his place. Kňažko's speech was an attack on the leadership of Public Against Violence, in which he said they were a "mere executor of concepts" formulated by federal (i.e., Czech) leaders and that Mečiar was the true defender of Slovak interests.[144] Thus Mečiar was deemed a Slovak nationalist.

On March 5, at an emergency meeting of the republican council of Public Against Violence, Gál proposed that Mečiar be recalled as prime minister in the face of the danger of the destabilization of society and the disintegration of the movement. In response, Mečiar, Kňažko, and thirteen other members of the council walked out and founded a new group called VPN-For a Democratic Slovakia. (Later they changed their name to Movement for a Democratic Slovakia, or HZDS.)[145]

But the split and the proposal to oust Mečiar were only the beginning. As federal prime minister Marián Čalfa pointed out, the new Mečiar group was supported by the spectrum of opponents of the government in power. On March 6, thousands of people demonstrated in Bratislava in support of the Slovak prime minister, and radical nationalist groups not belonging to VPN, including the Slovak National Party, expressed their support for Mečiar's new group.[146] The Slovak communists also saw the new group as favoring their interests in its opposition to some aspects of the economic reform.[147] Obroda—the organization of 1968 communists—also backed Mečiar on this account.

Mečiar's transformation seemed even more dramatic when just this moment was chosen for the issuing of a sovereignty declaration and for the first commemoration of the Slovak state since World War II.[148] The "declaration of the sovereignty of Slovakia" was drafted by five nationalist groups and signed by key intellectuals.[149] The commemoration of the Slovak state brought an estimated five to ten thousand people into the streets.

Mečiar manipulated the situation skillfully. He called for calm and did not associate himself with the crowds in the street. In a meeting with Havel, Mečiar told the president that he remained supportive of the federation and of Havel's proposal for a referendum on the future state setup.[150] Mečiar, at this time still against the more radical manifestations of Slovak separatism, made a statement saying the sovereignty declaration would not be approved by the parliament, arguing that "these opinions are not shared by the majority of Slovak citizens and therefore should not be taken seriously." He and Alexander Dubček issued a statement saying that Slovaks should not be influenced by extremism and that "possible manifestations of emotions, passions, and intolerance" would hinder Slovakia's democratic development.[151] In spite of the warnings, thousands of people went into the streets on March 10–11 in support of the declaration. Mečiar was thus able to take advantage of the fact that the crowd had found Mečiar rather than the other way around.[152]

Not only had Mečiar shifted his ideas, he also shifted his methods. Mečiar moved away from his criticism of the SNS and other small extremist groups of nationalists for appealing to crowds in the streets rather than staying within the legal process.[153] He now turned to the streets, saying that while democrats referred disparagingly to crowds in the streets, he believed that "a civic movement ought to proceed primarily from respect for the citizen."[154] He said that he no longer believed that differences could be solved in legal institutions; therefore he was going outside them.[155]

Mečiar was removed from the post of prime minister on April 23, 1991.[156] From that moment on, throughout the rest of 1991 and up until the June 1992 elections, he built an increasingly stronger following comprised of many of the groupings he had previously opposed. He effectively isolated the democrats and Catholic nationalists.

Mečiar's Success

Mečiar was able to use his credibility as a democrat who had spoken out against more radical manifestations of nationalism, and against KDH's clericalism and links with the fascist past, to take the lead in the nationalist camp. He picked up the idiom of SNS and Matica—the nationalists whom he had so recently attacked in fall 1990. He still claimed to be true to the VPN program, but was now aligned more and more with what had, until then, been the opposition in parliament: the SNS and SDL.[157] In a more general sense, he argued that VPN had lost votes in the fall 1990 election to the populist SNS, but he then virtually became SNS. He complained about power manipulations against him and the fact that he did not have access to StB files as minister of the interior, and then broadly publicized allegations about others' secret police backgrounds, for example, that of Ivan Čarnogurský, brother of the prime minister and key figure in KDH.[158] He strongly criticized Matica Slovenská for the language law, on grounds that it discriminated against Hungarians, and then came out strongly against Hungarians himself.[159]

He also was able to use the attacks against him within the VPN movement to bolster his support and discredit the democrats of VPN: he argued that they were controlled by Prague and unrepresentative of Slovakia, and were manipulating information against him. The argument that Czechs and democrats were manipulating information to blacken Slovakia's image in the world even became a main plank in Mečiar's new platform. In an appeal from the Mečiar wing of VPN issued on March 29 a key element was "we reject the campaign of misinterpretation abroad which describes current political events in Slovakia as a return to socialism, fascistlike nationalism, and so on. We will endeavor to clean up Slovakia's image abroad."[160]

The content of his position and the basis of his appeal came to be about what Slovakia was not and we will analyze the implications of this in the next chapter. Interestingly enough, Mečiar never even decisively favored splitting the country. Going into the 1992 elections he continued to advocate a form of common state, and it was only in response to Czech Prime Minister Václav Klaus that he opted for independence.[161]

The Democrats and Nationalists Remain True to Their Beliefs

It was hard for the democrats and the Catholic nationalists to respond to the mass-elite because neither party identifications nor policy positions nor idiom gave much of a clue as to the nature of the threat they posed. Mečiar was able to use the issue that divided them, the fascist past, against both. We have already seen how the division over the fascist past was an important factor in Mečiar's rise to prominence and the Obroda group's entry into VPN. Throughout 1990–92 the democrats and nationalists remained at odds over their historical divides and unable to see that the mass-elite threatened them both. There were several moments when this divide was pivotal.

The first moment came in July 1990 in the incident mentioned above in which a plaque to Tiso was unveiled in Bánovce-nad-Bebravou.[162] Democrats and Czechs were alarmed that KDH supported the unveiling of the plaque and simultaneously called for a reevaluation, if not outright rehabilitation, of Tiso.[163] The plaque was removed and a historian's commission convened. Meanwhile, KDH was uncomfortably aligned with the unknown mass-elite nationalists of SNS, who supported their position.[164] KDH leaders tried to distinguish themselves from the SNS and from others they associated with the communist past.[165] But this did little to allay the fears of the Czechs and democrats.

Czechs and democrats grew even more concerned a few weeks later when a commemoration of the anniversary of the birth of Andrej Hlinka, founder of the Catholic nationalist movement before World War II, was held.[166] At the Hlinka commemoration the more radical nationalists of SNS joined émigrés connected with the Slovak state to disparage KDH leaders and to shout slogans about restoring the Tiso state.[167] In the uproar that followed the incident, representatives of KDH were criticized for attending the commemoration.[168] The KDH again faced a dilemma. The Catholic nationalists had to dissociate themselves from the extremists and émigrés but could not drop their ideology, which compelled them, more than any other political group, to be there.[169] While they tried to do this in statements in the parliaments and the press, KDH remained, in the eyes of democrats and Czechs, linked to the fascist past.[170]

Next came March 1991 and the crisis described above. KDH, until the split of VPN, had remained the main opponent, having come out of the fall 1990 local elections as the most powerful political force. The Catholic nationalists did not join the democrats of VPN immediately in spring 1991 in the decision to oust Mečiar. VPN leader Fedor Gál contends that this contributed to the downfall of both groupings of ideological elites.[171] While KDH's reluctance to support the democrats was less directly due to the divide over the fascist past, certainly the March 14, 1991, commemoration of the Slovak state anniversary was partly at issue, and KDH was not willing to seem opposed to Slovak national interests.[172]

After a period of initial hesitation, KDH joined the democrats in their effort to oust Mečiar. KDH leader Ján Čarnogurský became the new prime minister. The fact that he was the beneficiary of the ousting of the popular prime minister, and that he was from a party that had not won the June 1990 elections, put him in a difficult position from the outset. The very unpopular remains of the VPN were left with the KDH to fight Mečiar.[173]

But again in August 1991 the democrats and nationalists clashed over the fascist past when it came up in negotiations over a treaty with Germany. Until summer 1991, the most controversial issue in the German negotiations had been how to evaluate the removal of the Sudeten Germans after World War II, and whether or not the Czech side would acknowledge it as an expulsion. The Czechs were pushing for a preamble to the treaty, which spoke of the invalidation of the Munich treaty and the continuity of the Czechoslovak state from 1918.[174] But at the end of summer 1991, Catholic nationalists František Mikloško and Ján Čarnogurský wrote a letter to foreign minister Jiří Dienstbier complaining that the wording about continuity in the preamble ignored the existence of the Slovak state of 1939–45. They said that while the political regime of the Slovak republic deserved condemnation, the preamble "does not correspond to the real development of Slovak history nor to the history of the common state of Czechs and Slovaks." They therefore proposed that the controversial part of the preamble be dropped. Although the preamble was never changed, there was a big debate.[175] Czechs and Slovak democrats argued that it was absolutely necessary to recognize the legal continuity of Czechoslovakia since 1918 and that a failure to recognize this continuity could lead to the breakup of the state. They contended that this recognition was not an attempt to ignore history, as the Catholic nationalists feared.[176] The statement from Mečiar's party on the treaty controversy was very vague.[177]

However, the dispute over the treaty again clouded the focus on the mass-elite as a threat and reconfirmed the divide between the ideological elites themselves. The debate on the German treaty took place just when a new grouping of mass-elite nationalists called "For a Sovereign Slovakia" was pushing the Slovak parliament to declare Slovakia's sovereignty and adopt a Slovak constitution. The grouping was comprised of figures from the Mečiar group, the Slovak National Party, Matica Slovenská, and some from KDH. Again this was a moment when KDH had to choose where to place itself and whether to align itself with the mass-elite nationalists.

Against the wishes of some in his own party, Čarnogurský opted to speak against the sovereignty declaration and nearly caused a split in the increasingly polarized KDH movement. The conflict with the democrats over the German treaty, and the conflict within themselves over the sovereignty declaration, weakened KDH's position as articulator of nationalist concerns.

Other conflicts continued to arise between the democrats and the nationalists, making any possible alliance fragile. One example was that the ideological elites could not agree on the definition of liberalism and KDH made statements criticizing liberalism as an ideology.[178] As fall 1991 began, VPN and KDH were increasingly isolated. A poll taken around the time of the sovereignty declaration showed support for HZDS at 31 percent versus KDH at 9 percent.[179] But the fascist past would not go away as an issue. It came up again, and again divided KDH and the democrats in an incident in October 1991.

This time the battle focused on an interview in which the Czechoslovak ambassador to the United States, Rita Klímová, suggested that there was "endemic anti-Semitism" in Slovakia, that there had been anti-Semitic speeches and rallies, and that Slovaks were having a hard time facing their fascist past. Klímová claimed that the word *endemic* was mistranslated.[180] Ján Čarnogurský led the effort to oppose her claim. He argued that there were no anti-Semitic demonstrations in Slovakia and that Klímová was acting irresponsibly in her role as representative of both republics.[181] While the debate revolved around whether or not she really meant that anti-Semitism was endemic in Slovakia, the controversy further prolonged the focus on the divide between the ideological elites. The Slovak democrats, though they might have seen insensitivity in Klímová's position, could not accept the claim that there was no threat of anti-Semitism or of rehabilitation of the fascist past in Slovakia. Klímová herself continued to focus on KDH as the real danger to democracy.[182]

However, this again missed the point about the threat of the mass-elite, assuming instead that the fascist past was the problem. In addition, the mass-elite nationalists were the true beneficiaries of this incident, as it contributed to an escalating campaign to oppose the blackening of Slovakia's image in the world press. More than thirty deputies to both federal and Slovak parliaments—mostly from SNS and HZDS—signed a petition calling on the United Nations to send observers to Slovakia to "ensure objective and unmanipulated information of the international community about the development of the political situation in Czechoslovakia with an emphasis on Slovakia." Signatories argued that the continuing propaganda campaign "deforms Slovakia's image and can be described as a deliberately organized attempt at a moral genocide of Slovaks in the eyes of the world public."[183]

KDH found itself increasingly torn between its attempt to stay loyal to the coalition with VPN and to avoid the more populist nationalist wave while staying true to its principles.[184] Ultimately it was unable to hold itself together. It split in early 1992, with the more radical half joining the Mečiar camp in opposing the draft state-treaty. A disagreement about concessions in negotiations with the Czechs was just the final event leading to the split of the party on March 7, 1992. There had, almost from the start, been a more radical wing in KDH. Led by Ján Klepáč, this wing became known as the Slovak Christian Democratic Movement (SKDH as opposed to KDH).[185] There had also been disagreements over the economy, with the Klepáč wing favoring more leftist economic policies, thereby bringing them closer to the Mečiar group. The Čarnogurský wing went on to become a European style, right-of-center Christian democratic party, which, after Czechoslovakia split in January 1993, joined forces with some democrats of VPN. Members of the SKDH became some of the most radical nationalists, pushing for rehabilitation of the wartime Slovak state. That party never received much electoral support and did not make it into parliament in June 1992. After the split of the movement, and in the face of its isolation from the Mečiar forces, KDH came nowhere near its previous strength, with 8.9 percent of the vote and eighteen seats in the Slovak parliament.[186] The democrats, by this time, were even more isolated and did not make it into parliament in June 1992.

While the democrats and nationalists clearly remained divided, there were moments when they seemed to have understood the common threat they faced. Certainly there was an awareness that there was a difference between those who made the revolution and the so-called dark forces, which included former communists. As we saw above, KDH deputy Ivan

Šimko warned that in the controversy over the Tiso plaque the democrats and nationalists were losing sight of their common enemy, the communists. There was recognition at the time that VPN split of the common threat that Mečiar posed. KDH leader Ivan Čarnogurský said: "And now, no longer a communist, [Mečiar] stands at the head of a movement supported unanimously by the Movement for a Democratic Slovakia, the Party of the Democratic Left, and the Slovak National Party. No matter how hard I try, I cannot find any common ground for these parties but the membership of a great part of their officials in the former Communist Party of Slovakia." His bafflement about the nature of this grouping led him to end the article: "Who are you Mr. Mečiar?"[187] In the fall of 1991 a VPN spokesman differentiated between KDH and the mass-elite nationalists: "KDH obviously realized that there is a difference between cooperation with political entities that were established in November 1989—and that are oriented in a politically forward-looking manner—and with forces that have a certain continuity with our totalitarian past. . . . some of them have formed new political groupings (SNS, HZDS) that are dependent on nomenclatura cadres located in industry and in state administration, to say nothing of state security informers."[188]

Democrats seemed to agree that they and KDH shared a commitment to principle. A commentator in the VPN daily *Verejnost'* asked why Čarnogurský and KDH joined in the ousting of Mečiar and "put their head in the noose of people's dissatisfaction with the economy, on the brink of an abyss." He answered: "Anyone who would do this only for the feeling of political victory and ecstasy over wielding power would have to be suicidal, which the new premier probably is not. Therefore, we cannot but believe his words that he did so for the benefit of Slovakia."[189] Čarnogurský himself talked about "not taking the popular route."[190]

However, there was never full recognition that Mečiar's danger came from his lack of commitment to anything. Even if there was such recognition it would have been difficult to respond, since the mass-elite were so pervasive, were able to act more successfully in this environment, and, as we will see in the next chapter, better reflected the electorate.

Mečiar got a great deal of mileage from the failure, particularly on the part of the democrats, to understand the nature of the threat he posed to their power and to democracy more generally. Most blatant and lasting was the 1991 decision, spearheaded by the Gál wing of VPN, to remove him from office, which they assumed would also eliminate the threat he posed. However, this assumption was based on the belief that he was threatening due to his communist past or to his link to advocates for the restoration of the fascist past. But because Mečiar as a mass-elite represented a much more diffuse threat, removing him from office did little to stop him. In fact, because he was now in opposition, he was able to criticize the increasingly isolated democrats and nationalists without himself being in a position of responsibility or accountability.

Conclusion

There were two important divides between the elites in Slovakia. One was a typical cleavage over issues and ideas—the divide between the democrats and the Catholic nationalists over history and competing national ideologies.[191] The other divide was between fundamentally different ways of operating in politics. The first divide was identifiable, but the second divide—between the ideological elites and the mass-elite—was very difficult to see, since the mass-elite differed from the ideological elites precisely in their lack of identifiability. The second divide was not visible because it could not be determined from the signals assumed to be readable and revealing: policy positions and party identification, idiom, and information about an individual's past.

By looking at postcommunist politics through the lens of these two divides, we have seen how the problem of the absence of historical consciousness among the elite played itself out in postcommunist Slovakia. The lack of cohesion or commitment in the mass-elite is highlighted by the contrast with the ideological elites, the only true bearers of national ideology, and the only actors for whom ideology was at stake. Nationalist idiom was picked up and dropped by the mass-elite in an opportunistic way. Rather than a process of socialization through democratic institutions, we see that the rules of the mass-elite—short-term opportunism and remaining uncommitted—came to dominate and marginalize both groups of ideological elites. With politics dominated by the mass-elite there is little prospect for an elite to develop which is driven by anything other than egoism.

That nationalist mobilization rested not on a resurgence of previously existing ideologies but on short-term resentments thus is integrally connected to the fragility of democratic institutions. However, in postcommunist societies this is not because nationalism is at odds with democracy. Instead, without either civic or ethnic national ideology, without ideology at all, democratic institutions cannot take root.

7 Politics in a Hall of Mirrors

Even if no ideology existed when communism collapsed, why was it so hard to build one? An examination of the attempt by the ideological elites to pursue a historical justice agenda shows why this attempt to build the missing ideology turned into a perpetuation of its absence. The historical justice agenda included a range of policies aimed at righting the wrongs of the communist past, from the screening policy to keep former collabora-tors out of public life to trying to reevaluate parts of history distorted by communism, particularly the fascist past. This agenda was pursued in a variety of arenas: court cases, debates about commemorations, and the naming of political threats. Three factors contributed to the difficulties. First, both society and elites were being called upon to make the necessary judgments without the necessary interpretive frameworks. Second, Lenin-ism had left a legacy of poor information and lack of historical precedent. Third, the historical issues on the agenda were intrinsically complex.

An Illustrative Case

We can see all of these factors illustrated in an attempt to bring a legal claim for propagation of fascism against the organizer of the rally celebrat-ing the fifty-second anniversary of the declaration of the wartime Slovak state on March 14, 1991. March 14 had been celebrated by émigré groups since World War II, but this was the first time since the war that it was openly celebrated in Slovakia.[1] Demonstrators carried posters of Jozef Tiso and called for Slovak autonomy. There were even some people wearing the uniform of the Hlinka guard—the shock troops who had carried out the

Nazi order to deport Slovakia's Jewish population. A recording of Tiso's speech declaring the founding of the Slovak state was played. The rally took on greater significance because President Václav Havel attended and was assaulted by participants. Some two hundred angry demonstrators attacked Havel and his entourage.[2]

Federal assembly deputy Ján Mlynárik brought a legal claim against Stanislav Pánis, also a federal assembly deputy, for organizing the March 14 rally.[3] The charge was that Pánis violated the law against propagation of fascism. Pánis had said in his speech at the rally that "the declaration of the Slovak state in 1939 was one of the greatest and most glorious events in the history of the Slovak nation." Mlynárik wrote in his letter to the general prosecutor that the Slovak state was "tantamount to the negation of the principles of a democratic parliamentary state, installation of totalitarian power which unleashed a genocide of Jews, and persecution and murders of Slovak patriots who resisted Nazism."[4] Interestingly, according to Mlynárik, once he took his claim to the courts he discovered that the investigators assigned to the case did not know anything about fascism and even asked him to give them a lecture about what fascism was. He said, "I did this with unwillingness, unhappiness, because this kind of case is too important to be investigated by ignorants."[5]

A month after this interview, he received a letter from the general prosecutor that the investigation was stopped because they had found no propagation of fascism. Mlynárik complained that because Pánis's activities had gone unchecked by the law he continued to be a dangerous political force. He pointed out that while the court was deciding, Pánis had led a disruption of a rally commemorating the founding of Czechoslovakia and had denied the Holocaust in a speech in Norway.[6] Mlynárik claimed that the prosecutor protected people like Pánis.[7] Pánis himself was one of the founders of the Slovak National Party and, like its other leaders, was an unknown figure. Many speculated about his "dark" past.[8]

This incident is illustrative of all three facets of the problem of building ideology. First it shows, through the contrast between Mlynárik and the investigators, the absence of ideology that characterized most of the elite and society. Mlynárik, a historian who wrote actively in samizdat, a Charter 77 signatory, and a deputy for VPN, fits the profile of ideological democrat.[9] The investigators who are charged with making the judgment are products of the communist socialization process, and have no ideology that would enable them to judge the meaning of fascism. The investigators, like the mass-elite and like the electorate, were at a loss when they were called upon to make judgments, since, as we know, the fascist period and its meaning were not debated during the communist period. What the Communist Party called fascist was, in many people's minds, vague.[10]

The legal process is a microcosm of the democratic process more generally, relying as it does on accountability—using information to assess the extent to which politicians are telling the truth and taking responsibility for their actions. The legal process assumes the ability to judge, as does Mlynárik, who is surprised to find out that the investigators do not share his understanding of history. What he does not initially understand is that they have no ideological framework at all.

While the legal process assumed the ability to judge—that is, that people had some sort of common ideological framework—it also assumed that reliable information could be found to assist in the necessary judgment. Information can be simply evidence; it can also be legal precedent. In the aftermath of communism, however, it was difficult to find evidence that would facilitate judgment. This is the second facet that made it difficult to build ideology.

History, in many cases, had not been written. The history that was written, abroad and in samizdat, was associated with the ideological elites or the Czechs. It was difficult to assess the multiplicity of new sources and articles that appeared with the end of communism.[11] Archives were being opened and witnesses were beginning to speak, but this information was often inconclusive or unreliable. This only exacerbated the problem faced by the investigator who, with no clear ideological framework, was trying to make a judgment about propagation of fascism.[12]

In addition, legal precedent did not accumulate during the communist period, infused as the legal process was by Party ideology. This was particularly true in a regime priority area such as propagation of fascism. The law against the propagation of fascism was a communist-era law. It had been used by the communist regime to condemn the Catholic Church and other signs of nationalism as "clerico-fascist." But it did not clarify why fascism was bad and what connection the wartime Slovak state had to fascism.

But even if most people had ideological frameworks, even if information was reliable, the third facet that this case illustrates is that the issues that were being considered were themselves complicated. While it was not hard to establish that Pánis was the one addressing the rally or that Havel was attacked, it was difficult to evaluate whether Pánis's activities amounted to propagation of fascism. It raised the difficult question of how to weigh the evils of fascism and the evils of communism, given the fact that the communists had been so important historically in defeating fascism. The parliament, at the time, was in the process of reconsidering the law against propagation of fascism, and there was discussion of whether to add communism to the law as a prohibited ideology.

Without common ideological frameworks, without frameworks at all, it was impossible to use the legal system. The claims of those who had ideologies would always be caught in a quicksand of competing claims. They would be pushed out of politics. There would be no opportunity to establish a system based on independent information that could be commonly agreed to be true.[13] Precedent would not accumulate.[14] The individuals involved would not themselves become any more committed to a framework to guide judgment. All claims would be equally open to manipulation.

The Electorate and the Unwillingness to Judge

In the Mlynárik case we see clearly that the investigators are not apologists for the fascist past but rather lack any ideology at all. Mlynárik concluded, when the case was thrown out, that someone was protecting Pánis, as if the threat was apology for the fascist past and whatever political behavior such apology would imply. We can see how problematic this type of assumption was in the very arena discussed in the last chapter. The attempt to name and identify who represented threats to the new democracy was part of the historical justice agenda. Making links to history did two things simultaneously: it helped identify and label policy orientations of dangerous political figures and it was a way of condemning aspects of the past that were symbolically at odds with democracy. But it would only work if the electorate actually had a point of view on the meaning of the fascist and communist pasts and on why these ideologies were dangerous. In fact, not only were the ideological elites wrong about the nature of the threats to the new democracy, but their defeat illustrates why it was difficult to develop society-wide judgments of history in the postcommunist context.

The example I will use here is also from March 1991. As we saw above, this was a turning point in the post-1989 politics of Czechoslovakia. It was the point after which Mečiar's rise was assured and the pattern of appealing to the electorate based on discrediting of the democrats and nationalists was set. After this moment, even though they still ran the government, the ideological elites were more and more isolated. March 1991 was a moment fraught with confusion for the democrats in trying to sort out the meaning of, and the correct response to, the variety of events that were happening at the time. These events included a split in their own movement, VPN, and Mečiar's move to join what had until then been identified as dark forces and radical nationalists.

Could they use their ideology which told them that the fascist and communist pasts constituted the major symbolic threats to democracy to account for the fact that Mečiar appeared to be on the other side and that he had a great deal of support in this new incarnation?[15] In the crisis of March 1991 we begin to see the costs of the democrats' assumption that threats to the new democracy were identifiable and, if identified, would help convince the electorate to use their new power to defeat these threats.

Naming and Blaming

In the major statements issued by the remaining democrats of VPN, after Mečiar formed a new wing, we can see their attempt to name, and thus interpret, Mečiar's behavior. A group of thirty-five VPN deputies from the federal and Slovak parliaments issued a statement on March 8 criticizing Mečiar for "appealing directly to the people," thereby alluding to his dictatorial tendencies and his breaking of what were assumed to be the democratic rules of the game.[16] In another statement regarding Mečiar's new splinter group they made a direct link to the fascist past: "This platform is guided by a fuehrer principle and instead of specific responsibility toward the democratically elected bodies, the idea prevails that the leader is answerable only to the people, and to no one else, for executing his authority . . . this . . . defies the principles of parliamentary democracy."[17] Although this statement did not call Mečiar a fascist directly, it suggested that the threat he represented was based on fascistlike behavior. Mečiar was able to twist these allegations in his favor.[18]

The statement that sparked the most controversy at this time was made by Havel's press secretary, Michael Žantovský, at a press conference on March 11. In trying to explain Mečiar's switch and the confluence of troubling developments, he said, "A new coalition of 1968 reform communists, separatists, and forces which reminisce about the 1939–45 Slovak state as a golden period of the Slovak nation is taking shape in Slovakia." He maintained that this coalition had its own notions of economic reform. Most controversial, he said that there was a revival of ideas of "national socialism" and called it dangerous and possibly destabilizing.[19] Many Slovak commentators and politicians alleged that the use of the words *national socialism* clearly suggested fascism. Žantovský claimed he was using these words to describe a nationalist standpoint with a leftist orientation.[20] Invoking the danger of a coalition of leftists, dark forces, and apologists for the fascist past was assumed to be a powerful weapon to delegitimize those forces in the eyes of the public and the international community. This assumed that not only would society see this danger, but also more fundamentally, that members of the electorate had a point of view.

The assumption that society had a point of view, and that politics was based on a contestation between diverse points of view, is evident in the following statement by Havel. Havel was addressing the Slovaks at the height of the March 1991 crisis about the choice that faced them: "For the first time in its history [Slovakia] has the chance to make a totally free decision about its future. . . . It depends solely upon you, the citizens of the Slovak Republic, how to decide to realize your aspiration for national statehood. It depends solely on you what future you will prepare."[21] He posed a choice: for the first time in history Slovaks could link national statehood with the "idea of legality, democracy, and the spirit of European civic society and political culture and thus open the way for yourselves to enter the family of the advanced European democracies." Alternatively Slovaks had the choice "of placing your national aspirations above all other values and of making a decision in a manner that would confirm that preference."[22]

But Havel's misunderstanding is also revealed in this statement. Havel was assuming a type of politics wherein society consciously chose to support one policy or another, when this was a society that was incapable of making any choice at all. He articulated a choice between two policies. But there was a third option, which is the one that Mečiar took, and the one that appealed to society. The third option was to blame others for focusing on Slovakia's fascist past and creating a poor image. This argument, about who was saying what about Slovakia rather than about who Slovakia was, essentially meant "none of the above." It implied a reluctance to admit there was a choice. It meant being on both sides at once, just like the mass-elite.

We see a similar misunderstanding in the case of the March 14 attack on Havel. Havel and federal premier Čalfa, citing letters they received from all over Slovakia, said that the people on the square who attacked Havel were not representative of the nation. Havel said the letters "all assured me that those fascist groups do not represent the Slovak nation and that the Slovak nation is for democracy and for the federation."[23] Čalfa said that he also heard from many Slovaks by phone and that callers said they were embarrassed about the incident and that demonstrators did not represent their point of view.[24] An opinion poll from the time gives a rough picture of the types of reactions to the attack on Havel at the rally: 81 percent said that the reaction of rally participants was rude; 75 percent thought that it was natural that the president would visit any gathering of citizens; 53 percent said the president generally shouldn't go to such a meeting; 45 percent answered that the president's attendance was a provocation; 23 percent said the reaction of the participants against the president was justified.[25]

While the electorate did not agree with the attack on the president, and disapproved of the actions of the demonstrators in the square, this did not mean that the democrats and Havel spoke to their concerns or *represented* their concerns in other ways. All the letters Havel received supporting him and expressing embarrassment over the people in the square were not necessarily an indication of support for his more general positions. Needless to say, only a tiny percentage of the population wrote him letters.

The problem was that the democrats did not adequately read the society they claimed to be representing. They misunderstood society just as they misunderstood the mass-elite. Like the mass-elite, society was not attached to one point of view or another. The average member of the electorate was informed only by family stories, not historical consciousness.

The Mass Elite and Reflection

By looking at Mečiar's response, we can see more fully that the appeal of the mass-elite was *reflective* of society's lack of commitment rather than *representative* of an alternative point of view.[26] It was easy to pick up on mistakes of the ideological elites and use them to discredit them. This was true with liberal economic reforms as much as with the historical justice agenda. But this particular mistake of the ideological elites and Mečiar's response is revealing of how his appeal was due to his lack of ideological commitment. He and his allies and most of the mass-elite were not linked personally to either the communist or fascist past. This made it easy to focus on manipulation of information in the present rather than the issue of responsibility for the past.

It did not matter to the electorate whether or not Mečiar remained consistent in his positions, which he switched on many issues including the fascist past. What mattered was the appeal of the position he now took, which was directly opposed to Havel's spokesman's naming of the new threat from a cabal of communists and fascists. In an interview as he was returning from a trip to Rome and the Soviet Union, Mečiar complained that in Rome reporters seemed to think that Slovak nationalists were rehabilitating the wartime Slovak state and that fascism was appearing in Slovakia. "Slovakia is not fascist. To call Slovakia fascist is to damage its name and the interests of the Slovak republic abroad because it casts doubt on Slovakia as a whole."[27] Referring to this at a later moment, he said: "This image of Slovakia as following a national socialist direction of development tarnishes our name abroad and obstructs the influx of investments. The prime minister sees the office of the president of the republic to be behind this misinformation."[28] Thus the main point is that the president's spokesman, Žantovský, was making allegations about Slovakia's past.

What was really telling about Mečiar's argument (in contrast to the democrats who framed it as a choice between two positions) was that it was an argument about being connected to neither the communist nor the fascist past. What appealed to Mečiar's audience was this ambivalence and Mečiar's objection to having to take responsibility for distant events.

Here again we see the legacy of a communist socialization process that left most of the population with family stories as a source of information about the past rather than a national ideology. People knew what their own families did or did not do; this was not necessarily connected to what they thought *Slovakia* did or did not do. Their response did not arise from denial of the link between Slovak nationalism and the fascist past. Instead, it was something more like ignorance. It was a condition like amnesia, in which suddenly information is being revealed about your own past but you do not identify with the information. In addition, the main legacy from World War II for the inhabitants of a small country caught between large powers, was collaboration. Collaboration is about what was not done—not resisting—more than about what was done, that is, actively supporting a regime.[29] While the communist view of the fascist past did not constitute an ideology, it was clear to anyone socialized in that system that fascism was something bad. Slovaks had a hard time seeing why everyone—namely the Czechs, the democrats, and the international community—cared so much about a fascist past with which they did not identify. This was because of the ambiguity of collaboration and the fact that fascism seemed distant and like a derogatory label that Slovaks did not perceive as applying to them. The variety of interpretations of the period of the Slovak state being offered in the postcommunist press, in bookstores, and in the classroom did not help in this regard. Newly revealed information that was used to support the link between Slovak nationalism and fascism *did* seem conspiratorial.

Mečiar was not trying to rehabilitate the fascist past.[30] There was no link between Mečiar and the fascist past because there was no link between Mečiar and historical consciousness as such. He shared this with society. Mečiar made the argument that he, like society, and like Slovakia, was neither a communist nor a fascist. The dynamic is well illustrated in the following exchange with the Czech daily, *Mladá Fronta Dnes*. The interviewer asks why he has not vigorously distanced himself from slogans like "long live Tiso" and "only Hitler can teach the Czechs, these Jewish pigs, a lesson," and so forth:

> *Mečiar:* My first reaction after I returned from abroad was to call on the prosecutor general to make criminally liable all those who violated the law at the aforementioned demonstration. What more can I do, as prime minister, than to demand that they be prosecuted and that a special investigative commission be established? There is only one possibility left—to go to the streets and slap the faces of those people.
>
> *Mladá:* You should distance yourself from these people. So far, you have only expressed regret over the incident but, in our opinion, it is necessary to say quite loudly that you condemn these fascist tendencies, which are unique in Europe today.
>
> *Mečiar:* There was a Tiso plaque in Banovce-nad-Bebravou. Who was the first, and the only one at that time, to have publicly spoken out against and to have publicly attacked fascists? Mečiar. Or let us take [the rally marking the anniversary of Hlinka in August 1990] in Ružomberok, for example, where the situation was dangerous and could have developed in all kinds of ways . . . Who was the first and the only one to speak out? Mečiar. *Why do I have to constantly prove that I am not a fascist?* (italics added)[31]

The emerging argument is clear: the image of Mečiar, and by extension Slovakia, is being deliberately tarnished by enemies who want to take power away from him. Yes, the fascists are bad but no one would notice them if the Czechs did not overemphasize that legacy to the foreign press. If he and, by extension, society are not personally to blame, why is Slovakia? Mečiar's argument was powerful for much of the mass-elite and society, who were convinced that they themselves were not personally linked to this history, and saw it only as an abstraction.

Another example of Mečiar's stance is apparent in the statement of his political ally, Milan Kňažko, who had recently also split off from VPN. Saying that Havel's attending a rally where he knew he might provoke an angry response was politically irresponsible and that it threw a bad light on all of Slovakia, Kňažko continued:

> We do not want to follow up on the traditions of the Slovak state, which was established in the known historical context and which was negatively marked by this context. The Slovak government and the Slovak national council, too, have presented official apologies for some of their political attitudes, but am I to be ashamed for a state that ceased to exist in the year in which I was born? Am I to be ashamed for an isolated demonstration by a small group of little importance? Am I to be ashamed for a demonstration that I oppose, which I have not initiated, and in which I have not participated? Are we supposed to succumb to a collective shame?

Likewise, ignorance and not denial was evident in the response of Jozef Markuš, head of Matica Slovenská. In response to an interviewer who asked about the presence of flags of Hlinka Guards at the foundation's rallies, he said that until very recently, he did not even know what the flag looked like.[32]

Mečiar and What He Is Not

The absence of historical consciousness that defined the mass-elite meant that while they had personal histories these were not linked to a national ideology. Mečiar was successful at using the fact that he was not associated with any ideology, whereas the democrats and nationalists were, to discredit them. Interestingly, in an interview around this time, Mečiar said in answer to a question about his popularity: "I have never sought popularity. If I am very popular today, this popularity is not linked only with Mečiar as a person but also with the fear of the program of the others. *That is, I am not popular because I am Vladimír Mečiar and because I am the way I am but, rather, because the others are the way they are*" (italics added).[33]

Again we can see Mečiar's success at this strategy in his use of the argument about the conspiracy to blacken Slovakia's image in the world press. This argument, in fact, came from the Catholic nationalists, but when deployed by Mečiar and the mass-elite it had different implications. Mečiar could use the fact that the Catholic nationalists had called for reconsideration of the meaning of the Slovak state against them. He had joined the democrats in doing this in July 1990, as we saw in the previous chapter, when Mečiar had been the strongest critic of KDH's failure to condemn the unveiling of a plaque to Jozef Tiso. The fact that by 1991 he was using the discredited KDH argument, which included the claim that that history could not yet be judged, was lost on the population. He could sell himself as standing up for Slovak autonomy without the link to the fascist past. Interestingly, other mass-elite nationalists also distinguished themselves in this way from KDH while simultaneously making the conspiracy argument about Slovakia's image. For example, in an interview with SNS leader Miškovský, he said that the problem with KDH, as opposed to SNS, was its link to the fascist past. Yet frequently that same party issued statements very similar to KDH's. In a journal that came to represent the views of the mass-elite nationalists, KDH's position was described as simultaneously traitorously federalist *and* as an apology for the fascist past.[34]

It was even easier to use the conspiracy argument against the democrats. In the statement by Havel's press spokesman, Žantovský, the democrats and the Czechs were making direct allegations about the ghosts of the fascist past. But for Mečiar, the argument that there was a deliberate conspiracy to malign the image of advocates of Slovak autonomy took advantage of the fact that he was not committed to any position on this matter and the democrats were.

Fedor Gál is a good example of how the democrats were undermined by their principled stances. Gál had clear ideas about, and wanted to call attention to, Slovakia's fascist past. He could not abandon this focus even when he saw the legitimacy of Slovak complaints about Czech insensitivity. The fact that he was a Jew and a longtime opponent of the regime defined his positions.[35] Gál could easily be maligned since he could be consistently identified with a policy. The easy identification of his stance was augmented by the fact that he (as well as the democrats more generally) was calling on the population to take responsibility for the actions of the wartime state to which most felt unconnected. Gál had also been vocal about asking society to accept the hardships of the economic transformations, and to take control over their own fates. After Gál led the campaign to oust Mečiar from the position of prime minister, he was painted as an enemy of Slovakia and was so harassed that he felt it necessary to leave his home in Bratislava and take refuge in Prague.[36] Whereas Gál was a poor politician and made many blunders that only strengthened the opposition to the VPN democrats, the way Mečiar maligned him is illuminating. Democrats in general, owing to their refusal to abandon their commitments, were painted as enemies of Slovakia, alleged to be committing "political racism" by continuing to point to Slovakia's fascist past.[37]

The obsession with the blackening of Slovakia's image is typical of the defensive positions of nationalists everywhere.[38] But the fact that this became such a central part of the program of the Mečiar group, coupled with the nature of its appeal, adds to the case made in earlier chapters.[39] The nationalism of the mass-elite and of the society that they mobilized was more a product of absence of historical consciousness than of existing identities. Democratic politics in that context only fostered the defeat of those who represented clear ideological positions, particularly on the difficult issue of deciding the moral and ethical principles on which society should be based.

The Problem of Unreliable Information and Complex History

Even if all of society and the elite had had historical consciousness, several characteristics of the postcommunist environment made it very difficult to make the kinds of judgments that were on the agenda about both the communist and the fascist pasts. As we saw in the Mlynárik case, the unreliability of information due to communist censorship and distortions and the lack of legal precedent made it difficult for investigators to assess competing claims. In addition, the historical issues on the agenda were themselves extremely complex. Both of these factors were important in undermining the entire historical justice agenda, a development that indicates a failure for a new society-wide historical consciousness to develop. This agenda was undermined in two ways.

First, it was easy to make legal claims which, in an environment where it was difficult to assess what was true, could be politicized and settled not through a legal process but based on popularity. At the same time that Mlynárik brought his claim to court alleging the propagation of fascism at the March 14, 1991, rally, another legal claim was made about the same rally with very different implications. The Matica Slovenská brought a claim against Havel's press spokesman Žantovský for defaming the good name of Slovakia by linking Slovak nationalism to the fascist past. The claim was never pursued. But the fact that these two claims were brought at the same time shows how easy it was to use legal claims in spite of the fact that it was difficult to judge. The multiplicity of legal claims would make it difficult for voters and even the press to know what to believe. The fact that it was difficult to judge and that information was hard to come by could call into question the claims made by those who were committed to a legal process and were using what might be considered reliable evidence. Not only did this proliferation of legal claims perpetuate the problem of coming up with agreed upon standards that would begin to constitute legal precedent. It showed how it was easy to undermine the legal process—and the democratic process—by simply operating within it. Legal institutions shaped the idiom that all actors used, but the actors themselves and the fluid environment undermined the functioning of these very institutions.

Second, it was easy for the mass-elite to discredit the process of trying to find historical justice because of the very real problems that accompanied this process. The fact that the 1989 revolution was nonviolent, and the new political institutions democratic, made the simultaneous attempt to pursue a historical justice agenda (removing communist collaborators from politics, restitution of property, changing political symbols) *and* to engage in a process of independent reevaluation of controversial issues, almost impossible. Because the political agenda included keeping antidemocratic symbols and behavior out, it appeared necessary to take moral stands regarding the crimes of communists and fascists. But the goal of making certain political judgments before history was written was at odds with keeping history nonpolitical and waiting for an independent scholarly process to correct communist-era distortions. However, this ambivalence provided opportunities for the mass-elite to discredit the democrats and Catholic nationalists in the area of their main claim to legitimacy.

The Case of Lustration

Nowhere is this better illustrated than in the case of lustration—the attempt to keep former collaborators with the communist secret police out of public life. Lustration was certainly an example of a decision based on an assumption by anticommunist elites of a shared commitment to punishing collaborators with the old regime. But the screening process ran into difficulties because of the nature of collaboration under the communist regime and the problem of unreliable information. Of course the ideological elites themselves were aware of these problems and were quite divided and reluctant about the process.[40] As we saw in the previous chapter, lustration was beset by the following problems: First, it was not clear what the STB files actually said about collaboration. Many individuals' names were in the files because they were forced to collaborate or were targeted by the regime as potential collaborators. Others were there because they had deliberately inflicted harm. Second, often the files themselves were unreliable and easy to manipulate. Many files were destroyed, the information was not all in one place, and the files could hold distorted or unreliable information. The files did not hold the key to the truth about the past.

We can see the ambivalence of the democrats about the screening process in the case of Ján Budaj—a founder of VPN. This case was alarming for two reasons. First, the possibility that their own movement was open to secret police infiltration was disturbing. Second, the case pointed to the problems inherent in the lustration process itself that would contribute to public loss of faith in the process. After looking at the Budaj case, we will then look at how effectively Mečiar was able to manipulate the very problems of judgment inherent in the process to discredit this fundamental pillar of the legitimacy of the ideological elites.

The Case of Ján Budaj

Ján Budaj, in addition to being one of the most visible VPN leaders and head of the Slovak parliament in the spring of 1990, had been one of the few dissidents in Slovakia. Having been the most active person in the stream of dissent that came from the environmental movement, he was asked to withdraw from VPN's June 1990 election list when the screening process showed collaboration in his past.

Most of the readers who were interviewed regarding the Budaj case stood by him as a reliable and committed political figure and pointed to the unreliability of the files. Budaj admitted that he had signed a document on collaboration during a period when he was trying to get a passport in order to maintain his contacts with Polish friends and was involved with the distribution of samizdat. But he claimed that when he returned home, and was actually pushed to collaborate, he never did. The problem was that evidence of whether or not he ever did collaborate after his return (as opposed to simply signing the initial document) should have been contained in his file. But, according to VPN leader Fedor Gál, the file had been taken from the StB archives in March by someone who must have thought that Budaj would become important politically and that it would be possible to use the information in the file to blackmail him.[41]

The VPN leadership decided to abide by the agreement to withdraw candidates who were positively screened even though many believed Budaj to be innocent. In addition, in the summer of 1990, the loss of Budaj as an elected official probably did not seem particularly consequential. Many VPN activists were not running for office, and continued to be active in politics anyway because of their involvement in the movement. They probably thought that Budaj would do the same.

Whether or not he was an StB plant, even before November 1989, as some more conspiratorially minded democrats think, this incident was a turning point after which the popular support began to shift away from the democrats and the anticommunist cause.[42] This incident clearly demonstrates how easy it was to abuse the information in the files. It was also hard to assess what the meaning really was of the fact that Budaj appeared in the files. Was he really a collaborator? Information was seen as unreliable because some alleged that the Budaj case was manipulated by Prague to discredit a popular politician who felt strongly about Slovak autonomy. The fact that anticommunism and historical justice were the main claims to credibility for the ideological elites, and that they could not deliver on this, became a real limitation in their popular appeal.[43] More than this, it was difficult for them to anticipate the opportunities that the foundering screening process would provide for people like Mečiar to appeal to a public whose support for the anticommunist elites was not as solid as it appeared in the June 1990 election. Obviously the democrats could have abandoned the process. But they were caught here as well. The fact that the Budaj case suggested that there might be more collaborators in their own ranks than they expected made them stick to the policy. But adhering to the screening policy also allowed Mečiar to successfully manipulate the process.

The Case of Vladimír Mečiar

Mečiar was, at first, one of the major advocates of anticommunism and screening. However, as time went on and the investigations of the November 17 commission continued, there began to be suspicions about his own past and whether he had been an StB agent. Some members of VPN, who were involved in the committee investigating former collaborators, began to suspect that he might have covered the evidence about his past during his tenure as interior minister and gathered information that would allow him to manipulate and blackmail others. Mečiar began to make the argument that the screening process was misguided and that it was being manipulated by Czechs who had demanded that Slovak files be moved to Prague.[44] As we saw in the previous chapter, the conflict in VPN in early 1991 focused on this issue, with Slovak deputy prime minister Jozef Kučerák alleging misuse of the ministry of the interior and protection of people associated with the StB.[45]

The truth about Mečiar's past was never established, which is characteristic of the mass-elite.[46] In several attempts, through the lustration process, to determine that he collaborated with the StB, and that he had manipulated the files to cover his past, no conclusions were ever drawn.[47] Attempts to establish links to a collaborationist past were so difficult that they left an easy opening for Mečiar to argue that the process of trying to attribute historical responsibility as part of politics was misguided. He had similar objections to the land restitution law. Some democrats were already making similar arguments.[48]

He used his lack of identifiability and the very real problems associated with the lustration process, including critiques by Western human rights organizations, to make a case that the electorate was willing to believe. This had two elements. First, conveniently, his critique sounded like a commitment to a legal process and to truth. Second, the appeal in his position came from the absence of a real position and his argument for leaving the past behind. While the democrats and Catholic nationalists continued to believe that establishing his guilt reliably would discredit him in the eyes of the voters, the real threat they faced was that very few people, even in the elite, really cared.[49]

As with the fascist past, the legacy of communist collaboration was complex. In some ways, everyone collaborated. The claim that it was impossible to judge was compelling. Lawrence Weschler, in his article on the case of the former dissident Jan Kavan, has an interesting interpretation of a similar response to the screening process in the Czech Republic.[50] Kavan was forced to resign from his position as deputy to the Federal Assembly after his name was found in the files. Weschler argues that the witch-hunting that characterized the approach to former dissidents was due to the desire to pin blame on those who resisted communism. This, according to Weschler, allowed nondissidents to deflect or avoid their own lack of resistance. My argument is slightly different. The dissimulation, and thus collaboration, that characterized most of the elite and society, and the absence of a collective identity opposed to communism, made the lack of position of the mass-elite appealing. However, this was not because most felt guilty. Rather, it was because most did not see themselves as responsible. Interestingly, in the Federal Assembly vote on the lustration law the mass-elite parties were indecisive.[51]

In the case of Mečiar, as in the Budaj case, we can see how easy it was for the historical justice agenda to go astray. Information again was inconclusive. Furthermore, as in the Budaj case, it was possible to make a case for Czech manipulation of the files as a way of discrediting Slovak nationalism. The meaning of collaboration was also unclear.

The argument that justice was not being served by lustration sounded like a democratic one and was persuasive. It paralleled the argument being made about the fascist past: the historians had not yet done the work. However, Mečiar and other mass-elite political figures of course continued to use legal claims themselves. They continued to use defamation of character suits. Mečiar used the collaborationist accusation against KDH leader Ivan Čarnogurský (the brother of Ján Čarnogurský), claiming to have a document to back up the accusation. This started in spring 1991 when KDH joined the democrats in ousting Mečiar. The conflict continued and reemerged in the election campaign of 1992. Allegations about both men's pasts were frequently in the press. In each case it was difficult to make the judgment because of the inconclusive nature of the documents. And Mečiar clearly came out the winner.[52]

This again gets back to democratization with no ideological underpinning. It was, in fact, unclear that the lustration law served justice or even its initial political purpose. But the positions taken by Mečiar and, more generally, the victory of the mass-elite meant that common standards for judging the past failed to develop. Once Mečiar came to power, the lustration law in Slovakia was ignored though never formally abandoned.[53]

A Minister with a Fascist Past

Another case that demonstrates that what should have been a process of ideology building was in fact a process of perpetuating the absence of ideology is a court case about defamation of character. A lack of reliable information and precedent and the complexity of the historical issues at stake again prove problematic. In this case the minister of culture, who was appointed by Mečiar after the June 1992 elections, brought a defamation of character suit against a group of former VPN democrats (now defeated politically) for pointing out that it was inappropriate to appoint a minister who had a fascist past.[54] The VPN group was led by poet Lubomír Feldek. The minister, Dušan Slobodník, had been a member of the Hlinka Youth organization, the youth wing of the fascist party, and had allegedly also enrolled in a course that trained Slovak youth to commit acts of terrorism against the antifascist resistance. Graduates of this course might have been involved in destroying a Slovak town in 1945. The case turned on whether or not his past could be called fascist: was he really part of these organizations? Were these organizations fascist?

To support the claim that Slobodník's past was fascist, it was necessary to establish that he was in the terrorist course and that he was a member of the fascist youth. Using historian Ivan Kamenec and documents newly available from the Soviet Union, Feldek and his supporters assembled a case to show that Slobodník, in fact, had a fascist past.[55] Slobodník argued that he was only briefly enrolled in the course and had enrolled in order to avoid endangering his family. He was only formally part of the Hlinka Youth, and joined that organization not because of interest in its activities but because he wanted to participate in a Ping-Pong tournament. He was forced to quit the terrorist course and never did participate in blowing up the town. He claimed that he was mostly a victim of the Soviet "liberation" of Slovakia at the end of World War II. The Soviets took him off to Siberia as an alleged fascist collaborator. He was amnestied in 1963.[56]

Lawyers on both sides were faced with potentially unreliable information. Both sides were stuck relying on Soviet documents, which might themselves have been false or doctored.[57] The period of time in question wan an incredibly confusing one between the defeat of the Slovak National Uprising and the arrival of Soviet troops (which were concerned not only with "liberation" but also with political control). Testimony from witnesses, after so many years, was also open to question.

But even if this information had been fully reliable, and Slobodník's involvement in the terrorist course was short-lived as he claimed, there was also the problem of the complexity of the historical issues themselves. Should the Hlinka Youth be called a fascist organization, as it was in the Beneš decrees against fascist collaborators used in Czechoslovakia after the war? The Beneš decrees were considered by some Slovaks to have been dominated by Czech revenge for Slovakia's 1939 deal with Hitler. In addition, the history that had been written of the time period at stake was written in a highly ideological context. It was either written by communist historians or by émigrés who had personal stakes in the events. Slobodník attacked the historian used by the democrats as a consultant, and as an expert witness, for his ideologically inspired falsehoods.[58] An added complexity was the fact that Lubomír Feldek, the poet who had been accused of defaming Slobodník's character, had himself been a communist writer, thereby tainting his claims to antitotalitarianism in many people's eyes.

This issue, which was now before the courts, had never been processed in any other forum. There were few reliable histories. The evidence used was unprocessed and possibly unreliable. And it was not clear how a judgment could be made. The case ended up hinging on whether or not Slobodník's membership in these organizations could be deemed fascist. No one disputed that he had been in these organizations. The question was for how long and how voluntarily. What constituted fascist behavior, and what connection should be made between the new Slovak state and the actions of the old one, could not be decided. Even if Slobodník lost the case, which he did in the first round, there was no consideration of the larger question: did it matter that Slovakia had a minister with a fascist past? The press focused on the same issue we saw in previous instances when the wartime past came up: why is everyone calling us fascist?[59] It did not focus on the deeper question of Slovakia's relationship to these events as a society.

In addition, the case went through two rounds and had a somewhat comical element to it. In the first round, in the city court of Bratislava, the minister himself did not appear at the trial (even though he had brought the suit). Eventually, Slobodník's claim was turned down. The court deemed that Slobodník had been in the organizations and that the organizations could be called fascist. Slobodník appealed to the Slovak supreme court and the case was heard in early 1994. In that round, Slobodník's claim was granted in a judgment that appeared to be a rehabilitation of the fascist state. Included in the judge's statement was the argument that the Hlinka Youth organization was no different from the communist youth organization, and that while the rest of the world thought it was a fascist organization, Slovaks knew that it was not.[60] The democrats brought an appeal to the international court of justice in the Hague, which would have to wait several years to be heard. The end result was that there was no real judgment, just as in the Mlynárik case discussed above.

Interestingly, in the decision to bring the case to the Hague, the democrats were acknowledging that these issues could not be judged in the Slovak context, and that somehow an international court with Western standards of evidence would do a better job. The fact that the democrats took the appeal to an international court in many ways replicated the same conflict we have seen all along: the democrats, who were so isolated in Slovakia, had a constituency only outside Slovakia in the West. While the Supreme Court judgment looks like a rehabilitation of the fascist state, it shows, instead, a continuing failure to judge and to make the link between individual experience and the activities of the wartime state. It is reminiscent of Mečiar's position: if I am not fascist then why is Slovakia being called fascist? If Slobodník was part of the fascist youth organization, yet was not fascist, how can this organization be fascist? How can the Slovak state be called fascist?

Of course, some of the debate that took place over this case—the use of documents, the attempt to interpret what constituted responsibility for the fascist past—was part of a genuine process of coming to terms with this past. This process will continue for years. The history writing process, in the postcommunist period, continues to exist on the margins. But this independent process of evaluation is constantly under threat of being closed down. While outright censorship has not returned, the process tends to be threatened by state withdrawal of funds or failure to approve licenses for publishing houses. It is not clear how this history writing process will come to substitute for the family stories which still inform most people's understandings of the World War II period. With the ideological elites marginalized, and the mass-elite dominating politics, the history writing process will not necessarily contribute to the building of public ideology.[61]

Conclusion

The lack of historical consciousness in most of the elite and society was perpetuated in the postcommunist period when common standards failed to emerge.[62] Democratic institutions introduced in a context in which most of the elite and society lacked common interpretive frameworks functioned to hinder the building of new ideology. Clearly Mečiar was a successful entrepreneur, a demagogue mobilizing fears and resentments in hard times. However, he did not mobilize a nationalism that had any possibility of integrating society. Instead, his victory and the demise of the ideological elites along with their historical justice agenda contributed to an odd continuity with the ideological absence of the communist period. The lack of legal precedent from the communist period remained, but for different reasons. In addition, the proliferation of information in the postcommunist period prolonged the difficulty of making political judgments. Whereas during the communist period a deficit of information was the problem, paradoxically, in neither context was it possible to use information to assess important public issues and to hold politicians accountable. In both the communist and postcommunist contexts, therefore, public debate never substitutes for rumor or information generated in private. There is no reason to expect that in the world of the mass-elite, and the society that it reflects, a new ideology will emerge.

8 Conclusion

August 29, the anniversary of the start of the failed 1944 Slovak National Uprising, was chosen, in September 1992, as the national day of the soon-to-be-independent Slovak state. It was seen as a day when Slovakia, whose leaders had collaborated with the Nazis, reclaimed its place within the Western—or democratic—world.

After less than three years of democracy, the 1992 elections brought to power prime ministers in both the Czech and Slovak republics who were more committed to their personal futures, built on rival ideas about the future of the Czechoslovak state, than they were to preserving that state. While the final decision to split the country was the doing of Czech Prime Minister Václav Klaus, Slovak nationalism and demands for autonomy were certainly major factors in the decision.

The vote on Slovakia's national day came just after a sovereignty declaration was finally approved by the Slovak parliament and just before a new constitution was issued.[1] But the debate over the national day, and vote on it, again illustrates the pattern we have seen throughout the book. While some members of parliament continued to reflect a divide over a history that was itself ambiguous, the mass-elite with no historical consciousness dominated politics.[2]

The first theme is apparent in the debate itself. While no one proposed the anniversary of the founding of the fascist Slovak state, proposals on the agenda included not only the Slovak National Uprising but also anniversaries of key events in the Slovak national revival of the nineteenth century. One deputy even proposed a day in the seventeenth century when someone in Slovakia had been the first to use explosives for peaceful purposes in the mining industry. This last event, it was argued, would put the new Slovakia onto the map of Western European industrialization.[3]

The Slovak National Uprising was a divisive legacy and an unclear one. Those Catholic nationalists who did not see it as a traitorous uprising against a legitimate state and a civil war still viewed the Uprising as an event that caused violence and that was not supported by all. It was also communist and its memory had been co-opted by the communist regime. As we saw in chapter 4, it was first suppressed in favor of a focus on the Soviet role in the liberation and then adopted as the key event in Slovak history under the leadership of Gustáv Husák. The few Catholic nationalist deputies left in parliament, from KDH, made eloquent pleas against using this day.[4] The Slovak National Party was also opposed. From outside the parliament, Alexander Dubček and some democrats continued to push for the Uprising as a day that symbolized Slovakia's resistance to dictatorship.[5]

Whereas these debates demonstrate the lack of unifying events in Slovak history, the lack of involvement by the mass-elite nationalists is more important for my argument. Those deputies and political groups who appeared to have been the main mobilizers of nationalism were surprisingly silent. Certainly a national day is one of the key symbols in a nation's self-perception and presentation of itself to the world along with flags, anthems, and names of public places. Interestingly, many from Mečiar's party were not present for the vote or abstained.[6] Mečiar himself did not appear for the vote. Nor had he attended the commemoration of the Uprising a few weeks earlier.

The inability to agree on the key moment of Slovak history demonstrates the weakness of Slovak national development. However, the tepidness of interest and even voting by these deputies, so recently at the head of an apparently nationalist mobilization, reveals the more important absence that was a product of Leninist domination. This lack of interest in the new Slovak state extended to society as well. Sixty percent said they would not have voted for separation if given an opportunity.[7]

The decision on Slovakia's national day engenders "politics without a past" in two ways: first, we see the lack of a historical event to unite Slovakia; second, this story demonstrates the eradication of national ideologies by the Leninist regime. The first made the second much easier. One totalitarian regime left a tainted and unusable past; the other one wiped out even the past that was there.

Comparative Implications

Leninism left a peculiarly deceptive political landscape both for analysts and for political actors. In a revealing statement in this regard, Fedor Gál said: "I think it will take many years before we will fully understand under what conditions we in fact lived."[8] The analytical debate over whether what we were witnessing in the postcommunist world was institution building, on the one hand, or disintegration and continuity with the past on the other, was the first attempt to make sense of this terrain. But as it happened so soon after communism collapsed, this debate will be relatively meaningless in understanding the long-term theoretical implications of these changes.[9]

Still, this early analysis of postcommunist politics did have political implications. The tendency to view unfolding events following 1989 as a transition to, and consolidation of, new democratic institutions was not limited to Western analysts. The assumption that democratization was taking place and institutions were being built informed the political actors who presided over the collapse of communism as well as their Western advisers. The ideological elites, as did Western analysts, misunderstood how little cohesion or ideological unity existed in these societies.

This book has offered a method to read this process differently. Based on a reexamination of the nature of Leninist domination, it presents a way to see and look for the challenges to reconstituting societies that are obscured by the dominant focus. More specifically, if we fail to put the pervasive lack of historical consciousness at the center of the explanation we are misreading the processes of democratization, national mobilization, and nation-building that appear to be taking place in the postcommunist world.

The extent to which the mass-elite dominates politics varies across cases, depending on how far communism went in each society to weaken or destroy precommunist ideologies. Thus, while Slovakia had a particularly pervasive mass-elite, and the ideological elites were divided over the fascist past, politics would operate somewhat differently in places where ideologies had been preserved in greater portions of the elite and society.[10] But I would argue that except in unusual circumstances, the problem of ideological weakness is important throughout the former communist world: the proportion between these elite types defines the particularity of alliances and the specifics of how politics plays itself out.[11]

This book has focused in detail on a single case. But clearly Slovakia as an emblematic case can orient analysis of other postcommunist cases in which the distinctions elucidated here are not as clear-cut. Awareness of the effects of the precommunist, as opposed to the communist, nation-building processes and the distinction between family stories and national ideology can help analysts even in much more difficult cases like the former Yugoslavia. Suspicion about ideological masks and party labels and an understanding of the significance of ideological weakness can guide our inquiry in all postcommunist transitions, including the crucial Russian case.

In the Serbian case it is harder to distinguish between mass-elite nationalists such as Slobodan Milosevic, who was the key mobilizer of Serb nationalism with such tragic consequences, and those nationalists who are linked to a longer-standing national ideology. In addition to the stronger sense of national identity in that society generally, the war that broke out with the collapse of communism intensified the nationalism of the mass-elite and blurred the distinctions between the mass-elite and anticommunist nationalists. However, we can fruitfully ask what the connection was between weak national ideology embodied by Milosevic and the society he reflected, on the one hand, and the kind of violent conflict we have witnessed in the former Yugoslavia on the other. Milosevic has commonly been understood as an opportunist (and here we can distinguish between a nationalist opportunist and an opportunistic nationalist), and many of the war criminals and leaders of paramilitary units were crooks rather than ideologues.[12] Not only did the war strengthen nationalist sentiment; it also exacerbated the nihilism that arose from the egoism left by Leninism.

Yugoslavia, however, is not the rule in the former communist world, where weak nationalism and egoism are more prevalent than intense ideologically inspired hatreds from the past. It is a mistake to assume a ubiquitous potential for intense ethnic conflict when the real story might be weak polities that can never consolidate. Two of the most important countries in the former communist world—Ukraine and Russia—are much more similar to Slovakia than they are to the former Yugoslavia.[13]

There are also comparative implications beyond the postcommunist world.[14] The processes that created the mass-elite are not limited to communism and can be seen in different forms in the postcolonial world. The devastating lack of ideology that we find in postcommunist societies is reminiscent of phenomena long observed in Africa—predatory and nihilistic elites presiding over societies that lack social glue. V. S. Naipaul's eloquent characterization of Mobuto's Congo in 1975 alerts us to similar phenomena to those discussed here, though, as I suggested in chapter 2,

Leninist regimes were more effective than were modernizing regimes in the third world in destroying traditional ties and meanings.[15] The collapse of states throughout Africa in the aftermath of the cold war is in large part a product of ideological weakness and the failure for historical consciousness to develop.

There is also a link to discussions about the waning of the nation-state in the advanced, industrialized West. The deficit of historical consciousness in the aftermath of communist regimes could corroborate the argument that the nation-state as a format is in decline throughout the world. Similar arguments are made about the decline of parties and ideologies. While the postcommunist world might very well be part of this trend, I would suggest that the factors highlighted in this study, which arose as a result of the particularities of Leninist domination, are independently contributing to this outcome. Obviously this book has not addressed the relative weight of these causes, and future research might fruitfully ask that question.

Pathways for Future Research

There are several other themes, not fully explored here, that suggest pathways for future research. First, there is a strong sub-theme of the continuing effects of World War II and its changing meaning. The collapse of communism also meant the collapse of the world defined by World War II. What will happen once the wartime generation passes from the scene completely? What will be the implications for the understanding of World War II of a newly empowered Germany in the European Union? While the legacy and lessons of World War II have been institutionalized through the European Union, through the international war crimes tribunal, and through international human rights norms and procedures, we can ask how strong that legacy will remain once power shifts in the post–cold-war period.

A second sub-theme that could benefit from more research and could be fruitfully explored by anthropologists is the distinction between family stories and historical consciousness. This book has only begun to embark on the kinds of fascinating studies that could be done examining the sources of information individuals had about the events of World War II: who knew what, when, and from what source? Who passed on family stories? Who did not and why not? Since, as I have argued, ideas about the past were not institutionalized and were carried in people, it is people who need to be studied. Collective biographies of the key networks in dissent would strengthen the claims I made here. Closer biographical studies of elites who were products of the dominant Leninist pathway would be useful.

A final sub-theme that could be developed further is the broad problem of democratization—specifically the implications of the fact that the basic judgments assumed to be possible when democratic institutions are set up continue to be so hard to make. Democratic institutions are fundamentally about the ability to make judgments. Judgment is necessary for holding elites accountable.[16] Elites need to be able to assess who their allies and opponents are, and even who their constituencies are. It is also necessary to be able to judge whether other political actors are even playing the same political game.[17] So much goes on behind the scenes in the postcommunist world and there is so little "transparency," that this lack of ability to judge is a critical dimension of politics in new democratic institutions. We saw how these problems of judgment undermine the building of a new society-wide ideology. How does this problem affect other areas of politics? What kinds of circumstances might lead to an overcoming of the egoism of the mass-elite? War? Crisis? A charismatic leader? Can this be done through democratic institutions? If not, what does this mean for the future of this region?

At the end of the century shaped by two highly destructive ideologies, in the part of the world profoundly affected by both of these, societies are impaired by a pervasive egoism. Orwell's proles have become the elites. This might well secure these countries from large-scale totalitarian mobilization in the future. The mass-elites and mass societies left by Leninism appear not to be, as Arendt worried, susceptible to such mobilization. However, what does threaten is the danger of state collapse due to egoistic politicians and fragility of institutions. Egoism is a more daunting challenge than is an ideological opponent and, especially when wearing nationalist garb, it is hard to pin down. The postcommunist transition might represent a move from a twentieth-century politics shaped by rival ideologies to a twenty-first-century politics dominated by a much messier condition, more difficult to overcome and, when it spawns violence, more problematic for Western countries to combat.

Appendix: List of Interviews

Many of these individuals have held multiple positions and have had several affiliations since 1989. I have listed their posts and affiliations during the period covered in the book: 1989–93.

Elite Types

Democrats

Martin Kvetko, November 4, 1992 (leader in the Democratic Party in 1945–48 period and honorary chairman of the restored Democratic Party in the post-1989 period)

Peter Marianík, November 10, 1992 (head of the organization HUMAN)

Jan Urban, November 19, 1992 (spokesman for the Czech Civic Forum)

Michal Žantovský, August 18, 1993 (Havel spokesman)

Zora Bútorová, September 25 and December 1992 (sociologist, VPN activist)

Soňa Szomolányiová, July 8, 1992; July 18, 1993; April 10, 1994; summer 1995 (founding member of VPN; sociologist)

Martin Šimečka, October 9, 1992 (founding member VPN; writer; son of dissident Milan Šimečka)

Ján Mlynárik, November 19, 1992 (historian, VPN Federal Assembly deputy, 1990–92)

Milan Žitný, April 7, 1993 (journalist)

Jan Kavan, July 13, 1993 (Czech dissident and Federal Assembly deputy)

Miloš Žiak, October 20, November 5, and December 10, 1992; July 16, 1993; March 25, 1994 (founding member VPN; Havel representative in Slovakia; writer)

Jaro Franek, November 5, 1992; December 18, 1992; March 28, 1994 (press secretary for Jewish community)

Miroslav Kusý, April 22, 1994 (founding member of VPN; Havel representative in Slovakia; rector of Comenius University)

Milan Zemko, April 7, 1994 (head of Slovak parliament from June 1990; VPN but became independent)

Fedor Gál, April 15, 1994 (sociologist; chairman of VPN)

František Šebej, November 9, 1992; April 25, 1994 (Federal Assembly deputy for VPN, 1990–92)

Martin Bútora, November 24, 1993 (founding member, VPN; adviser to Havel on human rights; sociologist)

Juraj Špitzer, October 16, 1992 and April 4, 1994 (former editor of *Kultúrny Život*)

Peter Zajac, April 11, 1994 (head of Institute of World Literature; founding member of VPN; ideologist for VPN)

Suzana Szatmary, October 15, 1992 (VPN; Charter 77 foundation)

Rita Klímová, November 18, 1992 (Havel associate; Czechoslovak ambassador to United States)

Anticommunist Nationalists

František Mikloško, April 20, 1994 (chair of Slovak parliament; Slovak parliamentary deputy for VPN and then KDH)

Július Porubský, April 8, 1994 (head of Confederation of Political Prisoners)

Ondrej Sýkora, March 26, 1994 (member of first presidency of KDH)

Ján Klepáč, April 6, 1994 (leadership of KDH; vice chair of Slovak parliament; chairman of SKDH)

Viliam Oberhauser, April 12, 1994 (KDH and then SKDH; minister of forestry, 1990–92)

Vladimír Záborský, December 1992 (local leader of KDH, Bojnice)

Stanislav Kirschbaum, summer 1996 (Slovak émigré; professor at York University)

Igor Uhrík, April 26, 1994 (Slovak émigré; adviser to several parties; Slovak National Party)

Bartolemej Kunc, fall 1992 (KDH and then SKDH)

Ján Čarnogurský, fall 1992 (founder of KDH; Slovak prime minister 1991–92)

Mass-elite

Jozef Rea, April 20, 1994 (Slovak parliament deputy, HZDS, 1992–94)

Anton Hrnko, December 1992; April 19, 1994 (founder SNS; historian, Slovak parliamentary deputy, 1990–94)

Vladimír Miškovský, April 21, 1994 (founder SNS; Slovak parliamentary deputy, 1992–94)

Imrich Mori, April 22, 1994 (Slovak parliamentary deputy, HZDS, 1992–94)

Peter Brňák, April 15, 1994 (Štúr Society; Slovak parliamentary deputy, SNS/SNDH/Independent 1990–94)

Vladimír Repka, April 26, 1994 (editor, *Nový Slovák;* Štúr Society; Matica Slovenská)

Jerguš Ferko, April 15, 1994 (editor in chief, *Koridor;* head of journalists organization to protect Slovakia's image)

Jozef Prokeš, November 25, 1992 (head of SNS; Slovak parliamentary deputy, 1990–94)

Juraj Mihalík, October 13, 1992 (VPN/HZDS; sculptor)

Ivan Laluha, April 18, 1994 (founder Obroda; leadership of HZDS; Federal Assembly deputy, 1990–92)

Marián Tkáč, April 12, 1994 (Slovak National Bank; Matica Slovenská; multiple parties)

Luboš Jurík, April 13 and 19, 1994 (editor, *Literárny Týždenník;* spokesman for chairman of Slovak parliament, Ivan Gašparovič of HZDS)

Milan Ftáčník, April 10, 1994 (leadership of Slovak Democratic Left; Slovak parliamentary deputy, 1990–94)

Dušan Dorotín, fall 1992 (leadership of Slovak Democratic Left)

Lubomír Fogaš, April 20, 1994 (leadership of Slovak Democratic Left, Slovak Parliamentary deputy, 1990–94)

Milan Kňažko, April 27, 1994 (founding member of VPN; HZDS; Federal Assembly deputy; Havel adviser in Slovakia)

Stanislav Bajaník, fall 1992 and April 14, 1994 (secretary at Matica Slovenská)

Marta Aibeková, April 26, 1994 (deputy to Slovak parliament for HZDS, 1992–94)

Other Players and Background Interviews

Dušan Kováč, March 21, 1994 (historian of twentieth-century Slovakia, Slovak Academy of Sciences, Institute of History)

Michal Barnovský, April 14, 1994 (historian of twentieth-century Slovakia, Academy of Sciences, Institute of History)

Viliam Kratochvíl, April 22, 1994 (pedagogy and history at Comenius University)

Lubomír Lipták, October 22, 1992 (historian of twentieth-century Slovakia at Slovak Academy of Sciences, Institute of History)

David Daniel, October 20, 1992; spring 1994 (Slovak émigré historian on democratic side)

Ivan Kamenec, October 16, 1992; April 25, 1994 (historian of holocaust in Slovakia, Slovak Academy of Sciences, Institute of History)

Herta Tkadlečková, October 13, 1992 and March 29, 1994 (historian, twentieth-century Europe, Comenius University history faculty)

Jozef Jablonický, October 23, 1992 (dissident historian of Slovak National Uprising)

Katarína Zavacká, April 8, 1994 (historian, Institute of State and Law)

Viliam Prečan, fall 1992 (historian, Institute for Contemporary History, Prague)

Yeshayahu Jelinek, June 1992 (historian of the wartime Slovak state, University of the Negev, Beersheva, Israel)

Livia Rothkirschen, June 1992 (historian of holocaust in Slovakia, Hebrew University, Israel)

Robert Kotián, October 23, 1992 (editor, *Smena*)

Štefan Hrib, October 21, 1992 (Radio Free Europe correspondent in Bratislava)

Pavol Demeš, fall 1992 (minister of education; foreign minister)

Fero Alexander, December 13, 1992; April 22, 1994 (head of Jewish community)

Cameron Munter, November 20, 1992 (U.S. Embassy, Prague)

Ján Husák, March 29, 1994 (head of Slovak Union for Antifascist Fighters)

Vladimír Bussa, spring 1994 (director currency issuing department, National Bank of Slovakia)

Kristína Gavalierová, July 18, 1995 (bibliographical-informational section of the
 Slovak Pedagogical Library)
Vladimír Michalička, July 18, 1995 (Museum of Schools and Pedagogy at Slovak
 Pedagogical Library)
Peter Salner (ethnographer)
Eva Salnerová (assistant to U.S. consul)
Ernest Valko, April 26, 1994 (lawyer for Lubomír Feldek; deputy in Federal Assem-
 bly for VPN)
Pavel Hagyari, fall 1992 (lawyer for Lubomír Feldek)
Jan Obrman, August 1993 (Radio Free Europe, Munich)
Petr Brod, June 1992 (Radio Free Europe, Prague)
István Rev, November 4, 1994 (Hungarian democrat, Central European University,
 Budapest)
Peter Zavarský, spring 1994 (architect, Bratislava Holocaust monument)
Mikuláš Gažo, April 18, 1994 (Bratislava commission on street names)
Jozef Šucha, fall 1992 (press secretary for Slovak Ministry of Culture)

Notes

1 The Legacy of Two Totalitarianisms

1 The idea of a return of history is often treated almost mystically. See, for example, Robert Kaplan, *Balkan Ghosts* (New York: St. Martin's, 1993). Those who argue that history has returned do not carefully identify the mechanisms through which ideas about the past were preserved or passed on during the communist period.

2 While most analysts admit that some of these countries are moving more quickly than others toward democracy, the predominant literature that has been used to analyze these countries has been the literature developed to analyze the transitions from authoritarianism in Latin America and southern Europe. Phillipe Schmitter and Terry Karl have been some of the main analysts to try to extend this literature to the postcommunist world. See, for example, Schmitter and Karl, "The Conceptual Travels of Transitologists and Consolidologists: How Far to the East Should They Attempt to Go?" *Slavic Review* 53, no. 1 (1994): 173–85.

3 I use the word *totalitarian* to describe these regimes, even though that term has been the subject of much controversy. I am emphasizing the particular aspect of these regimes which distinguishes them from authoritarian regimes—their utopian nature and their radical attempt to eradicate competing groups and ideologies along with the market. In addition, in the postcommunist period it has become common inside the countries themselves to refer to the communist period as totalitarian.

4 George Orwell, *1984* (New York: New American Library, 1981), pp. 74–79.

5 See Benedict Anderson, *Imagined Communities* (London: Verso, 1991).

6 Ernst Haas, "What Is Nationalism and Why Do We Study It?," *International Organization* 40, no. 3 (1986): 707–44.

7 Ibid., p. 710–11.

8 For typical role of intellectual elites in national movements, see Victor Zaslav-

sky, "Success and Collapse: Traditional Soviet Nationality Policy," in Ian Bremmer and Ray Taras, eds., *Nation and Politics in the Soviet Successor States* (Cambridge: Cambridge University Press, 1993), p. 36.

9 In using the term *elite*, I mean those who became the political and cultural and economic elite in the postcommunist period. Some of these postcommunist elites, but not all, were part of the elite during communism.

10 While the argument applies to societies as well as elites, in the postcommunist world the 1989 "revolutions" as well as the setting up of new institutions were mostly an elite affair. Societies remain very much on the sidelines, as they did during the communist period when politics was completely an elite affair.

11 Poland is a very different case, in this regard, than is Slovakia or even Russia. In Poland, the continuing strength of the Catholic Church, as well as the enormous role of the Solidarity movement, kept alive anticommunist alternatives in a more significant way than elsewhere in the communist world.

12 For a comparative perspective on the control of the revolutions by anticommunist elites and the dominance of the later democratization processes by communist elites, see John Higley, Judith Kullberg, and Jan Pakulski, "The Persistence of Postcommunist Elites," *Journal of Democracy* 7, no. 2 (1996): 133–47.

13 See Hannah Arendt, *Origins of Totalitarianism* (New York: Harcourt Brace Jovanovich, 1973), and William Kornhauser, *The Politics of Mass Society* (New York: Free Press, 1959).

14 This argument has been made particularly in the German case. See William Sheridan Allen, *The Nazi Seizure of Power* (New York: Franklin Watts, 1984).

15 As we will see in the more detailed discussion of Arendt in chapter 2, I do not see postcommunist elites and societies as open to totalitarian mobilization. Still, the concept is useful. I also want to harken back to the moral element of Arendt's argument.

16 The historical process of Leninist modernization and nation-building which will be explored here has interesting comparative implications particularly for postcolonial societies. For an argument about the weakness of postcolonial states and nations and the implications of this weakness, see Kalevi Holsti, *The State, War, and the State of War* (Cambridge: Cambridge University Press, 1996). For a description of a phenomenon like the mass-elite see V. S. Naipaul, *The Return of Eva Peron* (New York: Vintage Books, 1981), pp. 185–219.

17 Havel's description of the nature of the clash between the democrats and the Communist Party during the 1970s is apt. He says it "was not a confrontation of two differing political forces or conceptions, but two differing conceptions of life." Václav Havel, "The Power of the Powerless," 1978, in Jan Vladislav, ed., *Václav Havel: Living in Truth* (London: Faber and Faber, 1987), p. 3. I also have in mind here Robert Putnam's distinction between the cultures of the north and the south in Italy. Whereas civic traditions were a product of "social capital" in the north, the south was unable to develop these traditions due to an absence of social capital. National ideologies provide social capital. Robert D. Putnam, *Making Democracy Work* (Princeton: Princeton University Press, 1993).

18 This would include mafias. See Stephen Handelman's *Comrade Criminal* (New Haven: Yale University Press, 1995) on the mafia in Russia.

19 According to Jowitt, individualism arises out of norms of impersonalism in a society's institutions and the internalization of these norms; egoism (what he calls personalism) is what happens without either of these. See "The Leninist Legacy" in *New World Disorder: The Leninist Extinction* (Berkeley: University of California Press, 1992), p. 288.

20 Such an idiom made for a shallow nationalism. I cannot really make claims about beliefs, and I am not arguing that these individuals did not have any nationalist beliefs. I am arguing that self-identifications should be understood to be fleeting and ephemeral. The idiom they pick up can be nationalist or democratic but they can drop this idiom easily and are not likely to make personal sacrifices in its name.

21 Theory-developing cases must be distinguished from theory-testing cases. In the former, a case is used to develop a new set of ideas that can be tested elsewhere.

22 Some might argue that the term *fascist* does not describe the regime of Jozef Tiso; in fact, two separate types of observers make this point for different reasons. The first type of observer is politically motivated and has an interest in rehabilitating Tiso's legacy (as we will see in the historiographical discussions in chapter 4). In fact, the term has changed meaning depending on political context. Immediately before and during World War II fascism was just an ideology—albeit one perceived as threatening—which some people or parties adhered to. Only after the war was it vilified as synonymous with evil, largely because of the Holocaust. The term became politically suspect because the communist regime used it widely to refer to regime enemies. The second type of observer is academic. It is generally not clear in academic discussions what the difference is between extreme nationalism and fascism. Some analysts would categorize the Slovak regime between 1939 and 1945 as fascist and some would not. The label is controversial mostly because of what it means regarding the state's position on the Jewish deportations and the extent to which the regime actively followed Nazi policies. There were two wings of the ruling party, one associated with Tiso, who is regarded as having been somewhat less willing to deport Slovak Jews and arguably more pressured by circumstance, and a second associated with Vojtech Tuka and Alexander Mach, who were more clearly pro-Nazi and eager to dispense with the Jews. In this book I use the term *fascist* to refer to the Tiso regime while simultaneously calling attention to the distinctions between the Tiso wing of the party and the more radical and overtly pro-Nazi wing. For academic discussions of the meaning of fascism and its applicability to the Slovak regime see Bela Vago, "Fascism in Eastern Europe," in Walter Laqueur, ed. *Fascism: A Reader's Guide* (Berkeley: University of California Press, 1976), pp. 229–53. For a different view of the Slovak regime, see Stanley Payne, *A History of Fascism 1914–1945* (Madison: University of Wisconsin Press, 1995).

23 As we will see in the historiographical discussion in later chapters, Tiso imposed Hitler's anti-Semitic policies and ignored protests from the Vatican to

halt the Jewish deportations, which began in the spring of 1942. The Tiso regime imposed laws parallel to the Nazi anti-Jewish laws and redistributed Jewish property to Slovak regime supporters.

24 "Tak zmýšl'áme o dejinách," *Smena,* October 23, 1992.

25 This meant that even those who remained in the Communist Party had to have made an active choice, since the Solidarity movement and martial law affected the entire society. The widespread nature of Solidarity itself was largely due to the failure of the communist regime to repress the Catholic Church. I thank Carol Timko for this insight. In addition, as Tomek Grabowski points out, traditional society in Poland remained more intact than it did elsewhere. See Tomek Grabowski, "Breaking Through to Individualism: Poland's Western Frontier, 1945–95" (Ph.D. diss., University of California, Berkeley, 2000).

26 In the Czech case, Václav Klaus, who could be considered ideological since he was part of a group which met throughout the 1980s to discuss free market ideas, dominated the mass-elites around him. (In the Slovak case, mass-elites dominated and co-opted ideological elites.) However, his ideology, limited as it is to economics, is amoral when it comes to issues of historical justice.

27 Kathleen Smith reports that those who were victimized by the Stalinist period were more interested in individual compensation for their suffering than they were in joining together with others united by a common experience of suffering to try to effect political change. Conversation with author. Also see Kathleen Smith, *Remembering Stalin's Victims: Popular Memory and the End of the USSR* (Ithaca: Cornell University Press, 1996).

28 Steve Fish, *Democracy from Scratch* (Princeton: Princeton University Press, 1995), pp. 84–86.

29 While Alexander Lebed regularly switches idiom, Vladimir Zhirinovsky, for example, has remained fairly consistent since he landed in his current incarnation. There are sometimes incentives for mass-elites to stick with an idiom for fully opportunistic reasons. But we can still question the extent to which they have the capacity to be ideology builders. On Lebed, see "Soldier Turned Politician," *Transition,* no. 23 (August 1996): 16–20, and "The Strong Man Russians Crave," *New York Times Magazine,* October 13, 1996. On Zhirinovsky see David Remnick, *Resurrection* (New York: Random House, 1997). For a different view see Stephen Hanson, "Ideology and the Rise of Anti-system Parties in Postcommunist Russia" (paper presented at Conference on Party Politics in Postcommunist Russia, University of Glasgow, May 23–25, 1997).

30 The categories here can fruitfully be used to sort out the meaning of what we are seeing in postcommunist politics. However, it is too early to predict outcomes based on alignments of types of elites. Only after some passage of time will studies in the style of Gregory Luebbert's on the interwar period be able to be done for postcommunist countries. See Gregory Luebbert, *Liberalism, Fascism, or Social Democracy: Social Classes and the Political Origins of Regimes in Interwar Europe* (New York: Oxford University Press, 1991).

31 In the Ukrainian case, as in Slovakia, the anticommunist nationalists did surprisingly poorly relative to the newly born mass-elite nationalist Leonid Kravchuk. As Alexander Motyl explains in an analysis that shares many characteristics with this one, the anticommunist nationalists in Ukraine were isolated

and lacked a constituency. Most of the elite and the society was much more like the mass-elites (national ideology had been eroded, diluted, or never built) than they were like the anticommunist elites. See Alexander Motyl, "The Conceptual President," in T. Colton and R. Tucker, eds., *Patterns in Post-Soviet Leadership* (Boulder, Colo.: Westview Press, 1995), pp. 103–21.

32   These ideas were articulated by Czech and Slovak dissidents and by dissidents in other parts of east central Europe. See discussion in chapter 2.

33   The use of the word *group* in social science means something lasting and with identifiable traits over time that is larger than the sum of the individuals in it. Without consciousness—which in the case of my typology comes from a collective process of articulating a meaning of the past—we are left with a group in the sense of the simple descriptive word, that is, a collection of individuals at a particular moment.

34   The war also brought about social change of its own. See Jan Gross, "Social Consequences of War: Preliminaries to the Study of Imposition of Communist Regimes in East Central Europe," *East European Politics and Societies* 3, no. 2 (1989). The war was less traumatic in Slovakia than in many other countries: there were nowhere near the losses or displacements of population that there were in places like Poland; nor were mass killings carried out on Slovak territory as in Ukraine; nor were there hand-to-hand killings as in Yugoslavia.

35   This was not only relevant in a symbolic sense but was also important since there were parallels between the social instabilities in the postcommunist period and the conditions that led to the emergence of fascism in the 1920s and 1930s. The frequent reference to the Weimar Germany analogy to understand postcommunist Russia is only one example.

36   The Holocaust has come to stand as a warning against intolerance (as evident in the Holocaust Museum in Washington) and as a referent whenever egregious human rights abuses take place (for example, Bosnia and Kosovo).

37   While there has been a growing literature about the meaning of the fascist past in Germany, France, and other countries in Western Europe, little has been written about this issue in the former communist world. One exception is Randolph L. Braham, ed., *Anti-Semitism and the Treatment of the Holocaust in Postcommunist Eastern Europe,* Rosenthal Institute for Holocaust Studies and Social Science Monographs (New York: Columbia University Press, 1994). Some examples from the many works on West European cases are: Charles Maier, *The Unmasterable Past* (Cambridge: Harvard University Press, 1988), Peter Baldwin, ed., *Reworking the Past* (Boston: Beacon Press, 1990), on the German historians debate, and Henri Rousso, *The Vichy Syndrome* (Cambridge: Harvard University Press, 1991), on France.

38   See Jürgen Habermas's framing of the German historians' debate in Maier, *The Unmasterable Past,* p. 47.

39   Of course, there was a variety of groups in the émigré community. See Yeshayahu Jelinek, "The Slovak State in Post-war Historiography," *Slovakia* 28, nos. 51–52 (1978–79), and "The Ludak Exile, the Neo-Ludaks, and Revival of Anti-Semitism in Slovakia" (paper presented at International Seminar on Anti-Semitism in Posttotalitarian Europe, Prague, 1992).

40   The West also quickly took up this comparison between Stalinism and Nazism

as the cold war started. See Les Adler and Thomas G. Paterson, "Red Fascism: The Merger of Nazi Germany and Soviet Russia in the American Image of Totalitarianism, 1930s–1950s," *American Historical Review* 75, no. 4 (1970).

41 This was true in a slightly different but no less powerful way in Russia, where state legitimacy was restored after Stalin by the regime's focus on World War II. See Nina Tumarkin, *The Living and the Dead* (New York: Basic Books, 1994), on the Russian case.

42 Pavel Campeanu, "National Fervor in Eastern Europe: The Case of Romania," *Social Research* 58, no. 4 (1991): 806.

43 Historical institutional arguments have been made by Rogers Brubaker, Victor Zaslavsky, and Veljko Vujacic. See citations below. My argument should also be seen in contrast to a third common analytical approach—modernization theory. That discussion can be found in chapter 2.

44 Eugen Weber's study of nation-building in France shows that even in that country, which we ordinarily think of as an old, established nation, modern nationalism had not captured loyalty until the early twentieth century. See *Peasants into Frenchmen* (Stanford: Stanford University Press, 1976). See also Walker Connor, "When Is a Nation?" in Connor, *Ethnonationalism* (Princeton: Princeton University Press, 1994), pp. 210–26.

45 I assume here that traditional and modern ways of understanding history are different. For a peasant, unconnected to a nation, all wars are the same and affect him only in the sense that his village or family is affected. See chapter 2 for an elaboration of this point.

46 See Rogers Brubaker, "Nationhood and the National Question in the Soviet Union and Post-Soviet Eurasia: An Institutionalist Account," *Theory and Society* 23 (1994): 47–78. Also, Victor Zaslavsky, "Nationalism and Democratic Transitions in Post-communist Societies," in Stephen Graubard, ed., *Exit from Communism* (New Brunswick: Transaction Publishers, 1993).

47 This view can be seen in all university and secondary school history texts and in Jozef Klimko, *Tretia ríša a l'udácky režim na Slovensku* (Bratislava, 1986).

48 The movie "Shop on Mainstreet" was shown widely in the mid-1960s and was the first awareness that many had of the way in which the Slovak state really was involved in the deportation of the Jews. It did not, however, explicitly make the link to what happened to the Jews after they were deported, or to the fact that this was part of an all-European Nazi effort. Most of the Western literature interpreting the meaning of the war and the Holocaust came out after 1948 and did not reach the communist world.

49 This was true, ironically, for Jews *and* for former fascist party members; the latter were even more loyal to the Communist Party because of the threat that their pasts would be disclosed.

50 Ken Jowitt's notion of neotraditionalism is useful here. It describes the situation in late communism where Party cadres no longer put the interests of the Party above their personal interests, since the Party no longer had a set of goals that could claim the loyalty of its members, what Jowitt calls a "combat task." Part of what had made the Party's combat task viable was its association with antifascism. But once this was lost, the personal interests of cadres became confused with those of the Party, leading to abuse of privilege and position for

the sake of personal enrichment. Ken Jowitt, "Soviet Neotraditionalism: The Political Corruption of a Leninist Regime," *Soviet Studies* 35, no. 3 (1983).

51 Of course there is variation among postcommunist societies in terms of the strength and significance of the nationalism carried by communist elites. And this depends on the context into which Soviet-designed national institutions were imposed. But we still must ask: how significant is the nationalism created by communist institutions?

52 The argument can explain the orientations of some newly transformed nationalists such as those associated with Matica Slovenská, the Slovak cultural foundation, and with certain institutes in the Slovak Academy of Sciences, which tried to cultivate a Slovak culture. Most complicated for my framework are the 1968 nationalist communists like Gustáv Husák, who had an independent memory of the war and were the heroes of the Slovak National Uprising, were incarcerated during the 1950s, and achieved prominence in 1968. They were less decisively negative with regard to the Slovak state than would be expected. The role of these groups is discussed in chapter 5.

53 Akos Rona-Tas uses a similar type of approach to look at continuities in the formation of economic elites in Eastern Europe. See Akos Rona-Tas and Jozsef Borocz, "The Formation of New Business Elites in Bulgaria, the Czech Republic, Hungary, and Poland: Continuity and Change, Pre-communist and Communist Legacies" (paper presented at Workshop on East Central Europe at Harvard University in May 1996).

54 *Samizdat* refers to literature that was self-published by dissidents and circulated by hand.

55 Soňa Szomolányiová, Martin Bútora, and Vladimír Krivý, "Positive Deviance: The Career of a Concept in Czecho-Slovakia in the Late 1980s" (manuscript, September 1989).

56 The Nazi regime was obviously less effective in suppressing truth about the past since it was so short lived. However, the establishment of a Jewish museum in Prague, which was meant to be a museum to a vanished race, is an example of Nazi efforts to control the past. The Nazi regime was more noteworthy for its brutality. Beyond the group immediately surrounding Havel, democrats varied in their emphasis on the communist or fascist pasts.

57 Some interview subjects talked about the émigrés bringing "canned identity"; the hothouse of emigration had diverged from the reality of those who lived in the country.

58 In Croatia, Gojka Susak, who returned in 1990 and who became defense minister, was a nationalist émigré who left in 1967 and, along with other émigrés, became involved in Croatian politics around the first free elections. See "Pizza Magnate in Canada Is a Croatian King Maker," *New York Times,* January 16, 1994. On the role of émigrés in Croatia see Laura Silber and Allan Little, *Yugoslavia: Death of a Nation* (New York: Penguin, 1996), pp. 85–86.

59 Jowitt, "Leninist Legacy," p. 285.

60 This argument was first elaborated in Guellermo O'Donnell and Phillipe Schmitter, *Transitions from Authoritarian Rule: Tentative Conclusions about Uncertain Democracies* (Baltimore: Johns Hopkins University Press, 1986).

61 See Schmitter and Karl, "The Conceptual Travels of Transitologists and Con-

solidologists," p. 180. See also Michael McFaul, "Party Formation after Revolutionary Transitions: The Russian Case," in Alexander Dallin, ed., *Political Parties in Russia* (Berkeley: International and Area Studies Research Series, no. 88), pp. 13–14.

62 This same literature tends to address the importance of a society-wide ideology only in terms of the "problem of stateness." That is, they use the common quotation from Dankwart Rustow that the problem of the nature of the political community or boundaries of the state needs to be solved before democratization can be accomplished. Dankwart Rustow, "Transitions to Democracy: Toward a Dynamic Model," *Comparative Politics* 2, no. 3 (1970). See also Phillipe Schmitter, "Democratic Dangers and Dilemmas," *Journal of Democracy* 5, no. 2 (1994): 57–74. This is certainly true of democratization in societies where boundaries are contested. But the problem of stateness assumes the existence of competing ideas about the state. What happens if these ideas are weak or do not exist?

63 Discourse analysis, commonly used in studying nationalist mobilization and party development, fails to take into account who is uttering the words in the public debate. There is a clear difference, as we will see, between the idiom of the mass-elite, picked up and dropped opportunistically in a fluid postcommunist environment, and the ideology of the ideological elites which they brought with them after years of discussing and developing those beliefs. In discourse analysis, which sees all acts of speech as important, idiom might be analyzed and given a meaning when the point is precisely how little meaning it has.

64 The classic critique of democracy dominated by populists going back as far as Plato is apt in the postcommunist setting. Egoism as a driving force for elites can benefit only those elites, not the larger interests of society.

65 See Putnam, *Making Democracy Work*. See also, Jan Zielonka, "New Institutions in the Old East Bloc," *Journal of Democracy* 5, no. 2 (1994). This point is made well in Valerie Bunce and Maria Csanadi, "Uncertainty in the Transition: Post-Communism in Hungary," *East European Politics and Societies* 7, no. 2 (1993).

66 Here I am referring to authors who expected parties to emerge to represent naturally existing or emerging cleavages in society. See Herbert Kitschelt, "The Formation of Party Systems in East Central Europe," *Politics and Society* 10 (1992), pp. 7–50, and Geoffrey Evans and Stephen Whitfield, "Identifying the Bases of Party Competition in Eastern Europe," *British Journal of Political Science* 23 (1993): 521–48.

67 I also emphasize, as does Jowitt, that what we see in the postcommunist world are demagogues, not charismatics. Demagogues merely reflect the society to which they appeal, populist style. Charismatics, on the other hand, offer transformative ideologies.

2 Historical Consciousness, Family Stories, and Nationalism

1 Some do look at Leninist regimes this way. One example is Richard Lowenthal, "Development versus Utopia in Communist Systems," in Chalmers Johnson,

ed., *Change in Communist Systems* (Stanford: Stanford University Press, 1970), pp. 33–116; Ken Jowitt does also, though he cares about the distinction between the Communist Party and the nation as defining membership. These ideas can be found throughout Jowitt's work, but see in particular *The Leninist Response to National Development,* Institute of International Studies, Research Series no. 37 (University of California, Berkeley, 1978).

2   Ernst Haas, "What Is Nationalism and Why Do We Study It?"; Ernest Gellner, *Nations and Nationalism* (Ithaca: Cornell University Press, 1993); Karl Deutsch, *Nationalism and Social Communication* (Cambridge: MIT Press, 1966).

3   Functionalist theories like this one see no role for an agent but rather see social processes as unfolding with a logic of their own.

4   Haas, "What Is Nationalism," p. 710.

5   Ibid.

6   I am using the terms *civic* and *ethnic* as alternative types of modern definitions of political membership. Civic is an inclusive idea about membership: all can be tied to a nation no matter whether they share language, culture, and religion. Ethnic is an exclusive definition of membership: those who are included must be of the same ethnic group and cannot join by choice. Jowitt has an interesting definition of *ethnic* which is relevant here since it calls attention to the modern aspect of ethnicity and to why ethnic is often subsumed into traditionalism. He defines ethnicity as "that mode of affective security and identification typical of an individuated society" and points to ways in which ethnicity has characteristics that are both modern and traditional. Nation-building class, University of California, Berkeley, spring 1993.

7   Haas, in categorizing Marxism as a version of national ideology, considers the particular class or coalition of classes that resists imperialism in a specific territory to be the equivalent of the nation ("What Is Nationalism," p. 731).

8   See Zygmunt Bauman, "Social Dissent in East European Politics," *Archives Europeenes de Sociologie* 12, no. 1 (1971): 35, for the percentage increases in number of people employed in nonagricultural parts of the economy between 1950 and 1960 in Romania, Bulgaria, Albania, Hungary, and Poland. Slovakia could be added to this list; Slovakia's level of development in 1948 is discussed in chapter 3.

9   Gellner sees the development of a standardized new "high culture" through school systems as the key to modern nation-building (*Nations and Nationalism,* p. 52).

10 For example in Rogers Brubaker, "Nationalizing States in the Old 'New Europe'—and the New," *Ethnic and Racial Studies* 19, no. 2 (1996): 411–37. Also, Walker Connor, "Nation-Building or Nation-Destroying," *World Politics* 24 (1972): 319–55. This approach has also been criticized for its functional logic and for failing to acknowledge the possibility that nationalism drives the process of industrialization rather than simply arising as an outgrowth of it; see Liah Greenfeld, *Nationalism: Five Roads to Modernity* (Cambridge: Harvard University Press, 1992), p. 18.

11 As is often the case in intellectual history, modernization theory was disposed of too completely by scholars frustrated by its failure to help understand the

lack of development in postcolonial societies. But modernization theory asked important questions about the strength or weakness of nationalisms and the cohesiveness of elites. See, for example, Sidney Verba, "Comparative Political Culture," in Lucian Pye and Sidney Verba, eds., *Political Culture and Political Development* (Princeton: Princeton University Press, 1965). For the point about intellectual history see Andrew Janos, *Politics and Paradigms* (Stanford: Stanford University Press, 1986).

12   Cited in James Rupnick, "Totalitarianism Revisited," in John Keane, ed., *Civil Society and the State* (London: Verso, 1988), p. 269.

13   Societies obviously vary in their objective experiences. But they also vary in how they interpret or remember what happened and why. I am pointing to the distinction between modern and traditional societies in this regard. However, there are also cultural differences in how societies treat the past. Cultures can vary in the extent to which they are committed to remembering through interpretation. For example, Judaism is fundamentally committed to remembering. Other cultures are not: Central Europe is often seen as less committed to remembering or conflicted in this regard because of its place between great powers making change so frequent. An extreme example of a cultural approach to remembering that led eventually to the near extinction of the culture are the Yuqui tribe, who after fleeing to the Bolivian rain forest to escape from Spanish missionaries in the sixteenth century began to lose their knowledge base. Before fleeing they had been an agriculture society. They had a taboo against ever speaking the name of the dead after death and, partly because of this, "no oral history was passed from one generation to the next. Along the way, the Yuquis also lost their storytellers, those who could pass on the stories of their culture without violating any taboos. They built no homes, made no art, wore no clothes." See Sandy Tolan and Nancy Postero, "Accidents of History," *New York Times Magazine,* February 23, 1992, p. 42. For the Jewish approach to remembering see Yosef Hayim Yerushalmi, *Zakhor: Jewish History and Jewish Memory* (New York: Schocken Books, 1989).

14   I use this idea instead of memory, frequently used in discussions of identity. The term *memory* has generally been used to make a distinction between objective events and history writing in its more positivist version, as well as the more subjective aspects of the past to which societies actually pay attention. Memory comes with metaphors of repression and denial and the idea that history, with its attention to facts and sources, can be an antidote to the more irrational memory. But while the term *memory* tends to blur sociological distinctions and to refer more to culture, *history* brings with it more of a reference to modernity and politics. Historians are seen as agreeing on common standards of evidence or at least working in a modern social scientific idiom.

15   This could be moral precedent or more mechanical use of precedent. An example relevant to the postcommunist East European cases is drawing on earlier constitutions when drafting new ones.

16   In Central Europe the national awakenings of the eighteenth and nineteenth centuries, based on the idea of historicism, saw language as the distinguishing feature of "submerged" groups. However, history was the mechanism through which these cultures' unique natures were recounted. Historians were dis-

coverers of nations, using the authority of the historical method to establish the existence of nations. Historians and other cultural figures could establish a national existence based on whether they could establish that they had a history—a language and customs—that was lost. See R. W. Seton-Watson, *The Historian as a Political Force in Central Europe* (London: School of Slavonic Studies in the University of London, 1922), on the role of historians in Central Europe. Also see John Breuilly, *Nationalism and the State* (Manchester: Manchester University Press, 1982), pp. 335–51.

17   According to Weber, "the community of political destiny, i.e. above all, of common struggle of life and death, has given rise to groups with joint memories which often have had a deeper impact than the ties of merely cultural, linguistic, or ethnic community. It is this 'community of memories' which . . . constitutes the ultimately decisive element of 'national consciousness.' " In *Economy and Society* (Berkeley: University of California Press, 1978), p. 903. As cited in Veljko Vujacic, "Historical Legacies, Nationalist Mobilization, and Political Outcomes in Russia and Serbia: A Weberian View," *Theory and Society* 25 (1996): 763–801.

18   Gellner, *Nations and Nationalism,* p. 21, Haas, "What Is Nationalism," pp. 709–10.

19   Many have pointed to this commonality as the reason that communists could so easily make the transition to ethnic nationalism.

20   See Jowitt's discussion of the idea of the "correct line" in Leninism as an amalgam of charisma and modernity: "The correct line is simultaneously an analytic and empirical statement of the stages of national and international developments, a set of policy guides, and an authoritatively compelling and exclusive ideological political statement that must be adopted and adhered to" (*New World Disorder,* p. 10).

21   For the link regarding nation-building, the literature above is relevant. On class interests see Isaac Balbus, "The Concept of Interest in Marxist and Pluralist Analysis," *Politics and Society* 1 (1971). On elites, see Ralf Dahrendorf, *Society and Democracy in Germany* (New York: W. W. Norton, 1967). Dahrendorf's approach will be discussed more below.

22   For a good discussion of charisma see Charles Lindholm, *Charisma* (Oxford: Basil Blackwell, 1990).

23   But in the case of Slovakia it might be both the blocking of articulation during communism and the weakness of national consciousness before Leninism; Slovakia lacked a common crisis or struggle or a truly transformative charismatic leader.

24   Paul Connerton, *How Societies Remember* (Cambridge: Cambridge University Press, 1989).

25   This was a war in which brigands had fought against the army and government of the north.

26   Connerton, *How Societies Remember,* pp. 21–22.

27   Paul Lendvai, *Anti-Semitism without Jews* (Garden City, N.Y.: Doubleday, 1971).

28   Gellner elaborates this type in his imaginary "Ruritania" model (*Nations and Nationalism,* pp. 58–62). Haas, "What Is Nationalism," p. 722; Miroslav Hroch,

Social Preconditions of National Revival in Europe (Cambridge: Cambridge University Press, 1985).

29 See Gellner, *Nations and Nationalism,* p. 29, for modern versus traditional means of passing on ideas about membership, including ideas about history. Interestingly the networks of dissent and the mass-elite networks rested on personal ties but of different types. This could be a subject of a whole research project. Some, like Katherine Verdery, argue that ethnicity was preserved through networks that subverted the state economy—that is, black market networks. While black market networks most likely included both types of elites, the networks in dissent that revolved around articulating alternative meanings were of a different type and served a different function. See Verdery, "Nationalism and National Sentiment in Post-socialist Romania," *Slavic Review* 52, no. 2 (1993).

30 Elemer Hankiss, "The 'Second Society': Is There an Alternative Social Model Emerging in Contemporary Hungary?" *Social Research* 55, nos. 1–2 (1988).

31 This kind of transformation happened throughout the Left in both Eastern and Western Europe; Arthur Koestler is one famous example.

32 Albert O. Hirschman, *Exit, Voice, and Loyalty* (Cambridge: Harvard University Press, 1970).

33 Haas, "What Is Nationalism'; Gellner, *Nations and Nationalism.*

34 Haas, "What Is Nationalism," p. 723.

35 In *The Leninist Response,* Jowitt shows that in contrast to modernizing regimes in the third world Leninist regimes were particularly interested in reorganizing village life so that they could destroy political and cultural competitors to Party control. Modernizing regimes in the third world were not as committed to this transformative task. See also Lowenthal, "Development versus Utopia."

36 This becomes more complex in multiethnic societies like Czechoslovakia, but for now I am focusing only on the Party and not on the ethnic issue.

37 In Slovakia, the alternative national version of history did not simply compete with the Leninist one but was at odds with the central element of regime legitimacy: the defeat of fascism in World War II.

38 The most important critique of modernization theory is that middle classes were a product of a different type of industrialization, which did not include a market. Theodore Gerber, "In Search of the Soviet Middle Class: Scientists and Other Professionals in Post-Stalinist Russia" (Ph.D. diss., University of California, Berkeley, 1995), and Victor Zaslavsky, "From Redistribution to Marketization: Social and Attitudinal Change in Post-Soviet Russia," in Gail Lapidus, ed., *The New Russia: Troubled Transformation* (Boulder, Colo.: Westview Press, 1994).

39 I am referring to the argument that civil societies emerged naturally out of modernization of society. See numerous articles by Gail Lapidus, Fredrick Starr, and also Moshe Lewin's *The Gorbachev Phenomenon* (Berkeley: University of California Press, 1989).

40 Individualism means the moral primacy of the individual rather than the corporate group. For elaboration of this point see the work of Jowitt and Grabowski, "Breaking Through to Individualism," on the development of individualism in Poland. I do not discuss here how individualism does or could

develop or the social-psychological conditions favoring individualism. What is important for this argument is the distinction between egoism and individualism (see definition in chapter 1). Individualism is often understood to derive from human nature rather than being a product of unique historical/cultural factors.

41 Jowitt, "Political Culture in Leninist Regimes," in *New World Disorder,* p. 80.

42 Ibid.

43 Jowitt elaborates these ideas in several essays in *New World Disorder.* Of course the treatment here cannot do justice to the nuance and complexity of the ideas, particularly the great lengths to which Jowitt goes to show the ways in which Leninism was an amalgam of traditional, modern, and charismatic modes of authority, and a substitution for Western liberal modernity.

44 Jowitt, "Political Culture in Leninist Regimes," in *New World Disorder,* p. 80.

45 Václav Havel conveys this idea well in "The Power of the Powerless," p. 53.

46 According to Rupnick, "Totalitarianism Revisited," pp. 266–67, East European dissidents began to use the term *totalitarian* after 1968 and after they gave up on reforming socialism. Previously they had blamed Stalinism; now they blamed the whole system. According to Zdeněk Mlynář, "the chief characteristic of totalitarianism is the ongoing capacity to limit all scope for independent action in every possible sphere of social activity . . . it has nothing to do with the degree of violence or terror employed. Power remains 'totalitarian' even when the forms of repression are less visible." Quoted in Rupnick, p. 273.

47 Ibid., p. 269.

48 Orwell, *1984,* pp. 175–77.

49 Mlynář in Rupnick, "Totalitarianism Revisited," p. 273.

50 Milan Šimečka, "Black Holes," *Kosmas* 3/4 (1985): 23.

51 Ibid., p. 24.

52 Šimečka speculates that maybe one in one thousand in the younger generation would have the curiosity to penetrate the black holes the regime created, and this required a great deal of energy. Ibid., p. 27.

53 Ibid., p. 26.

54 Ibid., p. 27.

55 See discussion of the role of generations in chapter 5.

56 The question of whether the regime intended to give priority to control rather than legitimacy is, of course, hard to answer.

57 Šimečka, "Black Holes," p. 26.

58 This idea comes through vividly in the depiction of the children in Milan Kundera's *Book of Laughter and Forgetting* (New York: Penguin, 1985).

59 As Havel puts it, "this [living within a lie] is more than a simple conflict between two identities. It is something far worse: it is a challenge to the very notion of identity itself" ("The Power of the Powerless," p. 54).

60 Arendt, *Origins of Totalitarianism,* p. 310.

61 At one point she says, suggestively, that the selfishness of the bourgeois could turn into the selflessness of the mass, but she does not draw out the link. Ibid., p. 338.

62 Ibid., p. 315.

63 Allen, *The Nazi Seizure of Power.*

64 Putnam, *Making Democracy Work*. While Arendt's ideas are close to Durk-heim's notion of anomie, Putnam's are from rational choice theory and histor-ical institutionalism.

65 Putnam confuses civic with all social capital.

66 See Jowitt, "Political Culture in Leninist Regimes," in *New World Disorder;* Edward Banfield, *The Moral Basis of a Backward Society* (New York: Free Press, 1958).

67 Certainly other types of ties or networks can be considered social capital. I am interested in the lack of social capital at this fundamental level of the nature of political community. Haas says that a society rationalized by a national myth is one in which people know what to expect from one another because they recognize common rules and norms, understand and respect a common au-thority, and "are secure in their view of the scheme of collective life." This allows for putting off short-term gain in the interest of cooperation. Haas, "What Is Nationalism," pp. 709, 711. As we saw in chapter 1, the democratiza-tion literature sees agreement on the nature of the political community as a prerequisite for democratization.

68 Dahrendorf, *Society and Democracy in Germany* (New York: W. W. Norton), pp. 219–20. Jowitt also suggests there is an absence of established successor elites in postcommunist societies. Jowitt, *New World Disorder,* p. 294.

69 There is contradictory evidence on the nature of the ties between elites in the networks of "neotraditional" Leninist regimes. Clearly these ties had some continuity and trust was necessary. These elites recognized mutual benefit in these ties. However, there is also evidence of lack of trust and the ephemerality of these networks. The point is that these are instrumental networks and have little to do with common connections to a society-wide ideology.

70 Without an extensive anthropological study, it would be difficult to sort out all the reasons, including family structure, rural versus urban backgrounds, and regional differences, that would make an individual into a political figure who operates based on ideas more than opportunism.

71 While there is no inherent reason that public and private could not be reinte-grated, as we will see in the second part of the book, the postcommunist en-vironment perpetuates and prolongs the very same vicious circle.

72 Zaslavsky, "Nationalism and Democratic Transitions in Post-communist So-cieties," p. 105.

73 A slightly different version is made for Romania also. See Katherine Verdery, "Nationalism and National Sentiment in Post-socialist Romania."

74 See Valerie Bunce, "From State Socialism to State Disintegration: A Compari-son of the Soviet Union, Yugoslavia, and Czechoslovakia" (paper prepared for the conference on "Democracy, Markets, and Civil Societies in Post-1989 East Central Europe," Harvard University, May 17–19, 1996). Bunce also makes the argument about identities, but that is not the focus of her argument.

75 See Brubaker, "Nationhood and the National Question in the Soviet Union and Post-Soviet Eurasia: An Institutionalist Account."

76 Ibid., p. 53 and pp. 58–59. This position is reminiscent of modernization the-ory insofar as it does not look at the quality of the process but only at its function.

77 While the role of each of these types is well integrated in Veljko Vujacic's argument about Serbia, these important distinctions do not enter Brubaker's argument. Veljko Vujacic, "Communism and Nationalism in Russia and Serbia" (Ph.D. diss., University of California, Berkeley, 1995).

78 See Brubaker, "Nationalizing States in the Old 'New Europe'—and the New." See also Brubaker, *Nationalism Reframed* (Cambridge: Cambridge University Press, 1996).

3 Weak Nationalism in Slovakia:
The Precommunist Period

1 Other national ideologies existed besides ethnic nationalism but were less decisively Slovak. These were communism and a Czechoslovak-oriented civic ideology. When I refer to nation-building and national consciousness, these modern ideologies should be included. However, the civic stream was weak in Slovakia and eroded first by the fascists of the wartime state and then by the communists in the postwar period.

2 The communist regime also destroyed the civic-minded Czechoslovak-oriented intelligentsia.

3 Owen Johnson, *Slovakia 1918–38: Education and the Making of a Nation* (Boulder, Colo.: East European Monographs, no. 180, distributed by Columbia University Press, 1985), p. 29. James Ramon Felak, *At the Price of the Republic: Hlinka's Slovak People's Party, 1929–38* (Pittsburgh: University of Pittsburgh Press, 1994), pp. 6–7.

4 Johnson, *Slovakia 1918–38,* p. 30.

5 Carole Skalnik Leff, *National Conflict in Czechoslovakia* (Princeton: Princeton University Press, 1988), p. 15.

6 Ibid., p. 18.

7 Ibid., pp. 13–15.

8 Johnson suggests that there could have been more that were nationally neutral and immediately became nationally conscious Slovaks with the establishment of the First Republic. See Owen Johnson, "The Slovak Intelligentsia, 1918–38," *Slovakia* 28, nos. 51–52 (1978–79): 27.

9 Leff, *National Conflict in Czechoslovakia,* p. 15.

10 Ibid., p. 17; Felak, *At the Price of the Republic,* p. 17.

11 Johnson, "The Slovak Intelligentsia," p. 27.

12 Johnson, *Slovakia 1918–38,* p. 18.

13 See Leff, "National Conflict in Czechoslovakia," pp. 204–11.

14 Johnson, *Slovakia 1918–38,* p. 27.

15 Leff, "National Conflict in Czechoslovakia," p. 277.

16 Milan Kučera and Zdeněk Pavlík, "Czech and Slovak Demography," in Jiří Musil, ed., *The End of Czechoslovakia* (Budapest: Central European University Press, 1995), p. 26.

17 Johnson, *Slovakia 1918–38,* p. 265.

18 Ibid., pp. 215–65.

19 Ibid., p. 29, 35.

20 Ibid., p. 43.

21 Ibid., p. 321.

22 Ibid., p. 321. Bratislava was not a Slovak city, and thus the home of Matica was in Martin, a smaller town. But only Bratislava was large enough to support cultural or literary organizations by providing livelihood for enough members to ensure an active intellectual life. Ibid., p. 322.

23 Stanislav Kirschbaum, *A History of Slovakia* (New York: St. Martin's Press, 1995), p. 202. He also points to the addition of faculties at Comenius University and the establishment of a Slovak technical institute and a Slovak school of commerce.

24 Husák quoted in ibid., p. 203. Husák says: "On the basis of the experience of six years, Slovakia is able to exist as an independent unit economically and financially, can hold out on its own, has even today the necessary forces . . . for international competition. . . . The Slovaks are an independent nation . . . all the formal attributes of a nation are there." From "O vývoji a situácii na Slovensku," *Svědectví* 15, no. 58 (1979): 376–77.

25 Kirschbaum fails to mention the numerous positions vacated by Jews who were deported by the fascist regime. Ibid., p. 202.

26 Leff, "National Conflict in Czechoslovakia," p. 92.

27 Johnson, *Slovakia 1918–38*, p. 27.

28 In that same year 6.46 percent were Greek Catholic; 4.8 percent were in the Protestant reformed church; 4.54 percent were Jewish. Ibid., p. 27.

29 Yeshayahu Jelinek, *The Parish Republic: Hlinka's Slovak People's Party* (Boulder, Colo.: East European monograph, no. 14, distributed by Columbia University Press, 1976), p. 2.

30 Johnson, *Slovakia 1918–38*, p. 319.

31 Kirschbaum, *A History of Slovakia*, p. 2. Kirschbaum also mentions that there was a strong oral tradition. He says that the first works of Slovak history were published in the seventeenth century in Latin. Some general outlines came out in the nineteenth century. Kirschbaum is most concerned with the fact that no history was written in foreign languages; he thus makes the questionable assumption that Slovaks themselves know their own history (pp. 2–3).

32 See Richard Maršina, "Slovenská Historiografia 1945–1990," *Historický Časopis* 39, no. 4–5 (1991): 370–79.

33 According to Johnson, during the First Republic, historians generally took the approach that history was something that happened more than fifty years ago. The histories that existed tended to be written by journalists, not historians. Johnson, *Slovakia 1918–38*, pp. 449–50. Kirschbaum points to some work done during the First Republic by Daniel Rapant. He cites two surveys done by the end of the 1930s, by František Hrušovský and by František Bokeš. The Hrušovský text was highly ideological. He also complains that much of Slovak history was written by Czechs. Kirschbaum, *A History of Slovakia*, p. 3.

34 Johnson, *Slovakia 1918–38*, p. 449.

35 Johnson reports that it was only in 1956 that a Slovak archive on schools was organized separately from the one in Prague. He also found that key Slovak records were lost. Interestingly, not only were the records lost—which were not that reliable to begin with—but no one knows for sure how they were lost. These records may have been taken to Prague in 1938–39 or in the late 1950s,

or dumped in the Danube River before the arrival of Soviet troops in April 1945, or destroyed in the bombing of some government buildings at that time. Ibid., p. 463, n. 45.

36 Johnson found it difficult to assess the social composition of Czech and Slovak societies in 1918 since there was no statistical system; it did not operate normally until 1922. Ibid., p. 453.

37 At neither time was much work done on the key question of the formation of the intelligentsia in Slovakia. Ibid., p. 457.

38 The membership was 11,063 in 1930 and was up to 30,147 by 1936. Johnson, "The Slovak Intelligentsia," p. 38.

39 The leadership was teachers, small landowners and entrepreneurs, lawyers, and Catholic priests. The constituency for this party was made up of two broad groups: the smallholding peasants and the Catholic population of Slovakia's smaller and medium-sized towns. But the party also had support in other groups, including college students and graduates who were attracted by the prospect of the government jobs that a regime controlled by Slovaks would award to the Slovak (as opposed to Czech, Hungarian, or Jewish) intelligentsia. See Felak, *At the Price of the Republic*, pp. 31–33. Many have interpreted support for the HSLS as due to unemployment of the intelligentsia because of Czech dominance of key positions. Johnson points out that the intelligentsia was underemployed not unemployed. Johnson, *Slovakia 1918–38*, pp. 266–67.

40 Felak, *At the Price of the Republic*, pp. 59–72.

41 Support for Social Democrats went from a high of 38 percent in 1920 to 11.4 percent in 1935. Once the communists split off from the Social Democrats, one of the reasons for the falloff in support, there was a small Left which was dominated by ethnic minorities, getting 10 to 13 percent of the vote. The Agrarians received 17 to 19 percent in Slovakia during these years (their supporters were mostly Protestant). Ibid., pp. 59–72.

42 The communists, of course, had followed the Soviet line, which was pro-Germany, from the Molotov-Ribbentrop pact of 1939 until the 1941 Nazi invasion of the Soviet Union. The Soviet Union even recognized the Slovak state. This had to be justified later as a temporary strategic move taken to prepare and arm the Soviet Union for the real antifascist struggle, given that the "imperialist powers" were primarily anti-Soviet anyway and, early in the war, hoped that the Nazis and the communists would do each other in.

43 Michal Barnovský, *Na ceste k monopolu moci* (Bratislava: Archa 1993), p. 97. This book is a comprehensive account of these years.

44 While the postwar trials started before the communists came to power, many argue that there was communist influence in the whole retribution process. This is still a subject of dispute among historians.

45 For details on this see Kirschbaum, *A History of Slovakia*, p. 226, and Josef Mikus, *Slovakia: A Political History* (Milwaukee, Wis.: Marquette University Press, 1963). For the fate of the leadership, see p. 184.

46 František Mikloško, *Nebudete ich most' rozvrátit'* (Bratislava: Archa, 1991). Citations here are from an English translation that Mikloško gave this author in manuscript form (p. 26). The English version is called *You Can't Destroy Them* and was translated by Danielle Rozgon.

47 The 120 volunteers being trained for an information service called "Slovak Secret Defense" were to provide information on the Slovak situation to a Slovak government in exile or other Slovak political activists abroad. Mikloško writes that most of these remained in Slovakia after the war and did not emigrate. But the White Legion was more broadly based and rested on the idea of nonviolent self-defense of society. Anyone who opposed communism automatically became a member of the White Legion. The trials of the White Legion took place in 1949, after the communists came to power. The White Legion operated a radio station in Austria from 1950 to 1953. See Mikloško, *You Can't Destroy Them*, p. 26–27.

48 Mikloško points out that none of these were tried before the retribution trials, seeming to suggest that their activities did not qualify as collaboration and could be separated out as national feeling without its fascist links. Ibid., pp. 27–28.

49 The idea of autonomy, and even anti-Semitism, did not disappear with the fall of the Slovak state. One example of this was the residual anti-Semitism that led to pogroms after the war, inspired by the fear that Jewish survivors might get back their property. Lendvai, *Anti-Semitism without Jews*, p. 247.

50 There continue to be historiographical debates about the extent of public support for the Tiso regime even after the uprising. Mikloško suggests opposition to Tiso's execution in a description of a particularly large group of pilgrims from Bratislava to Marianka on May 11, 1947, who kneeled in silence at the presidential palace as they went by. Mikloško, *You Can't Destroy Them*, p. 23. Also see Mikus, pp. 175–77, for opposition to Tiso's execution. In 1947 there were several pilgrimages and other pro-Catholic actions in the face of execution of Tiso and impending communist rule. Also see Brad Abrams, "The Politics of Retribution: The Trial of Jozef Tiso," *East European Politics and Societies* 10, no. 2 (1996): 255–92.

51 Mikloško, *You Can't Destroy Them*, p. 5.

52 Ibid., p. 29. The bishops protested, and in June 1949 an organization called "Catholic Action" was formed which was an attempt by the state to co-opt the church and create a national church of Czechoslovakia separate from the Vatican. Priests who protested were sent to prison.

53 For details see ibid., pp. 34–35, and appendices that list names of priests arrested.

54 Leff, "National Conflict in Czechoslovakia," pp. 95–96, says that the Democratic Party won the votes of all the prewar supporters of the Agrarian Party and 70 percent of HSLS supporters. One of its real weaknesses in opposing the communists was that it united such a broad spectrum of beliefs.

55 Jozef Lettrich, *History of Modern Slovakia* (New York: Fredrick A. Praeger, 1955), pp. 238–40.

56 While he gives no evidence or citations for this claim, Steiner says that some of the worst types (who happened to be of working class or peasant origin) from the Hlinka Guard got high posts in the Party apparatus and survived Stalinist purges "unlike many reputable old party members." Eugen Steiner, *The Slovak Dilemma* (Cambridge: Cambridge University Press, 1973), p. 80. See also p. 97.

57 The Democratic Party tried hard to save Tiso from execution, publicly pro-

claiming that it would try to save him. This was not enough to avoid the execution. Lettrich, *History of Modern Slovakia,* pp. 244–60. In fall 1947 state security organs (dominated by communists but run by a noncommunist) started to investigate ties between leaders of the Democratic Party and fascist exiles Sidór and Durčanský and claimed to have found evidence. Steiner, *The Slovak Dilemma,* pp. 85–86.

58　On March 31, 1948, accusations were submitted to the state court in Bratislava against fourteen leaders of the Slovak Democratic Party. Mikloško, *You Can't Destroy Them,* p. 28.

59　For more detail on this see ibid. and Mikus, *Slovakia,* pp. 245–53.

60　Mikus, *Slovakia,* p. 251.

61　Imrich Kruzliak, "A Quarter Century of Slovak Culture," in Jozef Kirschbaum, ed., *Slovakia in the 19th and 20th Centuries,* Proceedings of Conference on Slovakia held during meeting of Slovak World Congress, June 17–18, 1971 (Toronto: Slovak World Congress, 1973), p. 189.

62　Maršina, "Slovenská Historiografia," pp. 370–79.

63　The most reliable national history, Lubomír Lipták's *Slovensko v 20. storočí* (Bratislava: Vydavatelstvo politickej literatury, 1968), was written during the 1960s and included the World War II period. It was removed from circulation after 1969.

64　Sharon Wolchik, *Czechoslovakia in Transition* (London: Pinter Publishers, 1991), p. 190. See also Michal Barnovský, *Socálné triedy a revolučné premeny na Slovensku v rokoch 1944–1948* (Bratislava: Veda, 1978), p. 119. Author's interview with Barnovský, April 1994.

65　Wolchik, *Czechoslovakia in Transition,* pp. 188–89. Additional evidence that the bulk of the elites in Slovakia came from peasant/worker backgrounds is the following: In 1967, 60 percent of nonmanual employees with secondary education came from worker or peasant families. In 1979, 32.3 percent of all students in general secondary schools leading to university came from worker/peasant backgrounds, as did 62.3 percent of those in secondary trade and trade schools. Wolchik, pp. 178–80. Of course by 1979 many families that would have qualified as worker/peasant when communism arrived would have already become part of the educated professional class created by communist modernization.

66　Johnson makes an interesting point about types of intelligentsia which is significant for the argument about which families passed on ideology. Drawing on the work of a Czech sociologist Arnošt Bláha, he sees four levels of the nationally conscious parts of the population: first are those who hold a high school diploma; second are the creative intelligentsia, scientists, artists, and writers; third is the "leading intelligentsia," the several thousand people in any nation who have high intellectual potential for leadership; and a lower intelligentsia who were culturally aware though possessing no secondary education, *Slovakia, 1918–38,* pp. 7–8.

67　The Jewish and German population almost disappeared, and the Hungarian proportion of the population went from 17.6 percent in 1930 to 10.3 percent in 1950. See Jaroslav Krejčí, *Social Change and Stratification in Postwar Czechoslovakia* (New York: Columbia University Press, 1972), p. 11. See also Ludvík Němec, "Solution of the Minorities Problem," in Victor S. Mamatey and Radomír Luža, eds., *A History of the Czechoslovak Republic, 1918–1948* (Princeton: Princeton University Press, 1973), p. 416.

4   Islands of History: The Democrats and Nationalists

1   Strongly communist families are included here.
2   One of the few written documents on World War II associated with this group was a response to a TV series put on by the regime on the fiftieth anniversary of the declaration of the Slovak state, which linked the Catholic Church to all the evils of fascism. See letter by Bishop Ján Korec, written April 7, 1989, in response to "The Cross in the Snares of Power." Translated by Stanislav Kirschbaum in *Slovakia* 34, nos. 62–63 (1989–90): 77–126. For the Slovak version of the letter published after the 1989 revolution, see "Na margo jedneho seriálu" serialized in *Výber*, numbers 5, 6, and 7 (1990).
3   Interestingly, this family also embodied another legacy of the past critical to postcommunist politics. Ivan Čarnogurský was accused of collaboration with the secret police. The communist regime often attempted to lure members of dissenting families into collaboration.
4   Later he became a deputy to the Slovak National Council.
5   Čarnogurský helped Husák during the Slovak state period and Husák helped Čarnogurský avoid imprisonment in 1945. See interview with Ján Čarnogurský in *Smena,* November 22, 1991, in FBIS-EEU-91-230, 11/29/91, p. 6.
6   He became a deputy to the Slovak parliament in March 1990 and chaired it from June of that year. After the elections of 1992 he was again a deputy to the parliament, now for KDH. He switched from VPN to KDH in February 1992 when he realized that the democrats of VPN/ODU would be unlikely to make it into parliament in June 1992 and after KDH lost its more radical nationalist wing. Author's interview with Mikloško, spring 1994.
7   Author's interview with Klepáč, April 6, 1994.
8   But he did come from a family that experienced political persecution and was "public minded." He was religious and was never a Communist Party member. Author's interview with Oberhauser, spring 1994.
9   Interview with Pavol Čarnogurský, "Priestory šťastnej Europy," in *Literárný Týždenník* 24 (June 6, 1992): 1.
10   See biographical information on back of Čarnogurský's book, *14. Marec 1939* (Bratislava: VEDA Vydateľstvo Slovenskej Akademie Vied, 1992).
11   He held several different positions during the period of the Slovak state, including one that was more controversial, involving removing Jewish and Czech teachers and replacing them with Slovaks displaced from the land given to Hungary in 1938; when it came to the deportations, he boycotted the vote in the Slovak parliament in May 1942 but would not vote against them, since he claims to have believed that the legislation allowed for presidential exceptions. For more on Pavol Čarnogurský see Alan Levy, profile of Ján Čarnogurský in *Prague Post* 2, no. 21 (1992): 10; "Koniec jednej legendy?" an interview with Pavol Čarnogurský in *Pravda,* June 28, 1991, p. 3, and "Obludnosť'

legislativnej mašinérie," a response by legal historian Katerína Zavacká in *Pravda,* September 27, 1991, p. 5.

12 Oberhauser, interview.

13 Mikloško, *You Can't Destroy Them,* p. 62.

14 Ibid., p. 65.

15 Ibid., p. 67.

16 For example, the memoirs of T. Gašpar were published. Gašpar was chief of propaganda during the Slovak state and was in prison for twenty years until the mid-1960s.

17 Stanislav Kirschbaum said that émigrés were still not welcome during this period. Author's interview with Stanislav Kirschbaum, July 19, 1996. Kirschbaum, son of Jozef Kirschbaum, a major figure in the government of the wartime Slovak state, is a professor of political science at York University in Toronto and has written widely on Slovakia.

18 But in the only book on the topic published after 1989, by František Mikloško, there is no mention of the Kolakovic group's opposition to the Catholic hierarchy associated with the regime.

19 Controversy about whether the Vatican sufficiently opposed the Nazis' extermination of the Jews continues. There is also controversy specifically about the Slovak church, since the Slovak state was led by a Catholic priest and priests were active in its politics. Clearly the church opposed anti-Jewish policies and was important in stopping the deportations after they had already commenced. It is not clear how strong the church opposition was from the *beginning* of the deportations. See Yeshayahu Jelinek, "The Vatican, the Catholic Church, the Catholics, and the Persecution of the Jews during World War II: The Case of Slovakia," in Bela Vago and George L. Mosse, *Jews and Non-Jews in Eastern Europe, 1918–1945* (New York: Halsted Press, 1974), pp. 221–25; John S. Conway, "The Churches, the Slovak State, and the Jews, 1939–45," in *Slavonic and East European Review* 52, no. 126 (1974): 85–112, and Livia Rothkirschen, "Vatican Policy and the 'Jewish Problem' in 'Independent' Slovakia (1939–1945)" and "The Slovak Enigma: A Reassessment of the Halt to the Deportations," in Michael Marrus, ed., *The Nazi Holocaust,* vol. 4: *The 'Final Solution' Outside Germany* (Westport, Conn.: Meckler Corp., 1989), pp. 435–61 and pp. 473–83.

20 Born in 1924, and from a working class family, he was fifteen years old when the Slovak state was declared. This was just at the time he started religious education. Mikloško, *You Can't Destroy Them,* pp. 69–70.

21 Ibid., pp. 71–72.

22 Ibid., p. 72.

23 Ibid., p. 68.

24 Mikloško, interview; Klepáč, interview. Mikloško came from a religious family and was introduced to the main activists in the secret church through his brother Jozef Mikloško, who was also active in KDH after communism fell—as deputy to the federal parliament.

25 Mikloško, *You Can't Destroy Them,* p. 75–76.

26 Ibid., p. 74.

27 See *Lidová Demokracie,* May 23, 1990, p. 3, in FBIS-EEU-90-106, 6/1/90, p. 15.

28 Klepáč, interview.

29 One of the important pilgrimages, with mass attendance, took place earlier, in 1985, for the 1,100th anniversary of St. Methodius's death. In 1988, one hundred thousand pilgrims went to Nitra. Mikloško, *You Can't Destroy Them,* pp. 82–85.

30 Ibid., p. 93.

31 Ibid., p. 92.

32 Klepáč, interview. One of the obvious problems with interviews after 1989 was that there had been such rapid change that it was difficult for interview subjects to remember what they had known before 1989, and they naturally framed their ideas in terms of the post-1989 debate. Klepáč might not have made the comment about church and nation before 1989.

33 For example, see Mikloško, *You Can't Destroy Them,* p. 26: "It was difficult to separate things religious from things national in Slovakia."

34 His personal archive was confiscated in 1976. See Pavol Čarnogurský, "Teror," *Literárný Týždennik* 42 (October 18, 1992).

35 He received his law degree from Comenius University in 1969.

36 In the interview he said that his mother brought food to a Jewish family living in the cellar of a house to which his family had been evacuated. However, when talking about the totality of the wartime events he said, "It is a tragedy that during that period 57,000 Jewish inhabitants lost their lives." He thus avoided ascribing responsibility.

37 He found a book by František Hrušovský, official historian of the Slovak state. Carole Leff calls this text "almost sacerdotal." Leff, *National Conflict in Czechoslovakia,* p. 90.

38 Klepáč, interview.

39 See H. Gordon Skilling, "The Muse of History—1984: History, Historians, and Politics in Communist Czechoslovakia," in *Cross Currents, A Yearbook of Central European Culture,* no. 3 (Ann Arbor: University of Michigan, 1984), 29–47. Also by Skilling, "Independent Historiography in Czechoslovakia," *Canadian Slavonic Papers* 25, no. 4 (1983): 518–39.

40 In 1978 he received a review from a 1971 international seminar on Slovak history in Zurich. He said the book was transported and circulated at great risk. Klepáč, interview.

41 Mikloško said that he and fellow dissident Ján Langoš had frequent meetings with Jaro Franek and Boris Lazar. Franek became spokesman for the Jewish community after 1989. At these meetings they discussed the Jewish issue at great length. Mikloško, interview. Langoš, a VPN activist, served as federal interior minister and federal parliamentary deputy from 1990.

42 Jozef Jablonický, another dissident, was a historian of the Slovak National Uprising who provided information on that period.

43 See Mikloško, *You Can't Destroy Them,* pp. 95–97.

44 A particularly radical group was led by an émigré named Kollár in Munich. František Vnuk was another key émigré who was sympathetic to the wartime state, and who published widely in the postcommunist Slovak press. See *Liter-*

árný Týždenník in the years 1990–92 for numerous articles by Vnuk and other émigrés.

45 For example in Croatia, the Baltics, and Armenia émigrés served in governmental positions.

46 See Yeshayahu Jelinek, "The Ludak Exile, the Neo-Ludaks, and Revival of Anti-Semitism in Slovakia," pp. 1–2.

47 In the late nineteenth and early twentieth centuries, the Hungarians had repressed most Slovak cultural life, and the émigrés continued it in the United States. At the first Slovak congress in Cleveland in 1907 there were ten thousand delegates of various parishes and societies. Jozef Pauco, "Slovaks Abroad and Their Relationship with Slovakia," in Jozef Kirschbaum, ed., *Slovakia in the 19th and 20th Centuries,* Proceedings of Conference on Slovakia held during meeting of Slovak World Congress, June 17–18, 1971 (Toronto: Slovak World Congress, 1973).

48 This agreement, which became the source of much controversy, declared that Slovakia would have some autonomy within the common Czechoslovak state. Slovaks later felt the Czechs had gone back on this agreement. For the text of this agreement, see Lettrich, *History of Modern Slovakia,* pp. 289–90.

49 This is the claim of Jozef Pauco, who became a leader of the Slovak league. Pauco was a personal secretary to Tiso, chief editor of *Slovák,* the HSLS paper, and he emigrated before the liberation of Czechoslovakia. See entry in Jozef Chreno, *Malý slovník slovenského štátu* (Bratislava: Slovenská Archivná Správa, 1965), p. 141. As evidence of the bitter divides that remained between émigré supporters and opponents of the Slovak state, Pauco is particularly vilified in Jozef Lettrich's book, p. 223.

50 The Slovak National Council Abroad was founded by former Slovak state leaders Karol Sidor, Dr. Jozef Kirschbaum, Peter Prídavok, and Konstantin Čulen; the Slovak Liberation Committee was led by Dr. Ferdinand Durčanský; Stefan Polakovič; and Aloyz Macek and Dr. Stanislav Mečiar, also leaders in the Slovak state. Pauco, "Slovaks Abroad," p. 341.

51 Ibid.

52 This organization was founded by Canadian-Slovak industrialist Stefan Roman. For background on Roman see "Stefan Roman, Founder of the World Congress of Slovaks," *Europa Vincet,* no. 1 (1992): 36–37.

53 There were three: *Slowakei,* in German, *Slovakia* in English, and *Slovak Studies,* which was multilingual. See Kirschbaum, *A History of Slovakia,* pp. 4–5.

54 Ibid., p. 4.

55 Igor Uhrík, one of the most active Slovak émigrés in post-1989 politics, was from this wave and did not join any Slovak organization until just before the fall of communism. Even so, after 1989, he was acting on behalf of himself, not any organization. Author's interview with Uhrík, spring, 1994.

56 See František Braxator, "Slovaks Abroad and Their Relationship to Czecho-Slovakia," in Jozef Kirschbaum, ed., *Slovakia in the 19th and 20th Centuries,* pp. 348–49. Braxator says that the majority of this later emigration did not see aid to Slovakia as taking the form of an effort to revive the Slovak republic of 1939–45.

57 While some argue that they are trying to save the idea of Slovak statehood even

if the Tiso regime is tainted, the émigrés go further, to rescue and celebrate the reputation of the regime and particularly its leader Jozef Tiso.

58 For a brief, but incomplete, discussion of historiography see Yeshayahu Jelinek, "The Slovak State in Post-war Historiography," pp. 17–24.

59 See Stanislav Kirschbaum, "The Slovak Republic and the Slovaks," *Slovakia* 29, nos. 53–54 (1980–81): 14. Kirschbaum also says independence was "the best solution, not only under the circumstances, but also for the Slovak nation" (p. 16).

60 They tend to focus on the fact that compared to other European countries the Slovak currency was strong and goods were available. See Korec, letter, p. 122.

61 S. Kirschbaum, "The Slovak Republic and the Slovaks," pp. 22–23; Korec, letter, p. 122. They tend to cite communist authors to support these points, particularly Gustáv Husák. See Korec, pp. 109–11; Kirschbaum, p. 27.

62 S. Kirschbaum, "The Slovak Republic and the Slovaks," p. 17. Repression is mentioned vaguely: that "certain people suffered." For argument about lenience toward political opponents like communists, see Korec, letter, particularly p. 109.

63 Korec tends to underplay the role of the clergy in the politics of the Slovak state (pp. 92, 98–99). The Korec document in particular tries to exonerate the church, since it is a response to a communist attack claiming that the church was the root of the evils of the Slovak state.

64 In France, too, nationalists use this logic of displacing responsibility for the deportations from a popular national figure to others that could be labeled extremists. Marshall Philippe Pétain is portrayed as doing the best he could, while Pierre Laval is blamed for the deportations.

65 The Aryanization policy was justified by the idea that since Jews constituted only 4 percent of the population they should not own more than that percentage of property. According to some estimates, Slovak Jews owned 30 percent of property before the war. For a view that sees this policy as justified, see Mikus, *Slovakia: A Political History,* p. 96; František Vnuk argues elsewhere that Slovaks should not be blamed for the fact that Jews tended to associate themselves with the oppressors of Slovaks, namely the Hungarians. "Drahý pán Mňačko" in *Literárný Týždenník* 35 (August 31, 1990).

66 S. Kirschbaum, "The Slovak Republic and the Slovaks," p. 21.

67 Pavol Čarnogurský argues that the parliament never ratified these laws, which were issued as government decrees. He also tries to suggest that Tiso did not sign them. Pavol Čarnogurský, *Pravda* interview.

68 Emigrés argue that Tiso saved thirty to forty thousand Jews through exceptions, though others dispute the rationale and effects of the exceptions, as we will see. S. Kirschbaum, *A History of Slovakia,* pp. 199–200. Kirschbaum draws his information from another émigré historian, Milan Durica. See also Korec, letter, p. 103.

69 Mikus cites a much lower number of deported Jews, saying that the figure of 60,000 often given for the 1942 period is exaggerated, and he instead uses the figure 52,000. He bases this on testimony from the German in charge of Jewish issues. Mikus, *Slovakia: A Political History,* p. 98. Also see S. Kirschbaum, *A History of Slovakia.*

70 As Jelinek points out, through this sort of argument émigrés justify the deportations themselves if not the later extermination. See Jelinek, "The Ludak Exile," p. 8. For what was known see Korec, letter, p. 104.

71 They leave out the fact that the HSLS paid the Germans five hundred marks per Jew deported and that Slovakia was the only country not occupied by Germany to voluntarily give up its Jews.

72 For the conspiracy view see Mikus, *Slovakia: A Political History,* p. 148, where he argues that the Russians deliberately caused the Uprising to start too early, thereby inviting German occupation. He bases this view on the fact that once the Uprising started they did not send sufficient aid. This paved the way for their entry as liberators. The Slovak communists and other Slovak partisans were just pawns in this plot. A similar argument is made about the Soviet role in the Warsaw Uprising.

73 See Korec for an ambivalent view; he does point out that no one had been killed on Slovak territory during the war until the Uprising (p. 114). Also, S. Kirschbaum, *A History of Slovakia,* pp. 221–23.

74 Even the semidissident group around Václav Klaus that met since the 1970s to discuss alternatives to communist economics was a more constant and identifiable entity than any that existed among Slovak democrats. Leader of VPN, Fedor Gál participated in the Klaus group.

75 Part of this party was absorbed into the National Front in 1948 and became a satellite party during the communist period; its communist-era members went in a variety of directions after 1989. One grouping within the party was the young nationalists who formed the Štúr Society.

76 Lettrich, who was vice president of the council, says that there was an attempt to have equal representation from Czechs and Slovaks. Lettrich had been head of the Democratic Party and chairman of the Slovak National Council during the 1945–48 period. Lettrich, *A History of Modern Slovakia,* pp. 271–72.

77 Kvetko, born in 1912, had been a key figure in the Uprising and then commissioner for agriculture in Slovakia between 1945 and 1948. Author's interview with Kvetko in Bratislava, November 4, 1992.

78 In the interview he mentioned the following groups: Czech Council of America, Evangelical Pastors, Slovak Sokol, and Evangelical Synod.

79 However, the émigrés of stature that returned after 1989 were mostly Czech, as were the famous civic dissidents like Václav Havel and the writer Milan Kundera. The Czech émigré community had an extensive publication network that also gave them a presence in the West.

80 Czechoslovakia served as an assurance to Western analysts and political leaders that there was a democratic alternative to communism. Although the Western powers never came to the aid of Czechoslovakia, it remained a powerful symbol of the threat to democracy and the rise of totalitarian domination both by the Nazis and the communists. The 1938 Munich agreement, whereby Czechoslovakia fell into the Nazi sphere, and the communist takeover of 1948, whereby it fell into the Soviet sphere, were both key moments contributing to Western governments' understanding of the significance of these totalitarian regimes.

81 Jozef Lettrich's book, cited above, is the one émigré history of World War II that

was published in the postcommunist period by the press associated with the democrats of VPN.

82 This was a more typical pathway in the Czech Republic than in Slovakia; it was often taken by Jewish communists. While the Czech antifascist resistance was not as strong as the Slovak was, there were more communist victims of fascism in the Czech case; there were more communists in the Czech Republic in general.

83 Peter Hrubý, *Fools and Heroes* (Oxford: Pergamon Press, 1980), pp. 2–5. Leszek Kalokowski, expelled from the Polish Communist Party in 1968, and Milovan Djilas, expelled from the Yugoslav Communist Party in 1954, are parallels in other Leninist systems.

84 This is well characterized in the memoir by Heda Kovály, wife of one of the Jewish communists tried along with Rudolf Slánský. Her husband, Rudolf Margolius, was head of the office of the minister of foreign trade. Her memoir was published in two forms: as a straight memoir in *Under a Cruel Star* (New York: Penguin, 1986) and with more commentary, with Erazim Kohák, in *The Victors and the Vanquished* (New York: Horizon Press, 1973). Jews were disillusioned by the failure of "bourgeois" democracy to withstand the Nazi assault. They saw communism as the one force completely opposed to Nazism. They were also drawn to communism because the guilt of survival led to the desire to sacrifice themselves for the reconstruction of society. Of course there were many prewar Jewish communists also.

85 Charter 77 was a human rights movement, inspired by the Helsinki agreements, that called upon the government to adhere to its own laws and human rights obligations. Members became signatories to its founding document. It was established in 1977 and Václav Havel was one of its leaders.

86 In 1968, the goals of democratization and national autonomy for Slovakia were mixed. Jewish communists did not generally have the choice of staying in the Party and compromising. This was because they were persecuted by the regime's anti-Semitism; they also tended to be oriented more toward the civic Czechoslovak ideology and away from Slovak nationalism.

87 Kusý was a Slovak parliamentary deputy and member of the Slovak parliament's presidium; in 1990 he was appointed rector of Comenius University; in 1991 he became Havel's representative in Slovakia. See *Kto je kto na Slovensku* (Bratislava: Konzorcium Encyklopedia, 1992), p. 99.

88 All of above from author's interview with Kusý, spring 1994.

89 He is included in Hrubý's book as going through this typical transformation. He began to question in 1963. See Hrubý, *Fools and Heroes*, pp. 203–7.

90 Kusý, interview.

91 In my interview, Kusý said that he did not know until much later that so few Slovaks signed. In retrospect, he said that this knowledge might have kept him from signing.

92 One reason he was tied in with the Prague group was because of his contacts from his university days in Prague. Kusý, interview.

93 Kusý, interview; "Slovak som a Slovak budem . . ." published in the samizdat journal *Listy* in 1982, cited in Skilling, "The Muse of History," pp. 29–30.

94 See cites in chapter 2 to Šimečka's writings on organized forgetting. Šimečka

had a profile similar to Kusý's. Born in 1930, he specialized in history of philosophy. He was a Czech but lived in Slovakia from the 1950s. He was also removed from the Party in 1970.

95 Others from his generation who took somewhat similar routes were Šimečka, and writers Ladislav Mňačko, Dominik Tatarka, and Juraj Špitzer. Špitzer, a Jewish communist, for example, had been in important positions throughout the Stalinist period. He was a socialist realist writer and a partisan, but was later removed from the Party and turned to a more civic ideology. Author's interview with Špitzer, October 16, 1992.

96 Interestingly, among the few figures with stature from this generation three died during the 1989–92 period: Milan Šimečka, in summer 1991; Mňačko and Dubček in the fall of 1992.

97 For a discussion of this term, see Soňa Szomolányiová, "The Repolitization of Slovak Society" (paper presented at the Fourth World Congress for Soviet and East European Studies in Harrogate, July 21–26, 1990); also see Szomolányiová, Bútora, and Krivý, "Positive Deviance: The Career of a Concept in Czecho-Slovakia in the Late 1980s."

98 Some, like Jaro Franek and Milan Zemko, were not allowed to receive candidate degrees in their fields.

99 Szomolányiová et al., "Positive Deviance," p. 5. She also points out that this allowed for more contact with the rest of society than did the Prague dissidents, who were cut off. Author's interview with Soňa Szomolányiová, April 10, 1994; author's interview with Peter Zajac, April 11, 1994.

100 Szomolányiová, "The Repolitization of Slovak Society," p. 9. One thousand copies were published and then taken by the police.

101 Ibid., p. 10.

102 Slovaks were not willing to take risks on Havel's behalf and did not sign petitions demanding his release from prison; they were only willing to do so on behalf of local dissidents. Ibid., p. 11, and interview with Kusý.

103 Ibid., p. 12.

104 Fedor Gál, *Z Prvej ruky* (Bratislava: Archa, 1991), p. 18.

105 Gál was born in 1945; Zajac in 1945; Szomolányiová in 1946; Zemko in 1944; Bútora in 1944; Žiak in 1961. The information on these individuals is from interviews carried out by the author in 1992–94. Bútora interview, November 24, 1993; Gál interview, spring 1994; Žiak interviews, July 16, 1993 and March 25, 1994; Zajac interview April 11, 1994; Zemko interview April 7, 1994; Szomolányiová, April 10, 1994.

106 Gál, interview. This included Miloš Zeman, Karel Dyba, and Klaus. Gál collaborated with some of them through official projects and others through an unofficial group that began in 1974 with twenty-five to thirty people. This heterogeneous group included Pavel Machonin, the reform communist sociologist, and Klaus. Interestingly, this group operated out of a number of different official institutions over time, since it was occasionally closed down by the regime. Thus, again, the continuity was through people, not institutions.

107 This weak alternative information was strengthened by contact with the older generation that had ideologies. It was also bolstered by the fact that it was similar to the dominant Western/intellectual view of World War II and the

Holocaust and totalitarianism. This Western source of confirmation was particularly important after 1989.

108 The commitment to truth is often cited as a Czech tradition and is traced from Jan Hus to Tomáš Masaryk.

109 Havel often wrote how the West could learn from what he called the post-totalitarian form of domination in Eastern Europe. This, as opposed to the more violent Nazism, more totally penetrated people's lives. See, for example, "Between Ideals and Utopias," *East European Reporter* 3, 1987–88, p. 13. The more general view that developed among Central European intellectuals in the 1970s and 1980s was also influential. Interestingly, Milan Kundera has spoken of Jews as the "intellectual cement" of Central Europe and "a condensed version of its spirit." He talked about Central European intellectuals as being functionally Jews. For a discussion of this view, see Melvin Croan, "Lands In-between: The Politics of Cultural Identity in Contemporary Eastern Europe," *East European Politics and Society* 3, no. 2 (1989): 176–97 (comment about Jews on p. 184).

110 Interviewees mentioned Erich Fromm's *Escape from Freedom*, novels by Czech author Arnošt Lustig, stories by Slovak author Leopold Lahola, and writings by Martin Gilbert on the Holocaust.

111 The Kamenec book had been his dissertation, which he defended in 1971. It was published in 1991 as *Po Stopách tragédie* by Archa Press. Many of the citations below are from a shorter article by Kamenec that appeared in English in the conference proceedings for a 1992 conference on the Holocaust in Slovakia: "The Deportation of Jewish Citizens from Slovakia in 1942," in *The Tragedy of Slovak Jews: Proceedings of the International Symposium, Banská Bystrica, March 25–27, 1992* (Banská Bystrica: Datei, 1992), pp. 81–106.

112 The Archa Press also began to publish Western classics of liberal political theory.

113 Jablonicky's works were seen as problematic by the regime mostly because he wrote about the importance of soldiers in the Slovak National Uprising, suggesting that they were, in some cases, more important than the Communist Party. See Skilling, "Independent Historiography," pp. 533–34.

114 Lettrich, *History of Modern Slovakia*, pp. 94–95.

115 Ibid., p. 110.

116 Ibid., p. 185.

117 Ibid., pp. 155–56.

118 Ibid., pp. 171–73.

119 Lettrich, pp. 177–79.

120 As Lettrich recounts, as early as 1938 the HSLS declared its anti-Semitism in a manifesto; more radical leaders promised the Germans as early as 1938 that "the Jewish question will be settled in the same way as in Germany." Ibid., pp. 175–76.

121 Kamenec shows that the bureaucratic apparatus worked extremely efficiently in carrying out the deportations. Kamenec, "The Deportation of Jewish Citizens," pp. 97–98.

122 Ibid., p. 87.

123 Ibid., p. 102.

124 Ibid., p. 87. Lettrich also talks about the corruption of the presidential exceptions. Lettrich, *History of Modern Slovakia*, p. 185.

125 Lettrich, *History of Modern Slovakia*, pp. 200–201. Lettrich says that the Uprising was motivated by "the desire to liberate Slovakia by its own efforts . . . to throw out the Germans, to destroy the dictatorship of the Slovak People's Party, reintroduce Czechoslovak democratic institutions, spare Slovakia the suffering of war . . . assure it its just place in a free Czechoslovakia . . . a political and military contribution by democratic Slovakia to the allied war effort." Kvetko also expressed this as the meaning of the Uprising. Kvetko, interview.

126 This view was resented even by some Slovak participants in the resistance. President Eduard Beneš in particular, in his wartime broadcasts, expressed the Czech view: "Do you realize the moral horror of the situation? . . . Do you see how the dates of March 14–15, 1939 will appear in the history of Slovakia?" (cited in Leff, *National Conflict in Czechoslovakia*, p. 165). Slovaks complained that Czech collaboration through working in arms factories was viewed as forced and as slavery, while the actions of the Slovak state were seen as treason even though they were often also done under Nazi pressure. Leff, pp. 164–65.

127 Soňa Szomolányiová, interview.

128 See chapter 6 for how this played out; on the issue of not realizing in advance the differences between the groups, two VPN activists—Soňa Szomolányiová and Zora Bútorová—said in interviews that they did not realize until after 1989 that there was anyone in Slovakia who thought well of the Slovak state. Bútorová complained, for example, that Mikloško did not mention in his book on the secret church the full extent of many Catholics' connection with the Slovak state. Soňa Szomolányiová reports that the first time she realized that Slovak state supporters would resurface was when she received an anonymous letter referring to her uncle who was a major figure in the Slovak National Uprising as a traitor. The letter said that she, the daughter of a traitor (the author of the letter was confused as to the relationship), should not be involved in politics. Author's interview with Zora Bútorová, September 25, 1992; Szomolányiová, interview.

129 Martin Bútora, one of the few Slovaks in Havel's inner circle, suggested this, as did Soňa Szomolányiová. Bútora, interview; Szomolányiová, interview.

130 As Stanislav Kirschbaum pointed out in my interview with him, there was hostility between these organizations. He claims that the Czech émigré community prevented establishment of a Slovak section in organizations like Voice of America and Radio Free Europe. Kirschbaum, interview.

131 Obviously power concerns entered the U.S. approach to former Nazi collaborators due to their common cold war anticommunism.

132 Yeshayahu Jelinek, "Slovaks and the Holocaust: Attempts at Reconciliation," *Soviet Jewish Affairs* 19, no. 1 (1989).

133 According to S. Kirschbaum, when Čarnogurský spoke to émigrés in Toronto in 1990, they were unhappy with his position; there was little contact during communism between émigrés and Slovaks in Slovakia. Kirschbaum, interview.

134 Interestingly, in 1987 the Catholic nationalists and the émigrés came out with

very different declarations of apology to the Jews. No such declaration had come out in the forty-five years since the war. The one issued by dissidents was organized by František Mikloško, Bishop Ján Korec, and Ján Čarnogurský. Korec wrote the text and Mikloško and Čarnogurský finalized it. Mikloško, interview. They were all condemned by the regime in *Pravda.* The Slovak World Congress declaration came out at a time when Yad Vashem, the Holocaust memorial in Israel, was going to commemorate the forty-fifth anniversary of the deportations. Jelinek, "Slovaks and the Holocaust," pp. 64–65. While the Slovak dissidents were willing to take responsibility on behalf of Slovakia—"the deportations and other anti-Jewish measures were in Slovak hands"—and to clearly say that the policies of that state ran counter to the principles on which they hoped to build Slovakia's future, the émigré declaration was much less willing to take responsibility without qualification. Texts of the declarations can be found in Jelinek, "Slovaks and the Holocaust: Attempts at Reconciliation."

135 This was particularly true for the younger generation.

136 Author's interview with Jurík, spring 1994.

137 S. Kirschbaum, *A History of Slovakia,* pp. 2–10. This fits with the observation about ethnic nationalists that while their ideology can be shown to be constructed, they believe that it is a given and arises from primordial ties. See Greenfeld, *Nationalism: Five Roads to Modernity,* among others for this point.

138 Čarnogurský, interview.

139 Mikloško, *You Can't Destroy Them,* pp. 1–6.

140 Korec letter.

141 This ambivalence can be found in Havel's speeches from early 1990; see in particular his "New Years Address to the Nation," January 1, 1990. Translation of the speech can be found in Havel, *The Art of the Impossible* (New York: Fromm International, 1998), pp. 3–9.

142 As we will see below, support from the West was partly what kept the democrats focused on the fascist past and divided from the Catholic nationalists. They, like Western analysts and advisers, failed to distinguish between a conservative nationalist ideology and a dangerous populist appeal to ethnic hatreds. One reason for this was the complicated legacy of the fascist past; in many cases the conservative nationalists were ambivalent about that past and were heirs to the parties that collaborated with Hitler.

143 Ken Jowitt makes this point, saying, "In 1989 . . . ethics moved from the purely personal realm to the public realm . . . as an autonomous political criterion for public action, one that judges leadership in terms of its impact on and contribution to human dignity. However, liberal democratic polities do not rest primarily . . . on the charismatic impermanence of politically ethical leadership or the private ethics of its citizens. They rest on 'public virtues.' " "The Leninist Legacy," in *New World Disorder,* p. 292.

5 Organized Forgetting: Elites with No History

1 Building legitimacy was especially important for the Party in Slovakia, where it had fewer adherents before the war, than in the Czech lands. Communist

Party membership in Slovakia was twenty times higher after the war than it was before. See Steiner, *The Slovak Dilemma*, p. 80–81.

2 Different forces controlled the creation of the myth about the war at different times. Most of the time it was the Czech leadership of the Communist Party or the Soviets; at other points it was more in the hands of the Slovak Communist Party, specifically right after the war and in the 1960s.

3 See the fascinating book by David King, *The Commissar Vanishes* (New York: Metropolitan Books, Henry Holt, 1997), on the Soviet case.

4 The frequent switches in Party position had implications on a more personal level as well for the very careers of individual Party members. These shifts made it difficult to know how to evaluate the status of key figures like Gustáv Husák—at one time a hero of the resistance and at another "bourgeois national-ist" and enemy of the communist cause.

5 Of course many listened to Radio Free Europe. However, while it provided an alternative source of *information*, it did not necessarily contribute to building alternative ideology, since individuals listened to it in isolation and did not articulate any common meaning for the information they heard.

6 *The American Heritage Dictionary*, 2nd ed. (Boston: Houghton Mifflin, 1982).

7 There was already discontinuity in the elite in the years following the war and into the communist period. Much of the leadership was formed by the experi-ence of wartime exile. This meant that often the immediate postwar elite did not know or necessarily trust one another. Leff, *National Conflict in Czechoslo-vakia*, p. 213.

8 The generational divide in postcommunist Eastern Europe and the former So-viet Union is one of the most important cleavages because of the revolutionary transformation that took place; support for and opposition to marketization often coincides with age.

9 It is difficult to say which years should be considered formative from a psycho-logical perspective. The years when one acquires an independent identity, in the late teens, would likely be formative for one's approach to history. Tech-nically, a generation is more than ten years. Twenty years, the amount of time we ordinarily think of as a generation, did not sufficiently reflect the variety of experiences that shaped postwar Czechoslovakia. Of course, there is a differ-ence of almost twenty years between the younger in each cohort and the older in the previous cohort.

10 If their parents never integrated their individual experiences of World War II into a larger ideology, it would be difficult for their children to draw on their families for a source of alternative ideology, and even unintegrated family stories might have lost potency.

11 See the directory for the parliament, *Slovenská Národná Rada, X. Volebné obdobie* (Bratislava: Kancelária Slovenskej Národnej Rady), p. 102.

12 Šimečka, "Black Holes: Concerning the Metamorphosis of Historical Memory," p. 25.

13 Two examples are the Štúr Society, which appeared right after 1989 and was one of the first visible groups using nationalist symbols, and a group formed by Peter Brňák (born 1959) called the Slovak National Democratic Union. He was one of the most radical nationalist deputies.

14 Ivan Laluha was closely associated with Dubček and founder of the Obroda group. Others are economist Hvezdon Kochtúch; Vladimír Mináč; Roman Kaliský; Pavol Števček; Ladislav Ťažký; Milan Rúfus. Miroslav Kusý was one of the few to become a democrat, as we saw in chapter 4.

15 Prominent ones who became nationalists were Vladimír Mináč, Roman Kaliský, and Pavol Števček.

16 See Dušan Hamšik, *Writers against Rulers* (London: Hutchinson and Co., 1971), p. 15.

17 Leff, *National Conflict in Czechoslovakia*, p. 268. In the mid-seventies there were again warnings about "bourgeois nationalism."

18 It was early for such recent history to have entered the textbooks. In general, the textbooks from the first republic were used during the 1945–48 period. Author's interview with PhDr. Kristína Gavalierová, July 18, 1995. Gavalierová was in the bibliography and information section of the Slovak Pedagogical Library, which is part of the Institute of Information and Prognosis for Youth and Education.

19 Steiner, *The Slovak Dilemma*, p. 90.

20 One example was a picture book called *Tragédia židov na Slovensku* that was never published. Also, a brochure by J. Laník called *Tomb of Six Million* came out during this period. Author's interview with Dr. Ivan Kamenec April 25, 1994. The Laník account was important beyond Slovakia. It was written by a refugee from Auschwitz and documented the murder mechanism at Auschwitz in great detail. The account by these refugees was presented to the allies as reason to bomb Auschwitz around the time of the deportation of the Hungarian Jews.

21 This was the case even in Israel but also in the United States and other countries where the process of memorializing could not happen until later; this delay had little to do with the state or politics. See Hannah Arendt, *Eichmann in Jerusalem* (New York: Penguin Books, 1977).

22 Economic enemies were attacked as former fascists as well as capitalists. Author's interview with Martin Kvetko, October, 1992.

23 Leff, *National Conflict in Czechoslovakia*, p. 168.

24 Ibid., p. 169.

25 Ibid., p. 169.

26 Steiner, *The Slovak Dilemma*, p. 96.

27 According to Paul Lendvai, who sees the source of the anti-Semitism of the purge period as coming directly from the Soviet Union, in spring 1951 Soviet advisers began to change the ideological basis of the alleged plot from "bourgeois nationalism to Zionism." In 1951, a special department was formed in the security services that dealt with "Zionism." See Lendvai, *Anti-Semitism without Jews*, pp. 251 and 256. He thinks it was likely that the use of anti-Semitism had less to do with foreign policy than anti-Semitism and politics inside the Soviet leadership. Lendvai cites accounts of Soviet torturers and their virulent anti-Semitism (pp. 253–54).

28 Quote from Lendvai, p. 256. He also points out that this was parallel to the rhetoric used in the Polish anti-Semitic witch hunts in 1968.

29 Leff, *National Conflict in Czechoslovakia*, p. 169.

30 Steiner, *The Slovak Dilemma*, p. 100; also see ibid., 167.

31 In Prague's Military Historical Institute and the Institute for the History of European Socialist Countries. In these institutes, more than half of the historians concentrated on the history of the twentieth century. In addition there was research being done at the Prague Institute for International Politics and Economics, at the universities, and at regional museums and state archives. For example, much of the work on the Slovak National Uprising was done at the Museum of the Uprising in Banská Bystrica. Karel Bartošek, "Czechoslovakia: The State of Historiography," *Journal of Contemporary History* 2, no. 1 (1967): 144–47.

32 The "habilitation" is roughly equivalent to the American Ph.D. See Maršina, "Slovenská Historiografia 1945–1990."

33 Author's interview with historian Herta Tkadlečková, March 3, 1994.

34 Tkadlečková, interview.

35 Ibid.

36 Author's interview with PhDr. Vladimír Michalička, CSc., at the Museum of Schools and Pedagogy at the Slovak Pedagogical Library in Bratislava, July 18, 1995.

37 Julius Alberty, "Problémy výučby dejepisu na školách," *Historický Časopis* 39, nos. 4–5 (1991): 513.

38 According to a 1982 government plan, 15.2 percent of students were supposed to go to general secondary schools or gymnazia; 23.2 percent to secondary trade schools, and 58.7 percent to workers/apprentice programs. Wolchik, *Czechoslovakia in Transition*, p. 207.

39 As in other communist countries, provisions were made to favor children of workers and peasants in admission to higher education. The workers' courses were established to accelerate the educational process and enable workers to go to university. See Robert Roško, "Z výskumu absolventov robotníckych kurzov," *Sociologia* 6, no. 2 (1974): 170–92.

40 Although it is not from this time period, we can get an idea of this type of text from a 1983 version: there is no mention even of the word *fascist* connected with the Slovak state; no mention of the Jews, and, in general, the World War II period is covered in a few paragraphs. *Dejepis pre 2. ročník stredných odborných škol a 1. ročník stredných odborných učilišt'* (Bratislava: Slovenské pedagogické nakladatel'stvo, 1983/1987). For this textbook, and each one below, the first date denotes when the education ministry approved the book and the second date indicates when the book came out.

41 Kristína Gavalierová, interview.

42 *Dejepis pre 11. postupný ročník všeobecnovzdelávacích škol* (Bratislava: Slovenské pedagogické nakladel'stvo, Passed 24 July 1957; published 1959). *Dejiny ČSR učebný text pre 9–11. postupný ročnik všeobecnovzdelávacích škol a pre pedagogické školy* (Bratislava: Slovenské pedagogické nakladel'stvo, passed October 1955, published 1956). Translations from school textbooks cited in this chapter are the author's.

43 Kruzliak, "A Quarter Century of Slovak Culture, 1945–1970," pp. 190–93.

44 This was true for the elites, who had a stake in Party ideology, as well as for the masses, who had less of a stake.

45 The atomization among the Party elite reached the highest levels: Klement Gottwald was convinced to sacrifice his "oldest comrade in arms," Slánský. See Lendvai, *Anti-Semitism without Jews*, p. 251.

46 Heda Kovály was the wife of Rudolf Margolius, who was convicted in the Slánský trial. Her memoir is called *Under a Cruel Star* (New York: Penguin Books, 1986).

47 Milan Hauner, "Recasting Czech History," *Survey* 24, no. 3 (1979): 220.

48 The Czechoslovak purge period was known as the most virulent in communist Eastern Europe. Ibid., p. 221.

49 Kaplan is cited in Lendvai, *Anti-Semitism without Jews*, p. 258.

50 H. Gordon Skilling, "Stalin over Prague," in Skilling, ed., *Communism National and International* (Toronto: University of Toronto Press, 1964), pp. 90–91.

51 Bartošek, *Czechoslovakia: The State of Historiography*, p. 149.

52 J. M. Kirschbaum, "Slovakia in the De-Stalinization and Federalization Process of Czechoslovakia," *Canadian Slavonic Papers* 10, no. 4 (1968): 551.

53 See Stanley Riveles, "Slovakia: Catalyst of Crisis," *Problems of Communism* 18, no. 3 (1968): 2.

54 In 1963, Slovak historians publicly called for reevaluation of the Uprising. Hauner, "Recasting Czech History," p. 222.

55 Riveles, "Slovakia: Catalyst of Crisis," p. 4.

56 Carole Leff does well at capturing the ways in which the debate in the Party during the 1960s represented continuity in Czech-Slovak relations, with its theme of betrayal.

57 Galia Golan, *Reform Rule in Czechoslovakia* (Cambridge: Cambridge University Press, 1973), p. 186.

58 Ibid., p. 186. Golan cites Bratislava TV, 20 March 1968.

59 Ibid., p. 190. This was a revision of the communist version of the Uprising.

60 Ibid., p. 195.

61 Ibid., p. 195. Števček was editor of the cultural weekly *Kultúrný Život* in 1955–69, during the liberal period. This weekly was the main arena for liberal discussion. He reemerged in 1989 as a nationalist and key member of "Korene," the organization of "nationalist intellegentsia." He was born in 1932 and received his Ph.D. in 1956. Whether or not his statement about the pervasiveness of the memory of the wartime state was true, it is interesting that the communist intellectuals made this argument.

62 Ibid., p. 195.

63 Ibid., p. 188.

64 See chapter 4 on this point.

65 Stanley Z. Pech, "Ferment in Czechoslovak Marxist Historiography," *Canadian Slavonic Papers* 10, no. 4 (1968): 518.

66 *Dejepis pre kurzy z učiva Základnej Devatročnej Školy* (Bratislava: Slovenské pedagogické nakladatel'stvo, passed 1959, published 1962, 2nd ed.); *Dejepis pre 2. ročník odborných škol* (Bratislava: Slovenské pedagogické nakladatel'stvo, passed 1960; published 1964, 4th ed.); *Dějepis pro 9. ročnik Základní Devítileté Školy* (Prague: Státní pedagogické nakladatelství; passed 1962, published 1963, henceforth the Czech book).

67 This book even gives numbers of deaths: five million at Auschwitz; at Terezín they killed people from seventeen countries; in some places there were gas chambers, in others crematoria. It goes on to say that the camps were not large enough to accommodate the hundreds of thousands of "democrats" from all of Europe, and that trains with prisoners went there "with thousands from Czechoslovakia." Czech book, pp. 102 and 112.

68 1960/64 book, pp. 309–10. Though it is part of a paragraph about the general terror and attack on culture and Nazification of culture.

69 Ibid., p. 307.

70 The Western imperialists are also blamed for sacrificing Czechoslovakia to the Nazis, since the Western powers thought the Nazis would take on and defeat the Soviets. Ibid., p. 333.

71 1960/64 book, pp. 321, 322, and 323. Interestingly, there is a line that says that the Czechs did not fall under the influence of fascism because of democratic traditions and the activities of the Communist Party.

72 1959/62 book, p. 324. Overall the Germans controlled everything, the economy, government, army, police. 1960/64 book, p. 335.

73 1960/64 book, p. 341.

74 According to the Czech book, the fascists and clergy "spread hatred for other peoples and for communists" (p. 104).

75 1960/64 book, pp. 333–34.

76 Ibid., p. 335.

77 1959/62 book.

78 1959/62 book, p. 324.

79 1960/64 book, p. 355.

80 Czech book, p. 102.

81 1959/62 book, pp. 331–32.

82 1960/64, p. 361.

83 1959/62 book.

84 1959/62 book, p. 334; 1960/64 book, p. 359.

85 1959/62 book, p. 334.

86 Interestingly, in the 1959/62 book there is also mention that the Slovak resistance also "aided the popular liberation struggle in the Czech lands."

87 List provided to author by Vilém Kratochvíl, Comenius University.

88 The discussion below is based on an English translation of the book: Rudolf Jašík, *St. Elizabeth's Square,* translated by Margot Schierl (Prague: Artia, 1964).

89 *Shop on Mainstreet* was a movie version of a book of the same name, published in 1965 by Slovak author Ladislav Grosman. Even though the movie received international acclaim, the regime banned it after 1968, partially due to the main actor's political activities.

90 Soňa Szomolányiová and Herta Tkadlečková were only two of the many people who told me this.

91 The hoisting of the white flag was the common practice during the deportations. See Kamenec, "The Deportation of Jewish Citizens from Slovakia in 1942," in *The Tragedy of Slovak Jews,* p. 93.

92 For example, novels by the Czech author Arnošt Lustig.

93 Other books on the topic came out in emigration; see chapter 4.

94 Obviously the fact that there were so few Jews left was one element of this. Also, Jews have in certain cases, like in Austria, participated in the silencing of discussion about responsibility for the Jewish deportations because they wanted to integrate themselves into Austrian life.

95 See Ken Jowitt, *New World Disorder,* chaps. 3 and 4.

96 Pech points out how unusual it was when the 1963 Barnabite commission was set up to investigate the purges. For the first time the regime asked experts, historians, and other scholars to get involved in the policy making process. Pech, "Ferment in Czechoslovak Marxist Historiography," p. 511.

97 The purges have been covered extensively elsewhere. See, for example, Vladimír V. Kusín, from *Dubček to Charter 77* (Edinburgh: Q Press Ltd., 1978).

98 Even non-Jewish reformers were alleged to be Jews. See Lendvai, *Anti-Semitism without Jews,* pp. 260–97.

99 Hauner, "Recasting Czech History," p. 214.

100 This was especially true in the economy. See Wolchik, *Czechoslovakia in Transition,* p. 62.

101 Alberty, "Problémy výučby dejepisu na školách."

102 In a major educational reform begun in 1976, and not finished until the mid-1980s, the attempt was made to reform the school system to coincide with the "scientific technical revolution." More funding was allocated for technical universities. In addition, often students chose technical education, since the humanities and social sciences were so infused with ideology. Vladimír Michalička, interview. Also see Wolchik on technical education as the preferred educational pathway for the elite.

103 *Dejepis pre 3. ročník gymnázia* (Bratislava: Slovenské pedagogické nakladateľstvo, passed 1986; published 1987).

104 Ibid., pp. 111–12.

105 Ibid., p. 126.

106 Ibid., p. 153.

107 Ibid., p. 126.

108 Ibid., p. 127.

109 Ibid., p. 128.

110 Ibid., p. 129.

111 Ibid., p. 162.

112 Tkadlečková, interview; author's interview with Vilém Kratochvíl, April 1994.

113 Florian Sivák and Jozef Klimko, *Dejiny štátu a práva na území ČSSR* (Vysokoškolské Skripta, Právnická fakulta Univerzita Komenského, 1976), pp. 152–65. See especially, pp. 155, 156, 164.

114 See Maršina, "Slovenská Historiografia."

115 H. Gordon Skilling, "The Muse of History—1984: History, Historians, and Politics in Communist Czechoslovakia."

116 The 1960s in the United States is a good parallel. Some people's values and lifestyles were shaped in a lasting way. Many were caught up in it as a fad and were not affected in any fundamental sense except that they might have read what was in fashion, said what was in fashion, or remember where they were when important events took place.

117 They were, in many ways, tainted by the normalization period, in the sense that they could be manipulated in the postcommunist period on the threat that their pasts be exposed.

118 Czechs resented Slovaks for having benefited from Husák's tenure as Party secretary and his seeming willingness to punish fellow advocates of Slovak autonomy less harshly than advocates of democracy.

119 Though one could argue that economic issues were sometimes seen in nationalist terms, Hvezdon Koctúch, for example, a key economist in the reform communist group (born 1929) was active, in the post-1989 period, in Matica Slovenská.

120 The reform communist cohort fit the mass-elite in another way as well, as we will see in chapter 6. As Soňa Szomolányiová points out, even if they were removed from the Party after 1968, they were still communists and knew how to operate in an environment where opportunism and manipulation was the favored strategy for political survival. See Soňa Szomolányiová, "The Formation of the Political Elites in Slovakia," in *Eastern Central Europe 2000* (Bratislava, 1993), pp. 33–39.

121 Milan Šimečka, *The Restoration of Order: The Normalization of Czechoslovakia, 1969–1976* (London: Verso, 1984), pp. 15–16.

122 Even given her argument, she is somewhat skeptical about the lasting impact of the 1960s on elite identity. She points out that the normalization period was devastating. Whereas the purges of the 1950s, after less than ten years had led to the reform movement of the 1960s, twenty years or more passed between the late 1960s and the late 1980s, time enough for the passing of a political generation. Leff, *National Conflict in Czechoslovakia*, p. 263.

123 See Archie Brown and Gordon Wightman, "Czechoslovakia: Revival and Retreat," in Archie Brown and Jack Gray, eds., *Political Culture and Political Change in Communist Studies* (New York: Holmes and Meier, 1979).

6 Nationalism without Nationalists? Democracy without Democrats?

1 Transitions from authoritarianism hinge on bringing former authoritarian elites into a new government and convincing them to participate in elections. It requires persuading them to join a single political game. See Giuseppe Di Palma, *To Craft Democracies* (Berkeley: University of California Press, 1990).

2 With the collapse of the Communist Party, the groups whose interests might have been predictable did not remain intact and it was not clear what would be important in the new environment. (Even if these groups remained intact, i.e., the military, it was not clear how and whether their interests would transfer to the new environment.) For relative importance of group identifications see Terry Lynn Karl and Phillipe Schmitter, "Modes of Transition in Latin America, Southern Europe, and Eastern Europe," *International Social Science Journal* 128 (May 1991): 269–84.

3 What is important is the extent to which economic interests were translated into identifiable interest groups and parties. Several analysts have noted that even many years into the transition, parties remain unconnected to a social base and ideologically vague, in spite of the fact that there are clear losers of

economic reform. This is especially noteworthy in the Russian case. See Stephen Hanson and Jeffrey Kopstein, "The Weimar/Russia Comparison," *Post-Soviet Affairs* 13, no. 3 (1997): 271–75. For a fascinating study of why what should be economic interests (in this instance of workers) did not take politically significant forms in the postcommunist context, see Carole Timko, "Weakness in Numbers" (Ph.D. diss., University of California, Berkeley, 1997) on the Polish case. The one place an active labor movement should have developed was Poland, given Solidarity's legacy. But it did not.

4 I use the word *revolution* here to refer to the set of events that led to the collapse of communism in November 1989. While *revolution* suggests more intentionality on the part of the "democrats" than was the case, and the collapse of communism was due mostly to the changes in the Soviet Union, I use this word as shorthand.

5 While the World War II past was the clear dividing line, the First Republic also raised conflicting legacies for these groups: the prefascist party of Andrej Hlinka, a Catholic nationalist who fought for Slovak rights first against the Hungarians and then against "Prague centrism," was also controversial.

6 The five were Ján Čarnogurský, Hana Ponická, Miroslav Kusý, Anton Selecký, and Manák.

7 See *Lidová Demokracie,* May 23, 1990, p. 3, in FBIS-EEU-90-106, p. 15.

8 Ondrej Sýkora, who became a member of the first presidency of KDH and was active in the Lutheran Church during the communist period, was himself suspicious of KDH. While he happened to know others of its founders from his workplace, he did not know Čarnogurský and felt it necessary to determine Čarnogurský's position on the fascist past before getting involved. This is another example of the separation of the opposition networks from one another. Author's interview with Sýkora, March 26, 1994.

9 Sýkora, interview; author's interview with Čarnogurský, fall 1992.

10 Yeshayahu Jelinek, "Slovaks and the Holocaust: An End to Reconciliation?" *East European Jewish Affairs* 22, no. 1 (1992): 9.

11 Sýkora, interview. See chapter 4 for an elaboration of this position.

12 Sýkora reported that Ján Čarnogurský told him that he did not agree with his father but could not stop him. Sýkora, interview.

13 From the beginning, a moderating force for this party was its ties to the organizational and ideological network of Christian Democratic parties in Europe.

14 Sýkora, interview; author's interview with Igor Uhrík, spring 1994. The émigrés were kept from speaking in the formal part of the program but did speak later in the day.

15 Milan Žitný, a journalist and active figure in VPN, said that KDH already in January talked about Slovak independence, and at the founding meeting delegates showed that they saw the former Slovak state as a legitimating myth. He used the term "l'udáci" to refer to these people and said they scared both the democratic intellectuals and the former communists. Author's interview with Žitný, April 7, 1994.

16 By 1994 this organization had become extremely nationalist, as was evident in this author's interview with its head, Július Porubský, spring 1994.

17 While VPN had been the leading political force since the revolution, polls in the

spring of 1990 showed KDH with 26–29 percent support and VPN with only 10–14 percent. Polls can be found in ČTK 24 April 1990, in FBIS-EEU-90-080 and ČTK 22 May, 1990 in FBIS-EEU-90-101.

18 VPN activists Miloš Žiak, Martin Bútora, and Soňa Szomolányiová told me this in interviews. Szomolányiová said that her pre-election speeches focused on this. This point was also made by Sýkora in an interview.

19 Prague Domestic Service June 2, 1990 in FBIS-EEU-90-105, p. 25.

20 Several VPN activists and one important member of KDH told me pieces of this story. On general divides between VPN and KDH, see Vladimír Ondruš, "Slovensko, na moj povel . . . Part II," *Slovenský Dennik,* October 11, 1993, p. 3. Ondruš was deputy premier of the Slovak government from 1989 to 1991 and member of the Slovak parliament from 1990 to 1992 for VPN. Bútora, in an interview with this author, said fears of "ghosts of the past" led to the invitation to Dubček. Also Žitný, interview.

21 Šimečka from the beginning was concerned with equal partnership with the Czechs and had the ability to negotiate with them. It was a real loss when he died in the summer of 1990; Dubček died in fall 1992.

22 Author's interview with Miloš Žiak March 25, 1994. Dubček agreed to be candidate for VPN at meeting of Slovak assembly of VPN reported in Prague Domestic Service, March 24, 1990, in FBIS-EEU-90-058, pp. 16–17.

23 Žiak, March 25, 1994 and July 16, 1993 interviews.

24 For example see commentary by Július Sluka, former *Pravda* staff journalist, who blames the new leadership for an incident that occurred when university students cheered a speech by a "former member of the parliament of the wartime Slovak state" [probably Pavol Čarnogurský] and for equating Stalin with Hitler in the posters of the "gentle revolution." *Bratislava Pravda,* January 10, 1990, p. 3, in FBIS-EEU-90-011, p. 24. Also see statement by the Bratislava city committee of the Antifascist Fighters Union, which says that they protest the "steadily increasing number of publications, the aim of which is to rehabilitate the former clerico-fascist regime in Slovakia and its main representative, Dr. Jozef Tiso." The article demands that such publications be banned. The Antifascist Fighters Union was still very much intertwined with the Communist Party at that time. *Bratislava Pravda,* April 3, 1990, in FBIS-EEU-90-066, p. 21.

25 As Soňa Szomolányiová points out, the reform communists gave VPN name recognition. Also contributing to VPN's popularity were people who had recently been in communist structures but were involved in the caretaker government. Milan Čič, whose popularity rating in March was about the same as Dubček's, is an example. It was these same candidates who followed Mečiar and again won in 1992, suggesting a fair amount of continuity. Soňa Szomolányiová, "The Formation of Political Elites," in *Eastern Central Europe 2000* (Bratislava, 1993), pp. 34–35. Once these candidates joined the VPN lists, the numbers in the polls changed. As opposed to polls cited earlier showing KDH leading, in the final poll going into the election VPN's support was back up. The data was broken down for the different parliaments: Slovak National Council: VPN 26.1; KDH, 18.0; CPCZ (Communist Party) 12.1; SNS (Slovak National Party) 8.7; Federal Parliament: House of Nations: VPN 25.6; KDH 19.9; CPCZ 12.2; SNS 10.4; House of People: VPN 25.5; KDH 18.3; CPCZ 12.1; SNS 8.6. Poll by Method-

ological Research Commission of Slovak Radio May 30–31, 1990. Reported in *Verejnost'*, June 1, 1990, in FBIS-EEU-90-110.

26 According to Vladimír Ondruš, Budaj proposed an open competition for the position of interior minister. Dubček proposed Mečiar for this post. See Ondruš, "Slovensko, na moj povel," part 6, *Slovenský Denník*, November 8, 1993, p. 3.

27 The other candidates were Miroslav Kusý and Slavomír Stračar. Mečiar was chosen because of his energy, his ability to speak well, his experience in the caretaker government, and because he was acceptable to the coalition partners. Ondruš links the fact that these three were possibilities to the fact that many VPN activists withdrew from candidacy. Vladimír Ondruš, "Slovensko, na moj povel . . . ," part II, *Slovenský Dennik*, October 11, 1993, p. 3.

28 Žitný, interview. He was seen as an energetic politician and a good speaker, and this was also why he was chosen from three candidates for prime minister.

29 "While learning democracy we must not forget that responsibility is its constituent part." *Bratislava Pravda*, 25 January, 1990, p. 1, in FBIS-EEU-90-022, p. 24; we will see his position on anti-Hungarian activities below.

30 A manifesto from Obroda was published on December 1, 1989 in *Rudé Právo*, translated in FBIS-EEU-89-242, p. 43. The Democratic Socialist Party, set up at the end of November, lasted for about three months and was comprised of 1968 communists, including the controversial leader of the party Igor Cibula, as well as Jan Uher, Ivan Laluha, Ladislav Ťažký, Ján Sekaj, and Mečiar. In March Dubček joined VPN and this group disappeared from the political scene. Miloš Žiak, interview.

31 Kusý also expressed this view in this author's spring 1994 interview with him. Above quote from Kusý interview of November 24, 1989 with *Vienna Wochenpresse* in FBIS, December 1, 1989, p. 42.

32 Dubček is an example of someone known by reputation; Laluha was known through the professional network of sociologists working on a prognosis for Czechoslovak society.

33 A lot of the suspicions focused on Igor Cibula, who was said to be head of security during the 1968 period and emerged first as founder of the Democratic Socialist Party just mentioned. Cibula was an example of a mass-elite surveying the scene, guessing where to go, then changing when it became clearer where power would be. He became leader of the first party to be established in postcommunist Slovakia. But that party's prospects began to wane. Aside from Dubček's departure to VPN, this was indicated by Cibula's reported complaint on February 19 that his party was excluded from the roundtable talks on newsprint. See *Bratislava Pravda*, February 19, 1990, p. 2, in FBIS-EEU-90-037, p. 20. Cibula resigned as chairman of the Democratic Socialist Party in April, saying that he had instead accepted a position as deputy chief editor of the newly revived daily newspaper *Národná Obroda*. *Národná Obroda* had operated in the 1945–48 period. There he became a major voice articulating the new idiom of the Mečiar group. Resignation reported in *Bratislava Pravda*, April 13, 1990, p. 4, in FBIS-EEU-90-076, p. 15.

34 Roman Kaliský is an example of a key figure from 1968 whose leanings in the post-1989 period were difficult to predict. He was appointed to head the fed-

eral press and information office. It turned out that Kaliský became a strong nationalist voice. Ladislav Ťažký was linked to Obroda but also to the newly constituted Writers Union and the board of Matica Slovenská.

35 Peter Zajac, interview. Zajac, a VPN ideologist, went back to the literature institute after the 1990 elections.

36 As Soňa Szomolányiová points out, they were regarded as natural allies, and politicians recommended by the Obroda club naturally became a further substantial resource; their ties to one another were based on networks built in the communist youth organization in the 1950s or in the reform movement of the 1960s. Szomolanyiová, "The Formation of Political Elites," p. 36.

37 He also would have been at an advantage because he knew who the unknown political forces really were since they registered with the ministry. He knew more about who was who than did the ideological elites. They could have known more but chose to give him the position of interior minister.

38 Some of the 1968 communists did have commitments and followed Mečiar because of his increasing nationalism. However, they were the minority and were co-opted by Mečiar, who could use their ideas and 1968 reputations. It is difficult to find evidence that these people followed Mečiar because they knew that he could reveal their collaborationist pasts; however, many maintain that this was a key factor driving the alliance with Mečiar.

39 Most treatments of these problems have been from the perspective of whether or not it is possible to design an approach that is just and does not undermine the principles of democracy. *The Haunted Land* by journalist Tina Rosenberg took this approach (New York: Random House, 1995). Here I look instead at the practical problems posed by the attempt to come to terms with the communist past, which have been underemphasized.

40 Václav Havel speech to the Federal Assembly, January 23, 1990, in FBIS-EEU-90-019, p. 22.

41 According to one report, the Party still controlled 90 percent of newspapers and periodicals. See Prague Domestic Service February 2, 1990, in FBIS-EEU-90-024, p. 28.

42 The CPCZ report to their new congress said that the new leadership of the CPCZ identifies fully with the "inspiration sources of Prague Spring." Bratislava Domestic Service December 5, 1989, in FBIS 12/6/89.

43 Ján Čarnogurský in *Bratislava Pravda,* December 29, 1989, p. 2, in FBIS-EEU-90-007, 1/10/90, p. 40. Also, Petr Pithart, after becoming Czech premier, said: "The motives which people had for joining the CPCZ were so diverse that naturally the motives for their leaving it, too, are diverse. I would not like to judge in those matters." Interview with *Rudé Právo,* February 2, 1990, in FBIS-EEU-90-027, p. 26.

44 This has always been a problem for revolutionaries. V. I. Lenin faced this same dilemma in 1918.

45 Čič said his decision did not arise from careerism. He said this choice would enable him to be an effective leader through the complicated election period. He stood for the June elections on VPN's list. Prague TV, March 11, 1990, in FBIS-EEU-90-048, p. 16.

46 Interestingly, many of these people broke off and followed Mečiar later. Sýkora

spoke of KDH's decision to bring in experts without regard to personal knowledge of their political commitments. He also pointed out that overall those experts chose to join the wing of KDH that followed Mečiar in the spring of 1992. This is consistent with the argument here: not being ideological elites, they tended to want to follow a winner and preserve their personal positions. Sýkora, interview.

47 *Lidová Demokracie,* December 4, 1989, p. 4 in FBIS-EEU-89-242, p. 35.

48 *Mladá Fronta,* December 12, 1989, in FBIS-EEU-90, 1/3/90, p. 33.

49 Report from Civic Forum in Prague Domestic Service, FBIS December 1, 1989, p. 36.

50 The continuing list of incidents suggesting foul play included: allegations about the activities of former presidium member Vasil Biľák; the claim that bugging devices were found in the homes of several Civic Forum leaders. Most often dark forces were alleged to be trying to split and cause discord among the democratic forces. One scandal was called "operation wedge."

51 Sacher was from the People's Party, a traditionally Catholic party but also a communist satellite party. Sacher's leaks of information about Oldřich Hromádko, a senior Civic Forum official, and one of Sacher's most vocal critics, were seen as a campaign tactic. At the time the People's Party was attracting much of the Christian democratic vote. Other allegations against Sacher were his protection of General Alojz Lorenz, a deputy internal affairs minister from the previous regime, and the fact that after firing StB officers he kept them on the payroll for another six months. See Tim D. Whipple, ed., *After the Velvet Revolution* (New York: Freedom House, 1991), pp. 49–51.

52 Budaj made this statement soon after anti-Semitic and anti-Hungarian slogans had appeared in Bratislava. Statement broadcast by Bratislava Domestic Service, February 14, 1990, in FBIS-EEU-90-033, p. 27–28.

53 Prague Domestic Service, 12 January 1990 in FBIS-EEU-90-0010, p. 44.

54 See Havel's statement at a rally organized by VPN condemning the principle of collective guilt. ČTK, May 16, 1990, in FBIS-EEU-90-096, p. 14.

55 According to one commentator, as of the end of April, four fifths of the people listed in the nomenklatura still held their posts and hardly any members of OF or VPN were directors in enterprises. *Lidový Noviny,* in FBIS-EEU-90-087, 5/4/90, pp. 26–27.

56 The parties requested this. Interior Ministry statement, in ČTK, May 25, 1990, in FBIS-EEU-90-103, p. 14.

57 The Slovak National Party was not listed with the parties who decided to screen but later claimed to have gone through the screening with no casualties. For the list of parties planning to screen see Prague Domestic Service, June 5, 1990, in FBIS-EEU-90-110, p. 18; for SNS claim see FBIS 6/20/90, p. 12.

58 The law was designed to formalize a process that had been going on informally since the revolution. Those deemed collaborators were banned for five years from holding elected or appointed public or professional positions in state organizations; or in joint-stock companies in which the state held a majority of the capital. They were also banned from top positions in universities. They included members of the people's militia and students in KGB schools; "con-

scious collaborators" who were registered as "trustees" or "candidates for secret collaboration"; Communist Party functionaries from the township level up, except for those who served from January 1, 1968 to May 1, 1969. Collaborators fell into the following categories: agents, informers, and owners of "conspiratorial apartments." See Paula Bren, "Lustration in the Czech and Slovak Republics," *RFE/RL Research Report* 2, no. 29 (1993): 17, and Jozef Darski, "Police Agents in the Transition Period," *Uncaptive Minds,* no. 4 (winter 1991–92): 25.

59 Interior Ministry statement in ČTK, May 25, 1990, in FBIS-EEU-90-103, p. 14.

60 These problems are well covered in Rosenberg's *Haunted Land,* pp. 69–70; also see Lawrence Weschler, "The Velvet Purge: The Trials of Jan Kavan," *New Yorker,* October 19, 1992.

61 The Ministry of the Interior did not keep a separate file containing only collaborators of the former StB. Materials were not kept in one workplace but in various districts and various ministry archives. Interior Ministry statement of May 25, 1990.

62 "The Interior Ministry on investigation" in *Lidová Demokracie,* May 26, 1990, pp. 1, 3, FBIS-EEU-90-105, p. 17.

63 There was disagreement about this between VPN leaders like Miroslav Kusý and Petr Uhl, a Czech who was a member of the Committee for the Protection of the Unjustly Persecuted, who said that it was possible to distinguish in the files between opponents of the regime and collaborators. ČTK, June 10, 1990, in FBIS-EEU-90-113, p. 22.

64 It was an anomalous communist successor organization, that is, it had resources because it had existed under communism; at the same time it had legitimacy because of its historical role and reputation.

65 For background on Matica Slovenská see *Tri roky: Obnovenej členskey základne Matice Slovenskej 1990–92* (Liptovský Mikuláš: Vydala Matica Slovenská, 1994). Also, Stanislav Bajaník, "Matica, po valnom zhromáždení II," and Augustin Matovčík, "Osud zviazaný's Maticou" in *Literárný Týždennik,* October 17, 1992.

66 *Smena,* March 29, 1990, p. 2, in FBIS-EEU-90-048, p. 25.

67 Zajac, interview; author's interviews with David Daniel, October 20, 1992 and spring 1994.

68 Viliam Gruška, head of Matica before August 1990, was uncomfortable with the political wing and this was the reason he left the post. Zajac, interview; Daniel, interviews.

69 He was on the central committee of the Communist Party until the revolution; he was active in the national movement during the 1960s but then, when normalization came, followed Husák and stayed in the good graces of the regime rather than adhering to the ideology he had previously advocated. His biography was similar in this regard to Husák's.

70 He was appointed Slovak deputy prime minister, on December 12. See Bratislava Domestic Service, December 12, 1989, in FBIS-EEU-89-240, p. 31. He briefly stood in as minister of culture. See Bratislava Domestic Service, February 28, 1990, in FBIS-EEU-090-041, p. 18. On January 18 it was announced that

Markuš became chairman of the government national economic council for drafting and implementing state economic policy. See Bratislava Domestic Service, January 18, 1990, in FBIS-EEU-90-017, p. 37.

71 Zajac, interview; Gál, interview.

72 He had alienated the people he worked with in the caretaker government and therefore no longer had support from VPN. He applied instead to KDH. The policy at the time, before a lustration law was passed, was that appointees to government offices would be screened and if found to have collaboration in their past could remove themselves voluntarily, without the information being made public. See Ondruš, "Slovensko, na moj povel . . . part III," in *Slovenský Dennik,* October 18, 1993, p. 3.

73 Zajac, interview.

74 As deputy prime minister he addressed the constituent assembly of the national union of Slovaks, an émigré organization, and talked about a "return [of] Slovaks living outside the historical Slovak territory to the national womb." *Bratislava Pravda,* January 22, 1990, p. 2, in FBIS-EEU-90-017, p. 40. He also visited with émigrés in the U.S. and Canada on a trip sponsored by the World Congress of Slovaks in spring 1990. See Ondruš, part III, p. 3.

75 Interestingly, his brother, Štefan Markuš, remained in the democratic camp. The democrats claim that Markuš did not have any nationalism in his past; the leader of the Štúr Society, Vladimír Repka, claims that he did. Repka said that the fact that Markuš came from a family of ethnic Slovaks from Hungary motivated him to be concerned about the preservation of Slovak culture, especially in the face of Hungarian pressures for assimilation. Author's interview with Repka, April 26, 1994.

76 This law would have made Slovak the official language even in Hungarian areas. For an example of the complaints the democrats began to have about Matica, see the declaration issued in objection to the language law and other extremist behavior, which says: "Matica Slovenská once represented the true interests of the Slovak people. Today we ask with uneasiness if some of their leaders realize the results of hidden and open support by parties and movements which under the slogan 'for the nation' are taking Slovakia in reality against the nation to economic disaster, international isolation, the breakup of the Czech and Slovak republic and the emergence of a wave of violence and hatred." "Občania Slovenská!" in *Kultúrny Život* 24, no. 29 (1990): 1.

77 Ondruš points to the fact that Matica was "a state-financed cultural institution with a mass membership, tradition, a good name, equipment, and publications." But, Ondruš complains, Markuš used this for his own ends to begin an aggressive campaign for a language law instead of trying to work on improving the teaching of Slovak, or other educational or cultural goals. See Ondruš, part III.

78 In an example of another common objection to the screening policy that left open the question of who was responsible for the policy going wrong, Markuš said of allegations about his past, "The current vetting campaign is an attempt by the actual State Security collaborators to compromise the irksome people— even defying all human rights guarantees in the process." In *Smena,* March 23, 1991, pp. 1–2, in FBIS-EEU-91-059, p. 18.

79 Jan Budaj and Milan Kňažko are generally seen as the ones who pushed this.

80 They were from the normalization generation and even less tied in than the Mečiar group, which had connections through reform communism and through state positions that they stayed in after 1989.

81 In the June elections the SNS won 13.94 percent of the popular vote and fifteen seats in the federal parliament and twenty-two seats in the Slovak National Council. See Jan Obrman, "Civic Forum Surges to Impressive Victory in Elections," in *RFE Report on Eastern Europe,* June 22, 1990, pp. 113–16. With regard to the local elections, there are a number of different readings of the level of SNS success. SNS was cited as having 21 percent support in mid-October 1990 in an article by analysts at the Center for Social Analysis who do public opinion surveys. See Zora Bútorová and Tatiana Rosová, "The Slovak National Party: Myths, Rituals, Devotees," *Respekt* 381 (1990). On first glance they did poorly in the local elections, getting only 3.3 percent of municipal assembly seats. However, if the number of electoral districts in which they ran candidates (4 percent) is taken into account, they did very well, winning 41 percent of the municipal council seats they actually contested. See Jiří Pehe, "Growing Slovak Demands Seen as Threat to Federation," in *RFE Report on Eastern Europe,* March 22, 1991, pp. 1–10.

82 With the possible exception of Anton Hrnko.

83 They came from a shadowy group around an unknown figure named Marian Andel. They also had ties to the grouping of young nationalists called the Štúr Society.

84 This was in contrast to several parties that did have actual continuity with precommunist parties. In addition to KDH having links to Catholic nationalism, the Democratic Party had links to its roots in the 1945–48 period, as represented by their choice of chairman, Martin Kvetko, who was a member of the earlier party. Obroda had some links to 1968. The Czech social democrats also had continuity with their earlier incarnation.

85 He says that he quit the Communist Party in December 1989. He was the only historian from that institute to go into politics.

86 There is certainly evidence of his feelings on these issues from early 1990. See response to interview with Čalfa, "Uprímnost' nadovšetko," *Literárný Týždenník* 3 (January 1990), p. 4.

87 Author's interviews with Hrnko, December 1992 and April 19, 1994. He said the TV program was on January 31, 1990.

88 Several members of VPN told me this.

89 He was chosen as chairman of the independent trade union on March 2 and resigned at the beginning of April. See *Práce,* March 2, 1990, pp. 1–2, in FBIS-EEU-90-046, p. 20–21, and *Práce,* April 10, 1990, in FBIS-EEU 90-074, p. 15.

90 Author's interview with Prokeš, December 1992.

91 Author's interview with Miškovský, May 1994. Other important figures in SNS were Andel, a teacher; Stanislav Pánis, who we will see in the next chapter led efforts to celebrate the fascist state; and V. Moric. Rumor had it that SNS was initiated by the former central committee of the Communist Party.

92 The émigrés had been present from the first days of the revolution and appeared on the stage at the rallies organized by VPN. Their work began to appear in *Literárný Týždenník* and other publications.

93 Several people commented on Slovak National Party's reputation: particularly other nationalists saying it was not sufficiently intellectual or morally oriented. Repka, interview; author's interview with Peter Brňák, April 15, 1994.

94 Author's interview with Igor Uhrík, April 26, 1994.

95 The more successful ones acted on their own; the Slovak League decided not to get involved in politics formally as an organization. Uhrík, interview.

96 In interviews with this author, František Šebej of VPN (November 6, 1992) and Vladimír Repka of Matica Slovenská and the Štúr Society both, in different ways, said the same thing.

97 *Zemědělské Noviny,* May 11, 1990, p. 2, in FBIS-EEU 90-097, p. 10.

98 See Bútorová and Rosová, "The Slovak National Party: Myths, Rituals, Devotees," p. 33.

99 For example, they gave aid in the form of fax machines, telephones, and copiers. According to Hrnko, for the election they gave $5–10,000. Other émigrés funded the more extremist nationalist press.

100 While Hrnko claimed that the Slovak state was not part of his party's legacy, in an article from March 1990, he provocatively brought up the economic prosperity of Slovakia during the war as opposed to the Czech republic's valueless currency as a protectorate. "Nehoráznost' na pokračovanie" in *Smena,* March 22, 1990, p. 1.

101 Uhrík, interview. He did not say this, however, until much later, after independence was achieved and many former Mečiar allies had grown disillusioned with Mečiar.

102 See Janusz Bugajski, ed., *Ethnic Politics in Eastern Europe* (Armonk, N.Y.: M. E. Sharpe, 1994, 1995), p. 345.

103 *Bratislava Pravda,* December 29, 1989, p. 2, in FBIS-EEU-90-002, p. 36. They also had a historical claim from World War II: that Hungarians deemed fascist collaborators be rehabilitated.

104 Established during the last years of communism, they had existed under the rubric of Matica and had invited people from Matica Slovenská to educate them about their national heritage. The Štúr Society also had a link to what had been the Democratic Party between 1945 and 1948 and became a communist front party after 1948.

105 Regarding the leanings of *Nový Slovák,* see Yeshayahu Jelinek, "Slovaks and the Holocaust: An End to Reconciliation?" p. 12. Jelinek cites an anti-Semitic article attacking Fedor Gál, leader of VPN. This was from a later period, but the paper was founded in 1990. Jelinek also points out that its name was a reference to the HSLS newspaper called *Slovák.*

106 Repka, interview. By 1994 Repka had become head of the office for contacts with foreign Slovaks at Matica Slovenská. His position on Tiso, whose picture he had on the wall of his office, was also ambiguous. While he said he did not want to look backward to that state, he maintained that nevertheless Tiso was the president of the first Slovak state and deserved honor for that reason.

107 *Večerník,* January 8, 1990, p. 2, in FBIS-EEU-90-016, p. 29.

108 *Rolnické Noviny,* January 5, 1990, p. 3, in FBIS-EEU-90-016, p. 29.

109 For example in FBIS-EEU-90-031, 2/14/90, p. 24.

110   Čič address to the government on minority rights in *Bratislava Pravda,* March 6, 1990, p. 4, in FBIS-EEU-90-048, pp. 16–19.

111   Later Budaj had to take himself off VPN's election list after being deemed a collaborator through the screening process (see chapter 7 for details). Some of the same people who had condemned him in February 1990 later took up his cause, arguing that the Czechs knew about his record ahead of time and pursued the issue after the election because they thought Budaj was too nationalistic. The link to the Czechs was made by Juraj Mihalík in an interview with this author, October 13, 1992.

112   Štúr Society statement in *Smena,* March 12, 1990, pp. 2, 3, in FBIS-EEU-90-053, p. 28.

113   Ibid.

114   See statements by Mečiar and Čič in Bratislava Domestic Service, March 14, 1990, in FBIS-EEU-90-051, pp. 16–17.

115   Sýkora, interview.

116   Miškovský, interview. See also Miroslav Pekník, "Bola to šanca pre Slovensko," *Literárny Týždenník,* June 6, 1992, pp. 12–13.

117   A proposed name—"The Czech and Slovak Federal Republic"—was one of ten points in their initial program of February 28. This name was close to the final choice, made after much debate. See "Introducing the Slovak National Party," in *Smena,* February 28, 1990, pp. 2, 3 in FBIS-EEU-90-045, p. 27.

118   The Civic Forum and VPN proposed a reintroduction of state emblem of 1920 as early as December. See *Bratislava Pravda,* December 13, 1989, p. 2, in FBIS-EEU-89-242.

119   Prague Domestic Service January 23, 1990, in FBIS-EEU-90-019, p. 20.

120   See "Odlišný názor jazykovedcov," in *Smena,* March 3, 1990, and "Výzva slovenským poslancom vo Federálnom zhromáždení," in *Smena* March 14, 1990.

121   "Hladovka za rovnoprávnost'," in *Smena,* March 23, 1990, p. 1.

122   Anton Hrnko, "Nehoráznost na pokračovanie," in *Smena,* March 22, 1990, p. 1.

123   As Ján Čarnogurský points out, while *czecho-slovakia* with the hyphen was the reference used in the Pittsburgh agreement of 1918 and appears in the international treaties signed in Paris at the end of World War I, it also became the country's legal name in October 1938 after the Munich agreement and lasted until March 1939 with the declaration of the Slovak state. Ján Čarnogurský, "Physics, Psychology, and the Gentle Revolution," in Tim D. Whipple, ed., *After the Revolution,* pp. 111–12.

124   ČTK, March 29, 1990, in FBIS-EEU-90-062, p. 22.

125   ČTK, March 30, 1990, in FBIS-EEU-90-063.

126   Uhrík, interview. See also "Do Europy pod vlastným menom," an interview with Uhrík on Slovak TV, reprinted in *Smena,* February 16, 1990.

127   See, for example, Slovak Prime Minister Čič's discussion with representatives of the Heavy Engineering Works Combine in which he agrees that "the federal government decided on a more radical conversion" than expected and "did not decide on a fair socioeconomic solution to the consequences." *Bratislava Pravda,* February 19, 1990, in FBIS-EEU-90-037, p. 12.

128 Hrnko, interview.

129 Sýkora, interview. He said that at the first KDH council many wanted the hyphen, while Čarnogurský advocated a compromise solution.

130 Čarnogurský, interview; Pekník, "Bolo to šanca."

131 Reported by ČTK, April 2, 1990, in FBIS-EEU-90-064, p. 18.

132 Ján Budaj and Roman Zelenay, both of whom later followed Mečiar, made statements with more nationalist content: "Majme zapálené srdcia, ale chladné hlavy," in *Smena*, March 31, 1990, p. 2.

133 Soňa Szomolanyiová, interview; Martin Bútora, interview. Author's interview with Michal Žantovský, August 18, 1993.

134 I deliberately underplay the negotiations over the future setup of the state in favor of the symbolic side of the divide between the ideological elites. Obviously both were issues. Proposals for greater Slovak autonomy coming from the KDH would not have seemed as threatening had that party not represented continuity with the fascist Slovak state.

135 The term *federalist* came to refer to those who favored a continuation of a strong role for federal bodies. Slovaks continued to propose other versions of federation and confederation. For a good treatment of the debates about this see Abby Innes, "The Partition of Czechoslovakia" (Ph.D. diss., London School of Economics, 1997), and Václav Žák, "The Velvet Divorce—Institutional Foundations," in Jiří Musil, ed., *The End of Czechoslovakia* (Budapest: Central European University Press, 1995), pp. 245–70.

136 Reprint of Mečiar's weekly address to Slovak television viewers on July 14, 1990, in *Národná Obroda*, July 16, 1990, p. 1, 2, in FBIS-EEU-90-142, pp. 12–13. There was a span of opinion in the Slovak government, with some strongly condemning the plaque and others advocating rehabilitation of Tiso. KDH ministers objected to the strength of Mečiar's statement, as did some members of the Democratic Party and even some from VPN. Ondruš, "Slovensko, na moj povel," part III.

137 This was in response to a Czech government statement; Boehm argued that Tiso was not on the list of war criminals and that the unveiling of the plaque did not violate the law prohibiting propagation of fascism. Boehm statement in Federal Assembly transcript, *5 Spoločná Schúze SL a SN*, July 20, 1990, pp. 231–33. Other KDH leaders also were ambivalent or outrightly favored rehabilitation of Tiso. Slovak interior minister Anton Andráš was quoted as saying that it was too early to unveil such a plaque but that eventually an approach to the Slovak state would be decided. This left open the possibility that the current judgment should be reconsidered. Andráš emphasized that he simply meant that the subject needed study and that he was not advocating rehabilitation. Reported in *Národná Obroda*, July 19, 1990, p. 2, in FBIS-EEU-90-142, p. 13.

138 Further evidence of Mečiar's intentions was that he ousted interior minister Andráš, with the support of the democrats of VPN. Later this move by Mečiar was seen as part of an attempt to gain more control over the interior ministry, which he would use to blackmail other politicians. Ondruš, part III.

139 There was a series of articles making this argument in fall 1990. The position is summed up in a declaration issued by the democrats: they argue that the

actions of some organizations are reminiscent of the coming of "totalitarianism" in the 1930s and 1940s and complain of the manipulation of Matica Slovenská by people who would rehabilitate Tiso. "Občania Slovenska!" published in *Kultúrný Život,* October 31, 1990, p. 1.

140 See Jan Obrman, "Language Law Stirs Controversy in Slovakia," in *Report on Eastern Europe,* November 16, 1990.

141 While SNS won only 3.3 percent of the available seats, that party won 41 percent of the seats it actually contested. KDH won 27.45 percent of local seats and Public Against Violence got 20.3 percent. Communists won 24.2 percent of mayoral positions, KDH, 19.8 percent, VPN, 17.4 percent. See Jiří Pehe, "The Local Government Elections," in *Report on Eastern Europe,* December 14, 1990.

142 Mečiar had taken strong positions in talks with the Czechs in August 1990 and some Czechs began to label him a nationalist at that time.

143 In an interview on March 6, 1991, Mečiar said he was not associated with this group until that point. He claimed that they had approached him recently after being told by the leadership of VPN that they no longer belonged in the movement. There was a general complaint about the leadership of the Fedor Gál wing of VPN that they were so committed to unity in the movement that they alienated those who had more nationalist views. Mečiar interview with Bratislava Domestic Service, March 6, 1991, in FBIS-EEU-91-045, 3/7/91, p. 15.

144 Pehe, "Growing Slovak Demands Seen as Threat to Federation," p. 3. Pehe cites Slovak TV, March 3, 1991. Mečiar also said that a process of differentiation had been taking place in the movement for a long time and that the leadership of VPN had tried to oust Mečiar from the prime ministership in October 1990. Kňažko's link to Mečiar arose from his personal differences with democrats.

145 Ibid.

146 Ibid., p. 4.

147 The Slovak communists of SDL also jumped on the nationalist bandwagon at this time, with SDL leader Peter Weiss saying that allegations "concerning a leftist coup, national socialism" were a victory for "Prague political and journalistic circles." He also complained that the Hungarians were overly involved in Slovak politics. *Bratislava Pravda* refers to ČTK report, April 25, 1991, p. 2, in FBIS-EEU-91-083, pp. 13–14.

148 This rally will be discussed more in the next chapter. Emigrés had celebrated the anniversary of the founding of the Slovak state since the war.

149 The groups were "Sovereign Slovakia," "Korene: Society of Slovak Intelligentsia," "Štúr Society," "Slovak National Democratic Movement," and "Synthesis 90." Among the signatories were several key artistic figures from 1968 like poet Milan Rúfus and writer Vladimír Mináč. Jozef Markuš, head of Matica Slovenská, called upon the Slovak National Council to adopt the declaration and called for a demonstration on March 10–11 to support it. The declaration laid out steps that would lead to full independence of Slovakia, starting with the demand that the Slovak National Council declare Slovak laws to have precedence over the laws of the federation. It proposed that Slovakia would become a fully independent state with its own army, cur-

rency, and foreign policy before deciding about signing a treaty for a common state with the Czech Republic. *Smena,* March 2, 1991, p. 4, in FBIS-EEU-91-049, p. 17; Pehe, "Growing Slovak Demands," p. 6.

150 Pehe, "Growing Slovak Demands," p. 5.

151 Ibid., p. 6.

152 On March 10, Havel expressed part of Mečiar's slipperiness: he said that Mečiar was by far the most popular politician in Slovakia, yet in the wave of demonstrations supporting him were people the prime minister did not associate himself with, "and many slogans that were heard there were not . . . too close to his heart either." Interview with Havel at Lány Castle, March 9, 1991, Prague Domestic Service, March 10, 1991, in FBIS-EEU-91-048.

153 This is quite different from his earlier responses to the behavior of SNS, for example at the commemoration of Andrej Hlinka in August 1990 or the demonstrations against the draft of the language law that was passed in fall 1990. For response to the Hlinka commemoration see speech by Mečiar to the Slovak National Council, Bratislava Domestic Service, August 27, 1990 in FBIS-EEU-90-169, p. 11. Mečiar criticizes the use of "slogans in the streets" and other undemocratic methods. For response to the language law, see Jan Obrman, "Language Law Stirs Controversy in Slovakia" *Report on Eastern Europe,* November 16, 1990, p. 15.

154 News conference in *Smena,* March 11, 1991, p. 1, 2 in FBIS-EEU-91-050, p. 20.

155 *Národná Obroda,* March 6, 1991, p. 2 in FBIS-EEU-91-046.

156 There were a number of reasons for his removal: first, were the accusations that led to an investigation of his manipulation of the Interior Ministry files and his secret meeting about arms sales to Russia. He was found to have had the meeting and not to have consulted parliament. The manipulation of STB files was not confirmed. He was also accused of making statements at rallies that called into question the foundations of parliamentary democracy. In addition, the government had ceased to function, given the conflict between the two wings of VPN. For details on the events leading to Mečiar's removal, see Jiří Pehe, "Political Conflict in Slovakia," *Report on Eastern Europe,* May 10, 1991.

157 Mečiar made this claim frequently. An example is in a speech published in *Verejnost',* April 2, 1991, pp. 1, 3, 14, in FBIS-EEU-91-066, p. 16.

158 Mečiar claimed that he had a file that proved Ivan Čarnogurský was an STB agent. See *Pravda* May 10, 1991, p. 2, in FBIS-EEU-91-094, p. 15.

159 In a commentary called "Dangerous Games" in the VPN newspaper *Verejnost',* the argument is made that it is impossible for citizens to make judgments because of the media, and Mečiar, in his skill at switching, took advantage of this. "He is able to declare a number of mutually conflicting attitudes and to worm himself into the favor of workers, the Slovak National Party, communists, and the VPN all at the same time." Jana Plichtová commentary in *Verejnost',* March 14, 1991, p. 3, in FBIS-EEU-91-053, pp. 22–23.

160 *Národná Obroda,* March 6, 1991, in FBIS-EEU-91-065, p. 11. One of Mečiar's complaints was that the people of the Gál wing "used the coincidence that the new platform was formed at the time of the anniversary of the World War II

Slovak state to label it as an association of chauvinists and separatists."
Mečiar speech in *Verejnosť*, April 4, 1991, pp. 1, 3, 14, in FBIS-EEU-91-066,
pp. 15–17.

161 Václav Žák, "The Velvet Divorce." Also see Miroslav Kusý, "Slovak Exceptionalism," in Jiří Musil, ed., *The End of Czechoslovakia* (Budapest: Central
European University Press, 1995), pp. 139–58.

162 The plaque was unveiled by graduates of the Roman Catholic teachers' institute, which had formerly been in a building, which was now the mechanical engineering college. It said that in that building, in the years 1934–1938,
there was a Roman Catholic men's teachers' institute that Jozef Tiso founded
and then ran. It identified Tiso as president of the Slovak Republic and a
successor to Svatopluk, leader of Great Moravian empire. In an interview in
Smena, Jan Turčan said that the plaque was approved by the district institute
for state preservation of monuments and the protection of nature in Bratislava, which suggests broader support. Interview in *Smena* 161 (1990), ex-
cerpted in *Výber* 32 (1990): 18.

163 See statements by Korec in ČSTK, July 8, 1990, in Výber 32 (1990): 18. For
statement of the council of KDH see *Slovenský Denník* 76 (1990) reprinted
in Výber 32 (1990): 18; Šimko statement in Federal Assembly transcript 5
společná schůze SL a SN, July 20, 1990, p. 234, and statements above in
discussion of Mečiar response.

164 SNS deputy Slota took a similar position to KDH in the Federal Assembly,
saying that this period needed to be reevaluated by historians and should not
be discussed in the federal parliament. He commented that it seemed "a little
strange that on this question mostly Czech deputies are expressing themselves." Federal Assembly Transcript, p. 239.

165 KDH deputy Ivan Šimko tried to play on the commonality between the democrats and nationalists in opposition to the communists. He argued that the uproar over the fascist past "serves the interests of those who want to divide us
against ourselves" (p. 234 Federal Assembly transcript). For the communist
view, which strongly condemned the plaque, see "Nebol porušený zákon?" by
Jozef Trepáč, a deputy in the Slovak National Council for the Slovak Democratic Left, in *Pravda,* July 17, 1990.

166 Hlinka founded and led the Slovak People's Party until his death in 1938. The
party was then renamed the Hlinka Slovak People's Party. His name was also
given to the paramilitary wing of that party, the Hlinka Guard, modeled on the
German SS. Most Slovaks agreed that he should be viewed as a positive figure,
though many thought he should be seen for the Catholic nationalist he was,
including his antiliberal and anti-Semitic views, and should not be embraced
as having left a legacy of democracy.

167 Examples include: "Beneš is a murderer" and "Slovak state" and others
openly favoring Tiso.

168 See commentaries by Peter Malár in *Národná Obroda,* August 28, 1990, and
Ondřej Neff in *Mladá Fronta,* August 28, 1990, p. 1. All in FBIS-EEU-90-172,
p. 17.

169 Members of the KDH leadership had, during the last years of communism,

gone on pilgrimages to Černova to commemorate Hlinka's stance there against a particularly brutal attack by Hungarians in 1906 against attempts to preserve Slovak culture.

170 See a KDH council presidium statement submitted to ČTK, printed in *Práce,* August 25, 1990, p. 2, in FBIS-EEU-90-172, p. 13. Also see speech by Ivan Čarnogurský, first deputy chairman of the Slovak National Council (SNR) in SNR transcript, *3. Schodza,* August 27–29, 1990, pp. 4–10. Mostly the KDH tried to show that they were committed to operating only within legal institutions.

171 In fact, at first KDH tried to use the VPN split against that party; see ČTK March 4, 1991, in FBIS-EEU-91-043, p. 21. KDH also refused to vote for the dismissal of Mečiar, saying they would decide after the commission's inquiry into allegations that Mečiar manipulated StB files and made secret agreements with the Soviets for arms sales. ČTK, March 18, 1991, in FBIS-EEU-91-053, p. 22. Fedor Gál said that by the time Mečiar finally was ousted it was already too late for the democrats to recover in the eyes of the public and Mečiar had succeeded in making Gál enemy number one. According to Gál, Čarnogurský had not realized that the downfall of VPN would also mean the downfall of KDH. Gál, interview.

172 KDH was split over the commemoration of the declaration of the Slovak state on March 14, 1991 and the attack by demonstrators on Havel. For some KDH statements on the events, see articles in the KDH newspaper *Slovenský Denník:* "Som nevinný . . . nic som neurobil!" March 12, 1991; "Na návšt'eve u kanadských Slovákov," May 27, 1991; "Bolo to potrebné?" March 16, 1991; "Poučovanie no pokračovanie," March 15, 1991; "Majme rozvahu a široké srdce," March 16, 1991, p. 1.

173 In an April report the Mečiar faction was supported by 30 percent of those polled and Gál's faction by a little over 4 percent. ČTK report, April 8, 1991, in FBIS-EEU-91-068.

174 This would have made the wartime protectorate in the Czech lands and the Slovak state in Slovakia invalid.

175 For a full background on the treaty debates see "Relations with Germany" by Jan Obrman in *Report on Eastern Europe,* November 15, 1991.

176 Statement by Jiří Dienstbier in *Mladá Fronta Dnes,* September 18, 1991, in FBIS-EEU-91-183, p. 13; Pithart interview with RFE/RL's Czechoslovak service in Munich, September 26, 1991; Presidium of the Slovak Council of VPN statement given to ČTK, September 19, 1991, in FBIS-EEU-91-186, p. 15.

177 ČSTK, October 9, 1991. The statement said that "the argument that the Slovak state arose under pressure does not remove the fact of its existence. Only in this context can we look at the political orientation of some of the representatives of the Slovak state and at the Slovak National Uprising, which had a clearly antifascist character."

178 There was also a small conflict over the issue of censorship, which arose when the intellectual journal associated with VPN, *Kultúrný Život,* published a short story construed to be offensive to Catholics. See "Running Up a Tab on the Last Supper" in *Prognosis,* Jan. 24–Feb. 26, 1992, pp. 12–14. On the debate over

liberalism see collection of articles "Liberalizmus spása či zatratenie?" in *Výber* 46 (1991): 24.

179 Poll carried out by the Slovak statistical office and published on September 17, 1991 in ČTK. From FBIS-EEU-91-182, p. 15. Clearly KDH had lost a considerable amount of support, which had been 25 percent in the fall 1990 elections.

180 Interview entitled "O špionech, antisemitismu a nemoci" in Czech magazine *Svět v obrazech,* October 3, 1991, pp. 6–7. It was a Czech translation of an interview done in English with Klímová by the magazine *Working Woman* but was never published there.

181 Čarnogurský statement reported in *Mladá Fronta Dnes,* October 24, 1991.

182 This was also the focus in a summary of the campaign against her that she had written up and that was in her files and which she gave me during my interview with her on November 18, 1992.

183 Report on petition in ČSTK, November 22, 1991, in FBIS-EEU-91-228, p. 11.

184 It did not have enough votes in the Slovak parliament to enforce its own policies and had to rely on the support of the VPN and the Democratic Party, both of which were federalist. See Jiří Pehe, "Slovak Nationalism Splits Christian Democratic Ranks," *RFE/RL Research Report* 1, no. 13 (1992): 14.

185 Eleven of the thirty-one KDH deputies in the Slovak parliament defected to the new party, as did five out of twenty-five federal assembly deputies and four members of the Slovak government. Ibid., p. 16.

186 They got 8.96 percent of the vote in the federal assembly House of People, winning 6 seats, and 8.81 percent of the vote in the House of Nations, winning 8 seats. See Jiří Pehe, "Czechoslovakia's Political Balance Sheet 1990–92," in *RFE/RL Research Report* 1, no. 25 (1992): 29.

187 "Confessions of an Adversary of Totalitarianism," *Národná Obroda,* May 13, 1991, p. 12, in FBIS-EEU-91-095, p. 12.

188 Interview with Peter Tatár, chairman of VPN deputies' club in the Slovak National Council in *Mladá Fronta Dnes,* September 17, 1991, p. 2; FBIS-EEU-91-182, 9/19/91.

189 This statement was made in trying to assess whether KDH would split over the above mentioned sovereignty declaration in September 1991. Reported by ČTK April 24, 1991, in FBIS-EEU-91-081, 4/26/91, p. 17.

190 Čarnogurský, interview.

191 Though this cleavage did not go very deeply into a social base.

7 Politics in a Hall of Mirrors

1 In 1990, it had been celebrated in Boston.

2 On March 13, five to ten thousand people had attended a ceremony in Bratislava cemetery to consecrate a cross at Tiso's grave. Jiří Pehe, "Growing Slovak Demands Seen as Threat to Federation," *RFE Report on Eastern Europe,* March 22, 1991, p. 8.

3 Pánis was a deputy in the federal parliament for Slovak National Party though he had, since the June 1990 election, broken off to found his own more radical

party. He was thought to be supported by émigré money from Germany or even by money from the Middle East.

4   Excerpt from Mlynárik letter cited in ČTK, March 15, 1991, in FBIS-EEU-91-054, 3/20/91.

5   Author's interview with Mlynárik, November 19, 1992.

6   At the October 28, 1991 commemoration of the birth of Czechoslovakia, Pánis was at the head of a group of skinheads that threw eggs at Havel.

7   It is not clear whether Mlynárik thought this because of Pánis's views or his connections.

8   He clearly fit the profile of mass-elite and is reminiscent of Zhirinovsky in the sense that his past is the subject of such speculation and he appeared in several different guises.

9   Mlynárik, a Slovak who lived in Prague, later became a frequent target for Slovak nationalists, particularly mass-elite nationalists. For example, in September of 1991 Ján Slota of the Slovak National Party commented, "I am convinced that in a few months' time we are going to have a Slovak state here. And all those who oppose this idea will be sentenced as traitors." In response to the demand by one VPN deputy that the parliament should censure Slota for this comment, Petr Brňák said that the same standard should apply to Mlynárik. This was a reference to Mlynárik's bringing to the legal claim against Pánis and his outspoken condemnation of signs of fascism. See series of press reports on the Slota incident in FBIS-EEU-91-188, September 27, 1991.

10 For a strikingly similar analysis applied to the lustration process in the Czech Republic, see Jiřina Šiklová, "Lustration or the Czech Way of Screening," *East European Constitutional Review* 5, no. 1 (winter 1996).

11 Some of these were previously banned but had circulated in samizdat; some were by unknown authors and publishers.

12 Many policy areas in postcommunist politics were affected by the unreliability of communist-era information. Journalists, who might have helped to hold politicians accountable, could not find out relevant information even if they tried; even if a freedom of information act had existed, it would often have led to files with fudged or inconclusive information.

13 For an argument that focuses on the critical role of independent information in postcommunist democratization, see Herbert Kitschelt, "Post-communist Democracies: Do Party Systems Help or Hinder?" (paper presented at Conference on Democracy, Markets, and Civil Societies in Post-1989 East Central Europe, May 17–19, 1996, Center for European Studies, Harvard University), p. 13. In contrast to the argument here, Kitschelt argues that independent information is increasingly available in postcommunist political life.

14 Other attempts to use this law, for example against the publishers of the Protocols of the Elders of Zion, ended with a failure to make a legal decision because the defendant did not appear on the appointed court date.

15 In spring 1991 his popularity ratings were at 81 percent. See Jiří Pehe, "Political Conflict in Slovakia," in *Report on Eastern Europe,* May 10, 1991, p. 2.

16 For example, deputy prime minister Kučerák said: "My belief is that each politician should be accountable to a specific group of people, to specific people or to groups that elect him, and must not refer to the anonymous mass of

people, to the nation. This is . . . playing a role of leader; . . . unfortunately, we have bitter experience of this." Bratislava Domestic Service, March 6, 1991, translated in FBIS-EEU-91-045, p. 13.

17 Statement translated in FBIS-EEU-91-049, 3/13/91, p. 22–23.

18 They brought the communist past in also, saying, "One of sources of destabilization in society is the fact that collaborators of former secret police still function in top state agencies." Pehe, "Growing Slovak Demands," p. 5.

19 Prague, ČTK, March 11, 1991, in FBIS-EEU-91-050.

20 Žantovský said he did not mean to offend the Slovak nation and that he was using a social scientific term. Statement in Prague Domestic Service, March 25, 1991, in FBIS-EEU-91-058, p. 20.

21 Havel address, March 14, 1991, in FBIS-EEU-91-051, pp. 16–17.

22 Ibid., p. 17.

23 Havel statement of March 17 before leaving for trip to Benelux countries, in FBIS-EEU-91-052, pp. 16–17.

24 Prague Federal 1 Television Network; March 15, 1991, in FBIS-EEU-91-052.

25 *Slovensko-Marec 1991,* Center for Social Analysis. Respondents were allowed to select more than one answer.

26 The topic of representation is complex and is beyond the scope of this project. I make the distinction between representation and reflection here to call attention to the difference between articulating a position that takes public opinion into account but also uses independent judgment, and a meer mirroring of what the public wants at a particular moment.

27 Interview with Mečiar by ČTK broadcast by Bratislava Domestic Service, March 15, 1991. Translated in FBIS-EEU-91-052, p. 18.

28 Mečiar news conference, March 18, 1991 reported in *Bratislava Pravda,* p. 1, 2. Translated in FBIS-EEU-91-058, p. 26.

29 Collaboration leaves a particularly confusing legacy. What is judged by victims, observers, and courts is outcomes, not intentions. But collaborators feel less responsibility because their intentions might have been fine but historical circumstances forced them to do what they did. See John Armstrong's article comparing collaboration in Slovakia and Ukraine, "Collaborationism in World War II: The Integral Nationalist Variant in Eastern Europe," *Journal of Modern History* 40, no. 3 (1968): 396–410.

30 The fact that a declaration of apology for the Holocaust was issued by the Slovak parliament in December 1990, when Mečiar was prime minister, shows that he had no particular tie to the fascist state. But it does not therefore show particular commitment to taking responsibility on behalf of Slovakia.

31 Interview with *Mladá Fronta Dnes,* April 2, 1991, FBIS-EEU-91-069, p. 18.

32 Interview in *Národná Obroda,* May 10, 1991, pp. 1, 8, 9, in FBIS-EEU-91-094.

33 Interview with Mečiar in *Bratislava Pravda,* May 6, 1991, pp. 1, 3, FBIS-EEU-91-091, p. 7.

34 It talks about KDH as having "manifested many signs of Catholic fundamentalism known from the times of the first Slovak Republic of 1939–45, whereby it repelled a considerable section of voters." The same article refers to the democrats as having engaged in "anti-Slovak racism," a reference again to the focus on Slovakia's fascist past. See Július Handzarík, "Slovakia's Road after the

Elections," *Europa Vincet,* nos. 3/4 (1992): 1–2. As we saw above, the term *federalist* referred to those who saw a strong role for the federal bodies as well as the republic level bodies.

35   It was much more his experience under communism than his Jewishness that led to his political views. Gál, interview.

36   While it is hard to link Mečiar directly to the anti-Semitic rhetoric that appeared in the nationalist press, Mečiar's attacks on Gál were indirectly linked to his Jewish background.

37   See, for example, "An Appeal by the Editorial Board," *Europa Vincet* 5 (1992): 17. This appeal was for readers to send in examples of the "disinformation campaign against Slovakia and the Slovak nation" which are often written by "citizens of the ČSFR."

38   It is an interesting version of ressentiment which usually is based on economic backwardness; here it is based also on a sort of moral backwardness regarding one of the key events that defined Western standards of morality in the postwar period—the Holocaust. See Liah Greenfeld, *Nationalism: Five Roads to Modernity,* for a discussion of the role of ressentiment in nationalism, pp. 8–17.

39   We saw in the previous chapter that this argument became a main plank in the Mečiar group program; in a list of Matica Slovenská's main actions on behalf of Slovakia's interests, opposition to the "distorted Czech-generated information about Slovakia and the alleged fascist elements in the national movement" is one of three. See Stanislav Bajaník, "The Slovak Foundation in the National Movement," *Europa Vincet* 3–4 (1992): 11.

40   See statement by Čarnogurský, who said that since there had not been time to "assess the entire period of totalitarianism" it was difficult to tell whether some people took "ethically tolerable" positions toward the state security. But he also says that he would "set the limit to moral acceptability" at agreement to collaborate with the state security. *Národná Obroda,* January 24, 1991, p. 13, in FBIS-EEU-91-020. František Mikloško said, "I view the whole issue as one gigantic avalanche which may be triggered into uncontrollable motion. For this reason I am reluctant and reserved about the screenings." Interview in *Smena,* January 22, 1991, in FBIS-EEU-91-017, p. 34. Havel expresses his reluctant support in an interview on March 31, 1991, FBIS-EEU-91-062, p. 23. For other examples see Tina Rosenberg, *The Haunted Land.*

41   See interview with Fedor Gál in Bratislava Domestic Service, June 10, 1990, in FBIS-EEU-90-113, pp. 22–23. Other political leaders also attested to their belief in Budaj's trustworthiness. Stanislav Pánis, of the SNS, did not, saying that if the public had known that Budaj was a collaborator, SNS would have gotten some of VPN's votes. Also Budaj briefing in ČTK June 10, 1990, in FBIS-EEU-90-113, p. 23.

42   It is likely that several from the original leadership of VPN, who were not part of the 1968 group, started to move toward Mečiar because of this incident, namely, Milan Kňažko. For conspiracy view, see writings of Milan Žitný and Miloš Žiak and author's interviews with Žitný and Žiak.

43   Though there was ambivalence about anticommunism in Slovakia to begin with.

44 He also complained that screening was a tool of political struggle and that much of the old regime remained intact. He pointed out that certain political groups could misuse the archives. He then specifically mentioned the fact that all the documents were taken to Prague. Mečiar speech in *Verejnost'*, January 14, 1991, pp. 1, 3, in FBIS-EEU-91-015, 1/23/91, p. 18. For another example of this argument see the commentary by Jan Fuele, "Darkness behind the Screenings Searchlight," in *Národná Obroda*, January 24, 1991, in FBIS-EEU-91-018, p. 23.

45 Kučerák questioned Mečiar's opposition to the screening legislation.

46 Neither of the two Slovak sociologists trying to find out biographical information about the new elites were successful. Milan Zemko said in an interview, "No one wants to talk about their pasts; they want to start again in 1989; you will have difficulty finding out biographical information." Zemko was a key political figure: deputy chair of Slovak National Council; later adviser to the Slovak president. He was one of the only people to walk the thin line between the democrats and the Mečiar group after they split. Author's interview with Zemko, April 7, 1994.

47 Allegations were that he spied on Dubček under the code name "Doktor." He allegedly arranged a raid in February 1990 on a villa in Bratislava where StB records belonging to the federal ministry of interior were housed to take the files. He also tended to appoint people who had been connected with the ministry of the interior in the past, which confirmed his manipulation of the secret police in the minds of many observers. There are many articles on this topic. Two in English are in *Prognosis:* "New Day, Same as the Old Day," October 12–15, 1992, p. 13, and "Mečiar StB Collaborator?" March 16–19, 1992, p. 7.

48 On the misguided nature of lustration, see statement of March 23, 1991, where Mečiar said that the announcement of the names of parliamentary deputies listed as StB collaborators was political and complained that the Council of Europe would deem the policy illegal and that Czechoslovakia's international reputation might be harmed. Statement in FBIS-EEU-91-058, 3/26/91. On restitution, he said that not only would the policy be expensive but that there were no reliable records and that the privatization policy was being placed at risk. He also complained that land would be returned to fascist collaborators. Statement reported by ČTK in FBIS-EEU-91-033, 2/19/91, p. 28.

49 Suggestive of this is a poll conducted in April 1991. In the poll one-third of the 1,032 people polled did not trust the results of the March screening of parliamentary deputies. One-third said they could not judge. While 40 percent of Czechs trusted the results, only 20 percent of Slovaks did and almost one-half of the Slovaks said they did not believe the findings. ČTK, April 18, 1991. Poll conducted by the Institute for Research on Public Opinion.

50 Lawrence Weschler, "The Velvet Purge: The Trials of Jan Kavan," *New Yorker,* October 19, 1992, p. 83.

51 Slovak mass-elite parties either abstained, were not present, or were divided, whereas ideological elites and communists had clear positions. Neither SNS nor HZDS had any deputies voting yes or no. Four SNS deputies abstained, while nine were not present. Seven HZDS deputies abstained and nine were not pres-

ent. The democrats of VPN were nearly unanimously in favor (with some not present), as was KDH. The communists were nearly unanimously opposed, with some not present. Vote breakdown in *Výber* 43 (1991): 17. In the Czech Republic there was a more complicated situation where the dissidents were genuinely divided on the correct approach to lustration, and this indecisiveness is registered in their voting results. This case is a good example of the need to look at the divide between ideological and mass-elites before evaluating something like a vote on legislation. Using this divide we can understand the indecisiveness on the part of the Czech dissidents to be a product of genuine disagreement about policy. The indecisiveness on the part of the mass-elites in Slovakia, which is reflected in the vote, was a product of lack of commitment.

52 For the competing allegations and defenses see Mečiar news conference in *Národná Obroda,* April 1, 1992, p. 9, and Čarnogurský position in *Slovenský Denník,* March 26, 1992, p. 2, both in FBIS-EEU-92-065, pp. 4–9.

53 See Paula Bren, "Lustration in the Czech and Slovak Republics," *RFE/RL Research Report 2,* no. 29 (1993).

54 The statement that led to the defamation of character complaint was sent to the Slovak News Service on July 29, 1992. The statement, by the writer Lubomír Feldek, was titled, "For a better image of Slovakia—without a minister with a fascist past." The complaint filed by Slobodník focused on the following line: "Mr. Slobodník became minister of culture and schools of the Slovak republic and immediately it became evident that he had a fascist past. . . . Does Mr. Slobodník suppose that Slovakia has some sort of specific exception and its own right to revise the philosophy of the Nuremberg process which is binding on all other countries?"

55 Another issue at stake in this case was the allegation that Slobodník had KGB connections. This allegation was deduced from his success as a scholar, including the fact that he traveled abroad many times after returning from exile in the Gulag. This is yet another example of the difficulties of establishing who elites were in postcommunist Slovakia. Miloš Žiak, interview.

56 See article making Slobodník's case, "Co o mne hovoria dokumenty," *Literárný Týzdennik,* 35 (August 22, 1992). See also "Slobodník's Traditional Vision" in *Prognosis,* October 2–15, 1992, p. 3B.

57 Author's interview with Feldek's lawyer Ernest Valko, April 14, 1994.

58 "Otvorený list historikovi Ivanovi Kamencovi," in *Literárný Týždenník,* August 13, 1993, p. 4.

59 See in particular articles in *Koridor,* the newspaper associated with HZDS. One statement by the presidium of the "HZDS Club for Science and Research" condemned the "shameless campaign against Dusan Slobodník, minister of culture and member of our club," as only "a small piece of a larger scenario for the defaming of the Slovak nation and its representatives both at home and abroad." *Nový Slovák,* August 26, 1992.

60 Decision published in *Sme,* March 30, 1994.

61 Of course new ideology could be created through authoritarian means. But this is just what is not happening, although Mečiar became increasingly authoritarian in his years as prime minister. Instead we see the perpetuation of absence of ideology within formally democratic institutions.

62 Šiklová makes a similar point about the lustration process in the Czech Republic. See "Lustration or the Czech Way of Screening."

8 Conclusion

1 The sovereignty declaration was adopted on July 17, 1992. The constitution was adopted on September 1, 1992. Demands for approval of sovereignty declarations were a constant part of Slovak political life from 1990 on. See chapter 6.

2 Once the ideological elites were marginalized, the main divide was between those who are more invested in the country's future—the technocrats—and those who are more opportunistic. While some elites seemed to be learning democracy as transitions-to-democracy theorists would expect, the opportunists continued to be favored. After Slovak independence in January 1993, power flipped back and forth between the followers of Mečiar and these more technocratic elites. But each side that took power during this short period engaged in radical personnel purges and undid what the other side had implemented in a matter of months. Among other things, this impeded the process of building up a knowledgeable civil service (a process which is already difficult because the establishment of a new state requires so many new positions to be filled by inexperienced people). It is important to keep in mind that the political defeat of Mečiar himself does not indicate the defeat of the mass-elite more generally.

3 Speech in Slovak parliament by Ján Fekete of HZDS; see transcript of Slovak National Council of September 29, 1992.

4 Speech in Slovak parliament by Anton Neuwirth; transcript of Slovak National Council, September 29, 1992.

5 For example, Martin Kvetko (one of few figures who returned to Slovak politics from the precommunist period), "Proti fašizmu, za spoločný štát," in *Národná Obroda,* August 28, 1992.

6 Among those who abstained or did not vote were key mass-elite nationalists from the Slovak National Party and Mečiar's party. Mečiar himself did not vote. The total was 89 in favor, 12 against, and 48 were not present or abstained (voting breakdown provided by Miloš Žiak). Interestingly, the same parties of mass-elite nationalists did not vote decisively for the main law condemning the communist past, the law on lustration; see chapter 7.

7 Poll on attitudes toward the split in October 1993 in "Aktuál'ne problémy po rozpade ČSFR" by Centrum pre sociálnu a marketingovu analýzu, Bratislava, October 1993.

8 Gál made this statement at a VPN news conference, recorded by Bratislava Domestic Service, June 10, 1990; in FBIS-EEU-90-113, p. 22. He was responding to the discovery that one of his close associates in the networks of dissent, Ján Budaj, appeared on the list of collaborators with the former secret police.

9 I am referring to the debate between analysts who wanted to use the transitions to democracy literature and those who insisted on taking into account legacies from the communist past. See Valerie Bunce, "Should Transitologists Be Grounded?" *Slavic Review* 54, no. 1 (1995): 111–27. On the other side, see

Philippe Schmitter and Terry Karl, "The Conceptual Travels of Transitologists and Consolidologists: How Far to the East Should They Attempt to Go?"

10 Poland is the most obvious counter example, with the remaining strength of the Catholic Church and the strength of the Solidarity movement. But even there the communist legacy dilutes the ability for this movement to function as a political force in the postcommunist period.

11 For example, in Croatia the symbols of the wartime fascist regime were rehabilitated to a greater extent than anywhere else. This was due to the importance of émigrés who embodied the legacy of that state and their alliance with Franjo Tudjman. It was also due, of course to the conflict with the Serbs. World War II left a different legacy in the former Yugoslavia than in Czechoslovakia, due to the ethnic violence that characterized the war in that region. Thus even family stories lent themselves to the mobilization of violence that we saw after 1990. A final factor was that once Serbia began to be perceived as the aggressor even by those Western powers reluctant to support the Croats due to their wartime past, there was not much effective Western pressure to abandon these symbols.

12 Milosevic, who had been a loyal communist and was outspoken in his opposition to nationalism, transformed himself into the mobilizer of Serb nationalism in 1987. Interestingly, when it seemed that he was not going to succeed in Bosnia, he transformed himself into peacemaker, seemingly leaving the Bosnian Serbs, and his intense nationalism, behind. He transformed again in the conflict in Kosovo. See Aleksa Djilas, "A Profile of Slobodan Milosevic," *Foreign Affairs* 72, no. 3 (1993): 81–96. A former secret police operative named Arkan is the most famous of the crooks/ethnic cleansers in the Yugoslav wars. See Laura Silber and Allan Little, *Yugoslavia: Death of a Nation* (New York: Penguin, 1996).

13 David Laitin tries to explain the appearance of ethnic violence in the Georgian case and the lack thereof in the Ukrainian case. Although the conditions existed for such violence in both cases, the difference in outcomes was due to the way in which communism preserved or wiped out traditional networks of village organization. Laitin argues that it is necessary to have a certain type of network out of which committed groups of self-sacrificing nationalists might come. Obviously, the lack of ethnic violence in the Ukrainian case is preferable, though it presents its own set of problems. See David Laitin, "National Revivals and Violence," *Archives of European Sociology* 36 (1995): 1–41.

14 Also inside the communist world: in China for example. Many analysts have pointed to the absence of any ideology and the short-term opportunism among Deng Xiaoping's successors.

15 *Return of Eva Peron,* pp. 185–219.

16 The problem of judgment is also often pointed out in discussions of the decline of civic culture. In the West these problems could well be a product of too much information rather than too little, as in the Leninist world. See David Shenk, *Data Smog* (San Francisco: Harper San Francisco, 1997), for a popular treatment of this idea.

17 The problem of information left over from the communist period coupled with the tremendous flux of the postcommunist period makes judgment particularly difficult.

Bibliography

Books and Articles in English

Abrams, Bradley. "Morality, Wisdom, and Revision: The Czech Opposition of the 1970's and the Expulsion of the Sudeten Germans." *East European Politics and Societies* 9, no. 2 (1995).

———. "The Politics of Retribution: The Trial of Jozef Tiso." *East European Politics and Societies* 10, no. 2 (1996).

Adler, Les, and Thomas G. Paterson. "Red Fascism: The Merger of Nazi Germany and Soviet Russia in the American Image of Totalitarianism, 1930's–1950's." *American Historical Review* 75, no. 4 (1970).

"After Communism, What?" *Daedalus* 123, no. 3 (1994).

Allen, William Sheridan. *The Nazi Seizure of Power.* New York: Franklin Watts, 1984.

Anderson, Benedict. *Imagined Communities.* London: Verso, 1991.

Arendt, Hannah. *Eichmann in Jerusalem.* New York: Penguin Books, 1977.

———. *Origins of Totalitarianism.* New York: Harcourt Brace Jovanovich, 1973.

Armstrong, John. "Collaborationism in World War II: The Integral Nationalist Variant in Eastern Europe." *Journal of Modern History* 40, no. 3 (1968).

Attitudes toward Jews and the Holocaust in Slovakia. Bratislava: Center for Social Analysis, March 1993.

Balbus, Isaac. "The Concept of Interest in Marxist and Pluralist Analysis." *Politics and Society* 1 (1971).

Baldwin, Peter, ed. *Reworking the Past.* Boston: Beacon Press, 1990.

Banfield, Edward. *The Moral Basis of a Backward Society.* New York: Free Press, 1958.

Bartošek, Karel. "Czechoslovakia: The State of Historiography." *Journal of Contemporary History* 2, no. 1 (1967).

Bauman, Zygmunt. "Social Dissent in East European Politics." *Archives Europeenes de Sociologie* 12, no. 1 (1971).

Bottomore, Tom. *Elites and Society.* 2nd ed. London: Routledge, 1993.

Braham, Randolph L., ed. *Anti-Semitism and the Treatment of the Holocaust in Postcommunist Eastern Europe.* Rosenthal Institute for Holocaust Studies and Social Science Monographs. New York: Columbia University Press, 1994.

Braxator, František. "Slovaks Abroad and Their Relationship to Czecho-Slovakia." In Jozef Kirschbaum, ed., *Slovakia in the 19th and 20th Centuries.* Toronto: Slovak World Congress, 1973.

Bren, Paula. "Lustration in the Czech and Slovak Republics." *RFE/RL Research Report* 2, no. 29 (1993).

Breuilly, John. *Nationalism and the State.* Manchester: Manchester University Press, 1982.

Brock, Peter. *The Slovak National Awakening.* Toronto: University of Toronto Press, 1976.

Brown, Archie, and Gordon Wightman. "Czechoslovakia: Revival and Retreat." In Archie Brown and Jack Gray, eds., *Political Culture and Political Change in Communist Studies.* New York: Holmes and Meier, 1979.

Brown, Michael, ed. *Ethnic Conflict and International Security.* Princeton: Princeton University Press, 1993.

Brubaker, Rogers. *Nationalism Reframed.* Cambridge: Cambridge University Press, 1996.

———. "Nationalizing States in the Old 'New Europe'—and the New." *Ethnic and Racial Studies* 19, no. 2 (1996).

———. "Nationhood and the National Question in the Soviet Union and Post-Soviet Eurasia: An Institutionalist Account." *Theory and Society* 23 (1994).

Bugajski, Janusz. *Czechoslovakia: Charter 77's Decade of Dissent.* New York: Praeger, 1987.

———, ed. *Ethnic Politics in Eastern Europe.* Armonk, N.Y.: M. E. Sharpe, 1994, 1995.

Bunce, Valerie. "From State Socialism to State Disintegration: A Comparison of the Soviet Union, Yugoslavia, and Czechoslovakia." Paper prepared for the conference on "Democracy, Markets, and Civil Societies in Post-1989 East Central Europe," Harvard University, May 17–19, 1996.

Bunce, Valerie. "Should Transitologists Be Grounded?" *Slavic Review* 54, no. 1 (1995).

Bunce, Valerie, and Maria Csanadi. "Uncertainty in the Transition: Post-Communism in Hungary." *East European Politics and Societies* 7, no. 2 (1993).

Burke, Peter. "History as Social Memory." In Thomas Butler, ed., *Memory: History, Culture, and the Mind.* New York: Basil Blackwell, 1989.

Butler, Thomas. "Memory: A Mixed Blessing." In Thomas Butler, ed., *Memory: History, Culture, and the Mind.* New York: Basil Blackwell, 1989.

Bútora, Martin, and Zora Bútorová. "Slovakia after the Split." *Journal of Democracy,* 4, no. 2 (1993).

———. " 'A Wary Approach': Attitudes toward Jews and Jewish Issues in Slovakia." *East European Jewish Affairs* 23, no. 1 (1993).

Bútorová, Zora, and Tatiana Rosová. "The Slovak National Party: Myths, Rituals, Devotees." *Respekt,* 381 (1990).

Campeanu, Pavel. "National Fervor in Eastern Europe: The Case of Romania." *Social Research* 58, no. 4 (1991).

Chirot, Daniel. "Ideology, Reality, and Competing Models of Development in Eastern Europe between the Wars." *Eastern European Politics and Societies* 3, no. 3 (1989).

Cohen, Asher. "Petain, Horthy, Antonescu, and the Jews." In Michael Marrus, ed., *The Nazi Holocaust*, vol. 4 (1983).

Commission on Security and Cooperation in Europe. *Human Rights and Democratization in Slovakia* (September 1993).

Commission on Security and Cooperation in Europe. *Report on Slovakia* (April 1992).

Connerton, Paul. *How Societies Remember.* Cambridge: Cambridge University Press, 1989.

Connor, Walker. *Ethnonationalism.* Princeton: Princeton University Press, 1994.

———. "National-Building or Nation-Destroying." *World Politics* 24 (1972).

Conway, John S. "The Churches, the Slovak State, and the Jews, 1939–45." *Slavonic and East European Review* 52, no. 126 (1974).

Croan, Melvin. "Lands In-between: The Politics of Cultural Identity in Contemporary Eastern Europe." *East European Politics and Society* 3, no. 2 (1989).

Dahrendorf, Ralf. *Class and Class Conflict in Industrial Society.* Stanford: Stanford University Press, 1959.

———. *Society and Democracy in Germany.* New York: W. W. Norton, 1967.

Darski, Josef. "Police Agents in the Transition Period." *Uncaptive Minds* 4, no. 4 (Winter 1991–92).

Deak, István. "A Fatal Compromise? The Debate over Collaboration and Resistance in Hungary." *East European Politics and Societies*, no. 2 (1995).

Deutsch, Karl. *Nationalism and Social Communication.* Cambridge: MIT Press, 1966.

Di Palma, Giuseppe. *To Craft Democracies.* Berkeley: University of California Press, 1990.

Djilas, Aleksa. "A Profile of Slobodan Milosevic." *Foreign Affairs* 72, no. 3 (1993).

Draper, Theodor. "The End of Czechoslovakia." *New York Review of Books,* January 28, 1993.

———. "A New History of the Velvet Revolution." *New York Review of Books,* January 14, 1993.

Evans, Geoffrey, and Stephen Whitfield. "Identifying the Bases of Party Competition in Eastern Europe." *British Journal of Political Science* 23 (1993).

Felak, James. *"At the Price of the Republic": Hlinka's Slovak People's Party, 1929–38.* Pittsburgh: University of Pittsburgh Press, 1994.

Fish, Steve. *Democracy from Scratch.* Princeton: Princeton University Press, 1995.

Frič, Pavol, Fedor Gál, Peter Hunčík, and Christopher Lord. *The Hungarian Minority in Slovakia.* Prague: Egem, 1993.

Friedlander, Saul. *When Memory Comes.* New York: Farar, Straus, Giroux, 1979.

Funkenstein, Amos. "Collective Memory and Historical Consciousness." *History and Memory* 1, no. 1 (1989).

Gambetta, Diego, ed. *Trust: Making and Breaking Cooperative Relations.* Oxford: Blackwell, 1988.

Geertz, Clifford. "Ideology as Cultural System." In D. Apter, ed., *Ideology and Discontent.* London: Free Press of Glencoe, 1964.

Gellner, Ernest. *Nations and Nationalism.* Ithaca: Cornell University Press, 1993.

Gerber, Theodore. "In Search of the Soviet Middle Class: Scientists and Other Professionals in Post-Stalinist Russia." Ph.D. diss., University of California, Berkeley 1995.

Gillis, John, *Commemorations.* Princeton: Princeton University Press, 1994.

Golan, Galia. *Reform Rule in Czechoslovakia.* Cambridge: Cambridge University Press, 1973.

Grabowski, Tomek. "Breaking Through to Individualism: Poland's Western Frontier 1945–1995." Ph.D. diss., University of California, Berkeley, 2000.

Graubard, Stephen, ed. *Exit from Communism.* New Brunswick, N.J.: Transaction Publishers, 1993.

Greenfeld, Liah. *Nationalism: Five Roads to Modernity.* Cambridge: Harvard University Press, 1992.

Griffiths, William. *Communism in Europe.* Cambridge, Mass.: MIT Press, 1966.

Gross, Jan T. *Revolution from Abroad.* Princeton: Princeton University Press, 1988.

——. "Social Consequences of War: Preliminaries to the Study of Imposition of Communist Regimes in East Central Europe." *Eastern European Politics and Societies* 3, no. 2 (1989).

Gyorgy, Andrew. "Comparative Patterns of Nationalism in Eastern Europe." *Canadian Slavonic Papers* 10, no. 4 (1968).

Haas, Ernst. "What Is Nationalism and Why Do We Study It?" *International Organization* 40, no. 3 (1986).

Hamšik, Dušan. *Writers against Rulers.* London: Hutchinson and Co., 1971.

Handelman, Stephen. *Comrade Criminal.* New Haven: Yale University Press, 1995.

Hankiss, Elemer. "The 'Second Society': Is There an Alternative Social Model Emerging in Contemporary Hungary?" *Social Research* 55, nos. 1–2 (1988).

Hanson, Stephen. "Ideology and the Rise of Anti-system Parties in Postcommunist Russia." Paper presented at Conference on Party Politics in Postcommunist Russia, University of Glasgow, May 23–25, 1997.

Hanson, Stephen, and Jeffrey Kopstein. "The Weimar/Russia Comparison." *Post-Soviet Affairs* 13, no. 3 (1997).

Hauner, Milan. "Recasting Czech History." *Survey* 24, no. 3 (1979).

Havel, Václav. *The Art of the Impossible.* New York: Fromm International, 1998.

——. "Between Ideals and Utopias." *East European Reporter* 3 (1987–88).

——. *Disturbing the Peace.* New York: Knopf, 1990.

——. "Letter to Dr. Gustáv Husák." In Jan Vladislav, ed., *Václav Havel: Living in Truth.* London: Faber and Faber, 1986.

——. "The Power of the Powerless." In Jan Vladislav, ed., *Václav Havel: Living in Truth.* Princeton: Princeton University Press, 1993.

——. *Summer Meditations.* New York: Knopf, 1992.

Higley, John, and Richard Gunther. *Elites and Democratic Consolidation in Latin America and Southern Europe.* New York: Cambridge University Press, 1992.

Higley, John, Judith Kullberg, and Jan Pakulski. "The Persistence of Postcommunist Elites." *Journal of Democracy* 7, no. 2 (1996).

Hirschman, Albert O. *Exit, Voice, and Loyalty.* Cambridge: Harvard University Press, 1970.

Hobsbawm, Eric, and Terence Ranger. *The Invention of Tradition*. Cambridge: Cambridge University Press, 1992.

Hochhuth, Rolf. *The Deputy*. New York: Grove Press, 1964.

Holsti, Kalevi. *The State, War, and the State of War*. Cambridge: Cambridge University Press, 1996.

Horowitz, Donald. *Ethnic Groups in Conflict*. Berkeley: University of California Press, 1985.

Hroch, Miroslav. *Social Preconditions of National Revival in Europe*. Cambridge: Cambridge University Press, 1985.

Hrubý, Peter. *Fools and Heroes*. Oxford: Pergamon Press, 1980.

Innes, Abby. "The Partition of Czechoslovakia." Ph.D. diss., London School of Economics, 1997.

Janos, Andrew. *Politics and Paradigms*. Stanford: Stanford University Press, 1986.

Jašík, Rudolf. *St. Elizabeth's Square*. Translated by Margot Schierl. Prague: Artia, 1964.

Jelinek, Yeshayahu. "The Ludak Exile, the Neo-Ludaks, and Revival of Anti-Semitism in Slovakia." Presented at International Seminar on Anti-Semitism in Posttotalitarian Europe, Prague, 1992.

———. *The Lust for Power: Nationalism, Slovakia, and the Communists, 1918–1948*. Boulder, Colo.: East European Monographs, 1983.

———. *The Parish Republic: Hlinka's Slovak People's Party*. Boulder, Colo.: East European Monograph, no. 14, distributed by Columbia University Press, 1976.

———. "Slovaks and the Holocaust: An End to Reconciliation?" *East European Jewish Affairs* 22, no. 1 (1992).

———. "Slovaks and the Holocaust: Attempts at Reconciliation." *Soviet Jewish Affairs* 19, no. 1 (1989).

———. "The Slovak State in Post-war Historiography." *Slovakia* 28, nos. 51–52 (1978–79).

———. "The Vatican, the Catholic Church, the Catholics, and the Persecution of the Jews during World War II: The Case of Slovakia." In Bela Vago and George L. Mosse, eds., *Jews and Non-Jews in Eastern Europe, 1918–1945*. New York: Halsted Press, 1974.

Johnson, Owen. "The Slovak Intelligentsia, 1918–38." *Slovakia* 28, nos. 51–52 (1978–79).

———. *Slovakia 1918–1938: Education and the Making of a Nation*. Boulder, Colo.: East European Monographs, no. 180, distributed by Columbia University Press, 1985.

Jowitt, Kenneth. *The Leninist Reponse to National Development*. Berkeley: Institute of International Studies, Research Series no. 37 (1978).

———. *New World Disorder: The Leninist Extinction*. Berkeley: University of California Press, 1992.

———. "Soviet Neotraditionalism: The Political Corruption of a Leninist Regime." *Soviet Studies* no. 3 (1983).

Kamenec, Ivan. "The Deportation of Jewish Citizens from Slovakia in 1942." In *The Tragedy of Slovak Jews: Proceedings of the International Symposium, Banská Bystrica, March 25–27, 1992*. Banská Bystrica: Datei, 1992.

Kann, Robert. *A History of the Habsburg Empire, 1526–1918.* Berkeley: University of California Press, 1974.

Kaplan, Robert. *Balkan Ghosts.* New York: St. Martin's Press, 1993.

Karl, Terry Lynn, and Phillipe Schmitter. "Modes of Transition in Latin America, Southern Europe, and Eastern Europe." *International Social Science Journal* 128 (May 1991).

Kavan, Zdeněk, and Bernard Wheaton. *The Velvet Revolution.* Boulder, Colo.: Westview Press, 1992.

Kirschbaum, J. M. "Slovakia in the De-Stalinization and Federalization Process of Czechoslovakia." *Canadian Slavonic Papers* 10, no. 4 (1968).

Kirschbaum, Stanislav. *A History of Slovakia.* New York: St. Martin's Press, 1995.

———. "The Slovak Republic and the Slovaks." *Slovakia* 29, nos. 53–54 (1980–81).

Kitschelt, Herbert. "The Formation of Party Systems in East Central Europe." *Politics and Society* 10 (1992).

———. "Post-communist Democracies: Do Party Systems Help or Hinder?" Presented at Conference on Democracy, Markets, and Civil Societies in Post-1989 East Central Europe, May 17–19, 1996, Center for European Studies, Harvard University.

Kohák, Erazim, and Heda Kovaly. *The Victors and the Vanquished.* New York: Horizon Press, 1973.

Korec, Bishop Jan. Letter written April 7, 1989 in response to "The Cross in the Snares of Power." Translated by Stanislav Kirschbaum in *Slovakia* 34, nos. 62–63 (1989–90). For Slovak version, published after the 1989 revolution, see "Na margo jedneho seriálu." Serialized in *Výber,* nos. 5, 6, and 7 (1990).

Kornhauser, William. *The Politics of Mass Society.* New York: Free Press, 1959.

Kovály, Heda. *Under a Cruel Star.* New York and London: Penguin Books, 1986.

Krejčí, Jaroslav. *Social Change and Stratification in Postwar Czechoslovakia.* New York: Columbia University Press, 1972.

Kruzliak, Imrich. "A Quarter Century of Slovak Culture." In Josef Kirschbaum, ed., *Slovakia in the 19th and 20th Centuries,* Proceedings of Conference on Slovakia Held during Meeting of Slovak World Congress, June 17–18, 1971. Toronto: Slovak World Congress, 1973.

Kučera, Milan, and Zdeněk Pavlík. "Czech and Slovak Demography." In Jiří Musil, ed. *The End of Czechoslovakia.* Budapest: Central European University Press, 1995.

Kundera, Milan. *Book of Laughter and Forgetting.* New York: Penguin, 1985.

Kusín, Vladimír V. *Dubček to Charter 77.* Edinburgh: Q Press Ltd., 1978.

Kusý, Miroslav. "Slovak Exceptionalism." In Jiří Musil, ed., *The End of Czechoslovakia.* Budapest: Central European University Press, 1995.

Laitin, David. "National Revivals and Violence." *Archives of European Sociology* 36 (1995).

Laqueur, Walter. *Fascism: A Reader's Guide.* Berkeley: University of California Press, 1976.

———. *The Terrible Secret.* New York: Penguin, 1982.

Leff, Carole Skalnik. *National Conflict in Czechoslovakia.* Princeton: Princeton University Press, 1988.

Lendvai, Paul. *Anti-Semitism without Jews.* Garden City, N.Y.: Doubleday, 1971.

Lettrich, Jozef. *History of Modern Slovakia.* New York: Frederick A. Praeger, 1955.

Lewin, Moshe. *The Gorbachev Phenomenon.* Berkeley: University of California Press, 1989.

Lindholm, Charles. *Charisma.* Oxford: Basil Blackwell, 1990.

Linz, Juan J., and Alfred Stepan. "Political Identities and Electoral Sequences: Spain, the Soviet Union, and Yugoslavia." In Stephen R. Graubard, ed., *Exit from Communism.* New Brunswick: Transaction Publishers, 1993.

Lowenthal, Richard. "Development versus Utopia in Communist Systems." In Chalmers Johnson, ed., *Change in Communist Systems.* Stanford: Stanford University Press, 1970.

Luebbert, Gregory. *Liberalism, Fascism, or Social Democracy: Social Classes and the Political Origins of Regimes in Interwar Europe.* New York: Oxford University Press, 1991.

Maier, Charles. *The Unmasterable Past.* Cambridge: Harvard University Press, 1988.

Mamatey, Victor S., and Radomír Luža, eds. *A History of the Czechoslovak Republic.* Princeton: Princeton University Press, 1973.

Marx, Karl. "On the Jewish Question" and "The Eighteenth Brumaire of Louis Bonaparte." In David McLellan, ed., *Karl Marx: Selected Writings.* Oxford: Oxford University Press, 1977.

McFaul, Michael. "Party Formation after Revolutionary Transitions: The Russian Case." In Alexander Dallin, ed., *Political Parties in Russia.* Berkeley: International and Area Studies Research Series, no. 88.

Mikus, Josef. *Slovakia: A Political History.* Milwaukee, Wis.: Marquette University Press, 1963.

———. *The Three Slovak Bishops.* Slovak Catholic Federation of America, 1953.

Motyl, Alexander. "The Conceptual President." In T. Colton and R. Tucker, eds., *Patterns in Post-Soviet Leadership.* Boulder, Colo.: Westview Press, 1995.

———. *Dilemmas of Independence: Ukraine after Totalitarianism.* New York: Council on Foreign Relations Press, 1993.

Naipaul, V. S. *The Return of Eva Peron.* New York: Vintage Books, 1981.

Němec, Ludvík. "Solution of the Minorities Problem." In Victor S. Mamatey and Radomír Luža, eds., *A History of the Czechoslovak Republic, 1918–1948.* Princeton: Princeton University Press, 1973.

Obrman, Jan. "Civic Forum Surges to Impressive Victory in Elections." In *RFE Report on Eastern Europe,* June 22, 1990.

———. "Language Law Stirs Controversy." In *Report on Eastern Europe,* November 16, 1990.

———. "Relations with Germany." In *Report on Eastern Europe,* November 15, 1991.

O'Donnell, Guellermo, and Phillipe Schmitter. *Transitions from Authoritarian Rule: Tentative Conclusions about Uncertain Democracies.* Baltimore: Johns Hopkins University Press, 1986.

Olsen, David. "The Sundered State." In Thomas Remington, ed., *Parliaments in Transition.* Boulder, Colo.: Westview Press, 1994.

Orwell, George. *1984.* New York: New American Library, 1981.

Pauco, Jozef. "Slovaks Abroad and Their Relationship with Slovakia." In Jozef Kirschbaum, ed., *Slovakia in the 19th and 20th Centuries.* Toronto: Slovak World Congress, 1973.

Paul, David. *The Cultural Limits of Revolutionary Politics.* East European Monographs, no. 48, distributed by Columbia University Press, 1979.

———. "Slovak Nationalism and the Hungarian State, 1870–1910." In Paul Brass, ed., *Ethnic Groups and the State.* London/Sidney: Croom Helm, 1985.

Payne, Stanley. *A History of Fascism, 1914–1945.* Madison: University of Wisconsin Press, 1995.

Pech, Stanley Z. "Ferment in Czechoslovak Marxist Historiography." *Canadian Slavonic Papers* 10, no. 4 (1968).

Pehe, Jiří. "Czechoslovakia's Political Balance Sheet, 1990–92." *RFE/RL Research Report* 1, no. 25 (1992).

———. "Growing Slovak Demands Seen as Threat to Federation." *RFE Report on Eastern Europe,* March 22, 1991.

———. "The Local Government Elections." *RFE Report on Eastern Europe,* December 14, 1990.

———. "Political Conflict in Slovakia." *RFE Report on Eastern Europe,* May 10, 1991.

———. "Slovak Nationalism Splits Christian Democratic Ranks." *RFE/RL Research Report* 1, no. 13 (1992).

Piekalkiewicz, Jaroslaw A. *Public Opinion Polling in Czechoslovakia, 1968–69.* New York: Praeger Publishers, 1972.

Przeworski, Adam. *Democracy and the Market.* Cambridge: Cambridge University Press, 1991.

Putnam, Robert D. *Making Democracy Work.* Princeton: Princeton University Press, 1993.

———. "Studying Elite Political Culture: The Case of 'Ideology.' " *American Political Science Review* 65 (1971).

"Reconstructing Nations and States." *Daedalus* 122, no. 3 (1993).

Remnick, David. *Resurrection.* New York: Random House, 1997.

Riveles, Stanley. "Slovakia: Catalyst of Crisis." *Problems of Communism* 18, no. 3 (1968).

Roksandic, Drago. "Shifting References: Celebrations of Uprisings in Croatia, 1945–1991." *East European Politics and Societies* 9, no. 2 (1995).

Rona-Tas, Akos, and Jozsef Borocz. "The Formation of New Business Elites in Bulgaria, the Czech Republic, Hungary, and Poland: Continuity and Change, Precommunist and Communist Legacies." Presented at Workshop on East Central Europe at Harvard University in May 1996.

Rosenberg, Tina. *The Haunted Land.* New York: Random House, 1995.

Rothkirschen, Livia. "Vatican Policy and the 'Jewish Problem' in 'Independent' Slovakia (1939–1945)" and "The Slovak Enigma: A Reassessment of the Halt to the Deportations." In Michael Marrus, ed., *The Nazi Holocaust,* vol. 4: *The 'Final Solution' Outside Germany.* Westport, Conn.: Meckler Corp., 1989.

Rousso, Henri. *The Vichy Syndrome.* Cambridge: Harvard University Press, 1991.

Rupnick, James. "Totalitarianism Revisited." In John Keane, ed., *Civil Society and the State.* London: Verso, 1988.

Rustow, Dankwart. "Transitions to Democracy: Toward a Dynamic Model." *Comparative Politics* 2, no. 3 (1970).

Sampson, Steven. "Rumours in Socialist Romania." *Survey* 28, no. 4 (1984).

——. "Toward an Anthropology of Collaboration in Eastern Europe." *Culture and History,* no. 8 (1990).

Schmitter, Phillipe. "Democratic Dangers and Dilemmas." *Journal of Democracy* 5, no. 2 (1994).

Schmitter, Phillipe, and Terry Lynn Karl. "The Conceptual Travels of Transitologists and Consolidologists: How Far to the East Should They Attempt to Go?" *Slavic Review* 53, no. 1 (1994).

Schopflin, George. "Nationalism, Politics, and the European Experience." *Survey* 28, no. 4 (1984).

Seton-Watson, R. W. *The Historian as a Political Force in Central Europe.* London: School of Slavonic Studies in the University of London, 1922.

——. ed. *Slovakia Then and Now.* London: Allen and Unwin, Ltd., 1931.

Sewell, William, Jr. "Ideologies and Social Revolutions: Reflections on the French Case"; and Theda Skocpol, "Cultural Idioms and Political Ideologies in the Revolutionary Construction of State Power: A Rejoinder to Sewell." *Journal of Modern History* 57 (1985).

Shawcross, William. *Dubček.* New York: Simon and Schuster, 1990.

Shoup, Paul. "Communism, Nationalism, and the Growth of the Communist Community of Nations after World War II." *American Political Science Review* 56, no. 4 (1962).

Šiklová, Jiřina. "Lustration or the Czech Way of Screening." *East European Constitutional Review* 5, no. 1, Winter 1996.

——. "The Solidarity of the Culpable." *Social Research,* 58, no. 4 (1991).

Silber, Laura, and Allan Little. *Yugoslavia: Death of a Nation.* New York: Penguin, 1996.

Šimečka, Martin. "The Unfinished Revolution." *Uncaptive Minds* 4, no. 2 (Summer 1991).

Šimečka, Milan. "Black Holes." *Kosmas* 3, no. 2 and 4, no. 1 (1985).

——. *The Restoration of Order: The Normalization of Czechoslovakia, 1969–1976.* London: Verso, 1984.

Skilling, H. Gordon. "Independent Historiography in Czechoslovakia." *Canadian Slavonic Papers,* 25, no. 4 (1983).

——. "The Muse of History—1984: History, Historians, and Politics in Communist Czechoslovakia." *Cross Currents, A Yearbook of Central European Culture,* no. 3. Ann Arbor: University of Michigan Press, 1984.

——. "Stalin over Prague." In Skilling, ed., *Communism National and International.* Toronto: University of Toronto Press, 1964.

Smith, Anthony. *National Identity.* Reno: University of Nebraska Press, 1991.

Smith, Kathleen. *Remembering Stalin's Victims: Popular Memory and the End of the USSR.* Ithaca: Cornell University Press, 1996.

Smolar, Alexander. "The Dissolution of Solidarity." *Journal of Democracy* 5, no. 1 (1994).

Stark, David. "Recombinant Property in Eastern European Capitalism." *American Journal of Sociology* 101, no. 4 (1996).

Steiner, Eugen. *The Slovak Dilemma.* Cambridge: Cambridge University Press, 1973.

Szomolányiová, Soňa, "The Formation of Political Elites." In Szomolányiová et al., eds., *Eastern Central Europe 2000.* Bratislava, 1993).

————. "The Repolitization of Slovak Society." Paper presented at the Fourth World Congress for Soviet and east European Studies in Harrogate, July 21–26, 1990.

Szomolányiová, Soňa, and Grigorij Mesežnikov, eds. *Slovakia: Parliamentary Elections, 1994.* Bratislava: Slovak Political Science Association / Friedrich Ebert Foundation, 1995.

————., eds. *The Slovak Path of Transition—To Democracy?* Bratislava: Slovak Political Science Foundation and Interlingua, 1994.

Szomolányiová, Soňa, Martin Bútora, and Vladimír Krivý. "Positive Deviance: The Career of a Concept in Czecho-Slovakia in the Late 1980s." Manuscript, September 1989.

Táborský, Edward. *Communism in Czechoslovakia, 1948–1960.* Princeton: Princeton University Press, 1961.

Taylor, A. J. P. *The Habsburg Monarchy, 1809–1918.* Chicago: University of Chicago Press, 1948.

Timko, Carol. *Weakness in Numbers.* Ph.D. diss., University of California, Berkeley, 1997.

Tolan, Sandy, and Nancy Postero. "Accidents of History." *New York Times Magazine,* February 23, 1992.

Tumarkin, Nina. *The Living and the Dead.* New York: Basic Books, 1994.

Ulč, Otto. *Politics in Czechoslovakia.* San Francisco: W. H. Freeman and Co., 1974.

Urban, Jan. "Nationalism as a Totalitarian Ideology." *Social Research* 58, no. 4 (1991).

Vago, Béla. *The Shadow of the Swastika: The Rise of Fascism and Anti-Semitism in the Danube Basin, 1936–39.* England: Saxon House. Published for the Institute of Jewish Affairs, 1975.

Vago, Béla, and George L. Mosse. *Jews and Non-Jews in Eastern Europe, 1918–1945.* New York: Halsted Press, 1974.

Verba, Sidney. "Comparative Political Culture." In Lucian Pye and Sidney Verba, eds., *Political Culture and Political Development.* Princeton: Princeton University Press, 1965.

Verdery, Katherine. *National Ideology under Socialism: Identity and Cultural Politics in Ceausescu's Romania.* Berkeley: University of California Press, 1991.

————. "Nationalism and National Sentiment in Post-socialist Romania." *Slavic Review* 52, no. 2 (1993).

Volgyes, Ivan. *Political Socialization in Eastern Europe: A Comparative Framework.* New York: Praeger, 1975.

Vujacic, Veljko. "Communism and Nationalism in Russia and Serbia." Ph.D. diss., University of California, Berkeley, 1995.

————. Historical Legacies, Nationalist Mobilization, and Political Outcomes in Russia and Serbia: A Weberian View." *Theory and Society* 25 (1996).

Waller, Michael, ed. *Party Politics in Eastern Europe.* Special Issue of *Party Politics* 1, no. 4 (1995).

Weber, Eugen. *Peasants into Frenchmen.* Stanford: Stanford University Press, 1976.

Weber, Max. *Economy and Society.* Berkeley: University of California Press, 1978.

Weidlinger. "After the Velvet Revolution." *Uncaptive Minds* 4, no. 4 (Winter 1991–92).

Weschler, Lawrence. "The Velvet Purge: The Trials of Jan Kavan." *New Yorker,* October 19, 1992.

Whipple, Tim D., ed. *After the Velvet Revolution.* New York: Freedom House, 1991.

Wolchik, Sharon. *Czechoslovakia in Transition.* London: Pinter Publishers, 1991.

Yerushalmi, Yosef Hayim. *Zakhor: Jewish History and Jewish Memory.* New York: Schocken Books, 1989.

Young, Crawford, ed. *The Rising Tide of Cultural Pluralism.* Madison: University of Wisconsin Press, 1993.

Young, James. *Holocaust Memorials and Meaning.* New Haven: Yale University Press, 1993.

Žák, Václav. "The Velvet Divorce—Institutional Foundations." In Jiří Musil, ed., *The End of Czechoslovakia.* Budapest: Central European University Press, 1995.

Zaslavsky, Victor. "From Redistribution to Marketization: Social and Attitudinal Change in Post-Soviet Russia." In Gail Lapidus, ed., *The New Russia: Troubled Transformation.* Boulder, Colo.: Westview Press, 1994.

———. "Nationalism and Democratic Transitions in Post-communist Societies." In Stephen Graubard, ed., *Exit from Communism.* New Brunswick: Transaction Publishers, 1993.

———. "Success and Collapse: Traditional Soviet Nationality Policy." In Ian Bremmer and Ray Taras, eds., *Nation and Politics in the Soviet Successor States.* Cambridge: Cambridge University Press, 1993.

Zielonka, Jan. "New Institutions in the Old East Bloc." *Journal of Democracy* 5, no. 2 (1994).

Articles and Books in Slovak and Czech

Aktuálne problémy Česko-Slovenska. Centrum pre sociálnu analýzu, Bratislava, January 1992.

Aktuálne problémy Slovenska po rozpade. Centrum pre sociálnu analýzu, Bratislava, March 1993 and October 1993.

Alberty, Julius. "Problémy výučby dejepisu na školách." *Historický Časopis* 39, no. 4–5 (1991).

Archiv Komisie Vlády SR pre analýzu udalostí rokov 1967–1970, materiály ÚV KSS, část normalizacia.

Augustin, Milan. *Krátké dejiny Židov na Slovensku.* Bratislava: Judaica Slovaca, 1993.

Barnovský, Michal. *Na ceste k monopolu moci.* Bratislava: Archa, 1993.

———. *Sociálne triedy a revolučné premeny na Slovensku v rokoch 1944–1948.* Bratislava: Veda, 1978.

Bartošek, Karel. *Dějepis pro 9. ročník základní devítileté školy;* Státní pedagogické nakladatelství. Prague, 1963.

Čarnogurský, Pavol. *14. Marec 1939.* Bratislava: VEDA, 1992.

Chreno, Jozef. *Malý slovník slovenského štátu.* Bratislava: Slovenská archivná správa, 1965.

Čulen, Konstantin. *Po Svatoplukovi druhá naša hlava.* Vydavatelstvo Garmond Partizánské a Priatelia Prezidenta Tisu v cudzine a na Slovensku, 1992.

Ďurica, Milan. *Jozef Tiso.* Martin: Matica Slovenská, 1992.

Florek, O., et al. *Dejepis pre 2. ročník stredných odborných škol a 1. ročník stredných odborných učilišt'.* Bratislava: Slovenské pedagogické nakadatel'stvo, 1983/87.

Frieder, Emanuel. *Z denníka mladého rabina.* Bratislava: Judaica Slovaca, Slovenské Národné Muzeum, Oddelenie Židovskej Kultúry, 1993.

Gál, Fedor, et al. *Dnešní krize.* Prague: Sociologické nakladatelství, 1992.

Gál, Fedor. *Z prvej ruky.* Bratislava: Archa, 1991.

Gál, Fedor, with Jana Klusáková. *Nadoraz.* Praha: Primus, 1992.

Gál, Fedor, et al. *Volby.* Prague: Nadace Film a Sociologii, 1993.

Golan, Karol, and Zdeněk Urban. *Dejepis pre 2.ročník odborných škol.* 4th edition. 1964.

Grosman, Ladislav. *Obchod na korze.* Prague: Mladá Fronta, 1966.

Hoffmann, Gabriel, and Ladislav Hoffmann. *Katolická církev a tragédia slovenských Židov v dokumentoch.* Garmond Partizánské, 1994.

Hnutí za Občanskou Svobodu, Dokumenty, 1988–89. Prague: MAXDORF, 1994 (Ústav pro soudobé dějiny, AVCR 1994).

Hrnko, Anton. "Obraz Slovenskej spoločnosti v rokoch 1918–38 v pracách Slovenských historikov." *Historický Časopis* 39, nos. 4–5 (1991).

Husák, Gustáv. "O vývoji a situácii na Slovensku." *Svědectví* 15, no. 58 (1979).

Jablonický, Jozef. *Glosy o historiografii SNP.* Bratislava: NVK International, 1994.

———. "Slovenské národné povstanie a tri etapy jeho hodnotenia." *Historický Časopis* 39, no. 4–5 (1991).

Józa, Jaroslav, František Posl, and Ladislav Varcl. *Dejepis pre kurzy z učiva základnej devatročnej školy.* 2d edition. Bratislava, 1962.

Kamenec, Ivan. *Po stopách tragédie.* Bratislava: Archa, 1991.

Kamenec, Ivan, et al. *Dejepis pre 3. ročník gymnázii.* Bratislava, 1987.

Kaplan, Karel. *Dva retribuční procesy, komentované dokumenty.* Praha: Nakladatelství R, 1992.

Ked' sme brali do rúk budocnost' (Chronology and documents connected with November 1989 revolution). Bratislava: Archa, 1990.

Klimko, Jozef. *Tretia ríša a l'udácký režim na Slovensku.* Bratislava, 1986.

Komisia vláda SR pre analýzu historických udalostí z rokov 1967–1970, vols. 1–3. Bratislava: Politologický Kabinet SAV, 1992.

Kováč, Dušan, ed. *Historia a politika.* Bratislava: Česko-slovenský výbor europskej kúlturnej nadacie, 1993.

Kováč, Dušan, and Lubomír Lipták. *Kapitoly z dejin pre stredné školy.* Bratislava: Slovenské pedagogické nakladatel'stvo, 1992.

Kronika demokratického parlamentu, 1989–1992. Prague: Cesty, 1992.

Kto je kto na Slovensku, 1969. Bratislava: Slovakopress/CSTK.

Kto je kto na Slovensku. Bratislava: Konzorcium Encyklopedia, 1992.

Kubín, L., et al. *Dva roky politickej slobody.* Bratislava: RaPaMaN, 1992.

Lahola, Leopold. *Posledná vec.* Bratislava: Slovenský spisovatel, 1968.

Leško, Marian. *L'udia a l'udkovia z politickej elity.* Prague: Perex, 1993.

Letz, Robert. *Slovensko v rokoch 1945–48.* Bratislava: Ústredie Slovenskej Krest'anskej Inteligencie, 1994.

Lipscher, Ladislav. *Židia v slovenskom štáte, 1939–45.* Bratislava: Print-Servis, 1992.

Lipták, Lubomír. "Slovenská historiografia obdobia po roku 1945." *Historický Časopis,* 39, nos. 4–5 (1991).

———. *Slovensko v 20. storoči.* Bratislava: Vydavatelstvo politickej literatury, 1968.

Machonin, Pavel. *Sociální struktura socialistické společnosti.* Prague: Svoboda, 1967.

Maršina, Richard. "Slovenská Historiografia 1945–1990." *Historický Časopis* 39, nos. 4–5 (1991).

Mesaros, Julius. "Reflexie o patdesiatých a šestidesiatých rokoch." *Historický Časopis* 39, nos. 4–5 (1991).

Mihálik, Juraj. *Spomienky na Zlyhania.* Bratislava: Príroda, 1993.

Mikloško, František. *Nebudete ich most' rozvrátit.* Bratislava: Archa, 1991.

Mináč, Vladimír. *Hovory M.* Bratislava: Vydavatelstvo spolku slovenských spisatelov, 1994.

———. *Návraty k prevratu.* Bratislava: NVK International, 1993.

———. *Odkial a kam Slováci?* Bratislava: Edicia Eseje, 1993.

Mňačko, Ladislav. *Súdruh Munchausen.* Cologne: Index, 1972.

Murín, Karol. *Spomienky a svedectvo.* Garmond Partizánské/Priatelia Prezidenta Tisu, 1992. First published by Zahraničná Matica Slovenská, Hamilton, Ontario, 1987.

Novák, Jozef. "Pomocné vedy historické na Slovensku po roku 1945." *Historický Časopis* 39, nos. 4–5 (1991).

Ondruš, Vladimír. "Slovensko, na moj povel," parts 1–10. In *Slovenský Denník,* October 4–December 20, 1993.

Rašla, Anton and Ernest Zabkay. *Proces s Dr. J. Tisom.* Bratislava: Tatrapress, 1990.

Roško, Robert. "Z výskumu absolventov robotníckych kurzov." *Sociologia* 6, no. 2 (1974).

Salner, Peter. "Tolerancia a intolerancia vo velkých mestách strednej Europy." Bratislava, 1993.

Sivák, Florián, and Jozef Klimko. *Dejiny státu a práva na území ČSSR.* Vysokoškolské Skripta, Právnická fakulta Univerzity Komenského, 1976.

Slobodník, Dušan. *Paragraf: Polárný kruh.* Bratislava: Slovenský Spisovatel, 1992.

Slovenská Národná Rada, X. Volebné obdobie. Bratislava: Kancelária Slovenskej Národnej Rady.

Slovensko na konci druhej svetovej vojny, Zborník materialov zo sympozia, November 1993. Bratislava: Historický ústav SAV, 1994.

Slovensko v politickom systéme Československa, 1918–38, materiály z vedeckého sympozia, November 1991. Bratislava, Historický ústav, SAV, 1992.

Slovensko v rokoch druhej svetovej vojny (Materiály z vedeckého sympozia, November 1990). Bratislava: Slovenská národná rada/Historicky ústav SAV, 1991.

Slovenský rodolub Dr. Jozef Tiso (18 Aprila 1992, 45 vyročie jeho smrti). Trenčín: Vydavatelstvo Ivana Štelcera, 1992.

Soják, Vávra, et al. *Dejepis pre 11. postupný ročník všeobecnovzdelávacích škol.* Bratislava: Slovenské pedagogel'stvo, 1959.

Starý národ, mladý štát: Prehlad slovenských dejin pre školy. Bratislava: Národná Banka Slovenska, 1994.

Tkáč, Marián. *Národ bez peňazi.* Bratislava: Bradlo, 1992.

Tkadlečková, Herta. *Všeobecné dejiny I, 1918–1945. Vysokoškolské Skripta.* Univerzita Komenského v Bratislave, 1990.

Tri roky: Obnovenej členskey základne Matice Slovenskej 1990–92. Liptovský Mikuláš: Vydala Matica Slovenská, 1994.

Trvanie a zmena na Slovensku: Sociologický výskum. Bratislava: Institut stredoeurópskych studií of Comenius University, September, 1992.

Urban, Zdeněk, et al. *Dejiny ČSR Učebný text pre 9–11 postupný ročník všeobecnovzdelávacích škol a pre pedagogické školy.* Bratislava: Slovenské pedagogické nakladel'stvo, 1956.

Vlk, Jan, Vendula Vaňková, and Jiří Novotný. *Minulost a dějiny v českém a slovenském samizdatu, 1970–1989.* Brno: Nakladatelství Doplněk, 1993.

Vnuk, František. *Neuveritelné sprísahánie.* Trenčín: Vydavatel'stvo Ivana Štelcera, 1993.

Czech and Slovack Sources in Translation

Foreign Broadcast Information Service, 1989–93 (FBIS)

Slovak and Czech Newspapers and Periodicals

Domino
Fragment
Koridor
Kultúrny Život
Lidové Noviny
Literárny Týždenník
Mladá Fronta
Národná Obroda
Novy Slovák
Práca
Pravda
Respekt
Slovenský Denník
Slovensky národ
Slovenské národné noviny
Slovenské Pohl'ady
Sme
Smena
Verejnost
Vyber
Zmena

Other Slovak and Czech Sources

Transcripts of Parliamentary sessions in Federal and Slovak parliaments, 1990–93

English-Language Periodicals

Europa Vincet
Prague Post
Prognosis
Radio Free Europe Research Reports; Report on Eastern Europe, 1989–1994

Index

Academy of Sciences. *See* Slovak
Academy of Arts and Sciences
Africa, 35–36, 180–81
Agrarian Party, 51, 203 n.41, 204 n.54
Allen, William Sheridan, 42
Andel, Marián, 90, 139, 231 n.83, 231
n.91
Andráš, Anton, 234 nn.137–38
anticommunism, ambivalence about,
242 n.43
anticommunist nationalists. *See* Catholic nationalists, Slovak; émigrés
Antifascist Fighters Union, 255 n.24
anti-Jewish laws, 68, 78–79, 210 n.65,
210 n.67. *See also* deportation of
Jews, from Slovakia
anti-Semitism: communists' use of, 32–
33; as endemic in Slovakia, 152; following Middle East war, 103; in Nazism, 103–4; and pogroms, 204 n.49;
in Poland, 218 n.28; and purges, 94–
95, 110, 218 n.27, 222 n.98. *See also*
anti-Jewish laws; deportation of
Jews, from Slovakia; Holocaust
Archa Press, 78, 214 n.112
archives/statistics, 52, 86, 159, 202
n.35, 203 n.36
Arendt, Hannah: on masses, 5, 41, 182,

188 n.15, 199 n.61, 200 n.64; on totalitarian regimes, 2
Arkan, 246 n.12
arms production, 144, 145
articulation, definition of, 27–28
Aryanization policy, 68, 78, 105, 210 n.65
atom bomb, 106
Auschwitz, 218 n.20, 221 n.67
Austria, 11

Bacílek, Karol, 94
Baltic nationalists, 10
Banfield, Edward, 42
Barnabite commission, 222 n.96
Belarus, 8
Beneš, Eduard, 54, 215 n.126
Beneš decrees, 54, 85, 174
Bernolák, Anton, 48
black market, 37, 198 n.29
Boehm, Tibor, 146, 234 n.137
Bokeš, František, 202 n.33
Bosnia, 246 n.12
bourgeois nationalists, 218 n.17, 218
n.27; and fascism, 102; of Husák, 93,
98–99, 101; of Novomesky, 98–99,
101; purging of, 94–95; rehabilitation
of, 100–101; textbook treatments of,
98–99

Shari J. Cohen, a political scientist, is currently Senior
Research Fellow at the National Jewish Center for
Learning and Leadership in New York City.

Library of Congress Cataloging-in-Publication Data
Cohen, Shari J.
Politics without a past: the absence of history in
postcommunist nationalism / by Shari J. Cohen.
Includes bibliographical references and index.
ISBN 0-8223-2378-8 (cloth: alk. paper).
ISBN 0-8223-2399-0 (pbk.: alk. paper)
1. Nationalism.   2. Post-communism.   3. History—
Philosophy.   I. Title.
JC311.C615   1999   320.54'094373'09049—dc21
99-28322 CIP